The Fiction of
George Gissing

ALSO BY LEWIS D. MOORE

Cracking the Hard-Boiled Detective:
A Critical History from the 1920s to the Present
(McFarland, 2006)

The Fiction of George Gissing

A Critical Analysis

LEWIS D. MOORE

McFarland & Company, Inc., Publishers
Jefferson, North Carolina, and London

LIBRARY OF CONGRESS CATALOGUING-IN-PUBLICATION DATA

Moore, Lewis D.
    The fiction of George Gissing : a critical analysis /
Lewis D. Moore.
        p.   cm.
    Includes bibliographical references and index.

    ISBN 978-0-7864-3509-8
    softcover : 50# alkaline paper ∞

    1. Gissing, George, 1857–1903 — Criticism and interpretation.
I. Title.
PR4717.M66   2008
823'.8 — dc22   2008034609

British Library cataloguing data are available

On the cover: George Gissing, New York Public Library
Historical and Public Figures; background ©2008 Shutterstock

Manufactured in the United States of America

McFarland & Company, Inc., Publishers
  Box 611, Jefferson, North Carolina 28640
   www.mcfarlandpub.com

For
Terry Flood

Acknowledgments

I wish to thank Dr. Priscilla Ramsey and Dr. John Springhall for listening to me discuss various problems in dealing with my research on Gissing and offering suggestions. I also wish to thank Professor Pierre Coustillas for his careful editorial comments on my articles that have appeared in *The Gissing Newsletter* and *The Gissing Journal*, of which he is the long-time editor. Dr. Bouwe Postmus generously sent me a copy of his meticulously annotated work on Gissing's notebooks.

Terry Flood and Rhonda Buckley have always responded with encouragement as I have progressed through this book. They also became readers of Gissing's fiction when I gave them some of his novels as Christmas presents. My sister, Shirley Moore Powell, has read my previous books with enthusiasm and patiently listened to me talk about Gissing. My wife Barbara and my sons Colin and Ryan are a constant support, and I thank them again for their indulgence in listening to my ruminations about Gissing's work and life.

An earlier version of Chapter 2 appeared in the *Gissing Newsletter* in 1987. Earlier versions of the following chapters were published in the *Gissing Journal*, a successor publication: Chapter 9 in 1999, Chapter 14 in 2007, and Chapter 15 in 2003. Chapter 3 was published in *A Garland for Gissing* in 2001 by Editions Rodopi. It has also been revised for the present book, and Rodopi has kindly granted permission for its inclusion.

Table of Contents

Acknowledgments   vi

Preface   1

Introduction   5

1. Gissing and the Imagination   9

Part One: The Social Imagination

2. The Triumph of Mediocrity: Gissing's *New Grub Street*   21
3. Deception, Violence, and the Criminal Act   29
4. New People: George Gissing's Rising Classes   40
5. The Loss of Innocence: Progress, Science, and Technology   50
6. The Failed Triangle: Marriage, Family, and Children   57
7. Politics, Work, and Business   71
8. Education Old and New   82

Part Two: The Personal Imagination

9. Money as Language and Idea   93
10. Discovery and Disintegration: Figures of Disquiet   104
11. Romantic Love, Sexuality, and Convention   114

12. The Dubious Sex: Women in George Gissing's Fiction   123
13. Conflicted Identities: The Individual and Society   132

Part Three: The Cultural Imagination

14. Against the Modern: Rural Idylls and Urban Realities   145
15. Gissing and Morley Roberts: The Life of Writing in
       Late-Victorian England   156
16. Nationalism, Imperialism, and the Idea of England   167
17. Religion and Morality   175
18. The Natural World in Human Time   185
19. The Late-Victorian Detective   197
20. Frontiers, Edges, and Boundaries   203
21. Conclusion   210

Bibliography   213
Index   219

Preface

I began reading George Gissing's fiction in the early 1960s when I bought second-hand copies of *New Grub Street* and *The Private Papers of Henry Ryecroft*. I could not have chosen two better works to start an exploration of his novels and the world he portrays. Once I read Jacob Korg's *George Gissing* some years later, I realized that not only his fiction but his life was of great interest, both testified to by the many subsequent critical and biographical works on him.

While Gissing studies did not begin in the 1960s, they certainly expanded considerably during that decade with the beginning of the *Gissing Newsletter*, later renamed the *Gissing Journal*, and publication of other critical biographies, collections of letters, critical works, a nine-volume edition of his letters, many academic articles, and dissertations. I wrote my dissertation on Gissing and social Darwinism for which I received my Ph.D. in Literature from American University in 1974. Two international conferences, one in 1999 in Amsterdam and the other in 2003 in London, have been held. A third conference will be held in Lille, France, in 2008. Along with the above, many new editions of his novels and short stories have appeared.

Gissing drew the attention of critics as well as reviewers during his lifetime. Pierre Coustillas and Colin Partridge's *Gissing: The Critical Heritage* (1972) reveals the interest he attracted by his novels, short stories, and nonfiction prose. However, it was not until 1912 when Morley Roberts' *The Private Life of Henry Maitland: A Portrait of George Gissing*, a biographical novel based on Gissing's life, and Frank Swinnerton's *George Gissing: A Critical Study* that any extensive attempts were made to assess his life and art. Unfortunately, Gissing's reputation declined for some years after his death in 1903, notwithstanding May Yates' *George Gissing: An Appreciation* (1922) and Mabel Collins

Donnelly's *George Gissing: Grave Comedian* (1954). In 1963, Jacob Korg's
George Gissing: A Critical Biography initiated a modern revival of interest in
Gissing's work. For the most part, the above works are critical biographies,
Gissing's life being a source of interest that at times rivals his novels and short
stories. In addition, Gillian Tindall's *The Born Exile* (1974) analyzes his work
in the context of his life while John Halperin's *Gissing: A Life in Books* (1982)
emphasizes the importance of Gissing's life in his fiction. Robert L. Selig's
George Gissing (1995) is a good introduction to Gissing's fiction with some
focus on his life. A shift occurs with Adrian Poole's *Gissing in Context* (1975),
John Goode's *George Gissing: Ideology and Fiction* (1978, 1979), Michael Col-
lie's *The Alien Art: A Critical Study of George Gissing's Novels* (1978, 1979), and
John Sloan's *George Gissing: The Cultural Challenge* (1989). Christina Sjöholm's
"The Vice of Wedlock": The Theme of Marriage in George Gissing's Novels (1994),
Simon J. James' *Unsettled Accounts: Money and Narrative in the Novels of George
Gissing* (2003), and Barbara Rawlinson's *A Man of Many Parts: Gissing's Short
Stories, Essays and Other Works* (2006) signal an increasing focus on his fiction
apart from his life. All of the above are in addition to the numerous journal
articles and collections of essays on Gissing's work. He also figures in critical
texts on nineteenth-century literature and culture. Finally, Pierre Coustillas's
editorial and biographical works and Bouwe Postmus's editing of Gissing's
occasional notes and poems deepen the critic's and scholar's understanding
of the forces that shaped Gissing.

    The present work naturally builds on what comes before it. Gissing's
fiction is the principal focus of this book and differs from the work of others
in its analysis of the role of the author's imagination as a means of understanding his culture, a culture that Gissing knows and struggles with on a
daily basis in writing his novels. Nearly all of Gissing's fiction centers on his
time period, and it is hoped that an examination of principal themes and
ideas in his novels and short stories will enable the critic and reader to recover
a sense of the lived feel of his world. This can never be complete, but his literary imagination gives one some awareness of late-Victorian culture. History, sociology, and painting help to bring the reader closer to that era, but
it is the imaginative engagement of the reader and critic that is crucial. Every
year that passes separates the present further from late-Victorian society. Yet,
the imaginative literature of the period still exists and offers a way to experience some vital sense of that world.

    Chapter 1 adds another fact that differentiates this book from other stud-
ies. It reminds one of the importance of the imagination in the Romantic poets'
criticism and poetry. Major earlier critics such as Sir Philip Sidney, John Dryden, Alexander Pope, and Samuel Johnson make statements about the
significant role that the imagination plays in literature. But no critic before

Samuel Taylor Coleridge, William Wordsworth, Percy Byshhe Shelley, and John Keats makes such strong statements about the absolute necessity for the active engagement of the imagination in the creative act. Wordsworth's process of composing poetry in *Preface to Lyrical Ballads* (1802) may not be identical to that of other poets, but his emphasis on the role of reason and emotion in that process underscores the important elements that the poet's imagination employs to achieve his ends. Readers and critics must bring the same intensity to their roles if they wish to engage Gissing's novels and short stories and through them his culture.

The libraries of American University, the University of the District of Columbia, Howard University, George Washington University, and, especially, Georgetown University have proven to be valuable sources for primary and secondary materials. The Library of Congress is always a good place for hard-to-find publications. In London, the British Library has been the best provider of necessary books and articles, especially their new facilities that opened in 1997. Located on Euston Road next to St. Pancras Station, it has by far the best environment in which to do research. Their efficient and helpful staff have always responded well to my enquiries.

Introduction

This book examines George Gissing's fiction and the function of the imagination in interpreting culture. Gissing wrote twenty-three novels, one of which, *The Private Papers of Henry Ryecroft* (1903), is an autobiographical novel. Starting from *Workers in the Dawn* (1880), Gissing focuses on his own time period with the exception of the posthumously published *Veranilda* (1904), a historical novel of sixth-century Rome. After his return from America in 1877, Gissing settled in London and lived precariously by tutoring. While he did not live in the worst East London slums, he frequented these areas and absorbed the desperation of the people living there. Five of his first six novels focus in whole or in part on the working-class poor. As the title suggests, *The Nether World* (1889) represents the nadir of his social and cultural vision. From 1890 on, Gissing wrote mainly about the middle class and the lower-middle class. An analysis of selected ideas that arise in his work allows one to perceive his world in detail.

The first chapter discusses the idea of the imagination and suggests ways of countering the post-modernist attack on individual consciousness and its ability to know anything. Rather than individual minds communicating primarily through language, post-modernist critics argue, somewhat mystically, that there is only language. However, this chapter demonstrates that we know of the existence of the imagination through its effects. Shakespeare wrote approximately thirty-seven plays, some considered works of the highest genius and others as much weaker in language and form. His reputation has gained in stature over the centuries and among people in many cultures. In the writing of plays like *Hamlet, King Lear, As You Like It*, and *Henry IV Part I,* something happens in Shakespeare's creative process that sharply distinguishes these from lesser plays such as *Two Gentlemen of Verona, Henry*

VI Part I, or *Titus Andronicus*. The power of his imagination is more strongly active in the former plays and is the cause of their effects. Lists of major literary artists and their works might vary, but certain writers appear over and over again. At the very least, the imagination is a convenient name given to this creative power. At the most, the concept of the imagination partakes of the qualities argued for by Romantic critics such as Samuel Taylor Coleridge, William Wordsworth, Percy Bysshe Shelley, and John Keats.

The remaining chapters are divided into three parts, i.e., "Social Imagination," "Personal Imagination," and the "Cultural Imagination." The first part focuses on groups, institutions, and class and explores Gissing's insights predominantly into the dramatization of the exterior lives of his characters. For example, Chapter 2, The Triumph of Mediocrity: Gissing's *New Grub Street*," contrasts the progressive failure of the novelist Edwin Reardon to the increasing success of the critic Jasper Milvain, the new man of the literary world who knows his market and the people who matter and works diligently to succeed. Chapter 6, "The Failed Triangle: Family, Marriage, and Children," reveals the dissolution of these crucial social structures. Part Two turns to the personal imagination as subject. These chapters concentrate on the individual's feelings, emotions, and ideas, the latter separately or as organized into coherent philosophies. Chapter 9, "Money as Language and Idea," investigates the role of money in people's lives, how they use it and view it. Chapter 13, "Conflicted Identities: The Individual and Society," shows Gissing's imaginative grasp of individual characters and their struggles toward self-awareness in an increasingly complex social structure.

Part Three explores the culture as idea and manifestation. Characters' understandings of their developing and changing world form these chapters. They reach for a broad understanding of the ideas that represent their culture. Chapter 14, "Against the Modern: Rural Idylls and Urban Realities," shows the opposition between city and country and the reluctant acceptance of the former as a dominant cultural model. Chapter 16, "Nationalism, Imperialism, and the Idea of England," analyzes the force of these concepts in characters' lives.

This work primarily examines Gissing's longer fiction. Unlike a good amount of recent Gissing criticism, this is not a critical biography. This is an important point since Gissing uses details of his life to fill some of his fiction, details that are transformed in the telling. Gissing argues on several occasions that his characters are not to be identified with him. However, in books like John Halperin's *Gissing: A Life in Books* (1982), attempts are made to connect events in his life to his work, not always unsuccessfully, that call into question Gissing's disclaimer. As one approaches his novels as imaginative works of art, Gissing earns the benefit of doubt regardless of how well the books seem to match up with his life. At most, he starts with his life and thoughts but changes them through the operation of his imagination in displaying their significance socially, personally, or culturally.

1

Gissing and the Imagination

George Gissing was both a conscious depicter of his society and an unconscious reflector of its manners and mores. Although arguing that "the novel of plot and character [usurps] the place of the novel of protest," Jacob Korg initially states:

> Most of George Gissing's social novels bear the mark of an allegiance divided between social reform and art. Each begins by addressing itself to some problem of nineteenth century civilization, such as poverty, Mammonism, socialism, rack-renting, educational reform, or the position of women, depicting evil conditions with powerful social realism ["Division of Purpose in George Gissing" 64].

One can argue that Gissing did not start out to be a creative artist and that it was only the Owens College crisis that opened up his life to other than academic prospects. It is of course quite possible that something else would have diverted him from his expected university career even if he had not met Marianne Helen Harrison and stolen money for her from the college cloakroom for which he served one month in prison. Gissing's letters and diary reveal someone with difficult emotional struggles, but these were not so serious that he could not, through prodigious efforts, maintain a rigorous work schedule and produce a large body of important fiction and nonfiction before his death in 1903. Through his many novels, short stories, essays, and critical works, the latter largely on Dickens, Gissing explores both his own thoughts and feelings as well as late nineteenth century cultural conflicts in British and European society. Except for *Veranilda: A Romance* (1904), all of Gissing's novels and short stories focus on his time period. Through the power of his imagination, this concentration creates a body of sustained narrative interpretation of late-Victorian culture and gives a lived feel of that world. As John Halperin demonstrates in *Gissing: A Life in Books* (1982), Gissing's life partially exists in his novels and stories, reflected on and evaluated over nearly thirty years. And, the broader culture is there as well.

Beginning with the practical assumption that Gissing's fiction is not life but like life, one can be fairly certain that the culture reflected in his work resembles what he saw and what actually existed. In *Bloody Murder* (1992), Julian Symons remarks on the Sherlock Holmes fiction of Gissing's contemporary, Sir Arthur Conan Doyle:

> We should remember, as most critics do not, that this was not "period" material for Doyle when the first three collections of short stories and three of the four novels were written. He was writing of the world around him, a world transformed by his imagination [85].

This raises the question of the perspective from which an author, at any narrative moment, explores his or her culture and how well he or she does it. Several categories of ideas are important in this context. One, the critic must be alert to the dominant ideas that Gissing's own interests reveal. For instance, the alienated or socially cut-off but educated young man who, because of his class position and/or poverty, finds difficulty in achieving and maintaining a place in society commensurate with his cultural level is an important focus throughout much of his fiction. This category reveals a great deal about Gissing's attitude toward society and bears a heavy emphasis in his fiction. Edwin Reardon in *New Grub Street* (1891), Godwin Peak in *Born in Exile* (1892), and Dyce Lashmar in *Our Friend the Charlatan* (1901) portray different facets of this character type. Second, Gissing employs other ideas about his culture that are not as central and figure in a secondary capacity. Education and its meaning and representation often function in this way. Harold Biffen's remarks in *New Grub Street* about the near futility of his tutoring and Emmeline Mumford's hapless attempts to make a lady out of Louise Derrick in *The Paying Guest* (1895, 1896) are only two examples of a minor educational theme Gissing works into his narratives. Of course, education is not always a minor theme. Helen Norman in *Workers in the Dawn* (1880), Walter Egremont in *Thyrza* (1887), and Mary Barfoot and Rhoda Nunn in *The Odd Women* (1893) contend with the need to elevate those either in the working class in the first two novels or the lower-middle and middle classes in the latter. In *The Odd Women*, their gender makes the need for educating "displaced" women crucial. Gissing argues that society will have no pity on them if, without family, marriage, or money, they have no training.

Much like concentric circles spreading from some point of energy, Gissing employs additional ideas that surround, invest, and give support to those in the first and second categories. Concepts relating to fashion and the social norms regarding clothing and dress in all areas are of this type. Food and drink and attitudes toward them also clarify the world in which the characters act. Of course, without these surrounding ideas, both the above primary and secondary concepts lack vitality and immediacy. They have a tendency to become abstract and lose their narrative effectiveness. A final category comprises those ideas that the critic raises in regard to Gissing's fiction because of their known importance to the culture. His work deals with them at some level, but they are not always immediately apparent to the reader. Nationalism, imperialism, and the idea of England are examples of this kind. Throughout, Gissing's continued, dramatic employment of an idea, not so much its specific content, determines the category in which it operates.

An exploration of the probable ongoing, dynamic development of these categories of ideas helps to understand their fluidity in his prose. Of course, the culture that Gissing portrays in his fiction is not the real culture that he knew and experienced although, as stated above, it resembles it. Rather, his fiction is an interpretation of the world in which he lived. John Spiers gives a succinct picture of this process: "Gissing sought documentary evidence, which he carefully noted and retained, and which he re-fashioned in imaginative literature" ("Introduction" 9). No one today can recreate that and put Gissing into it with all his uncertainties, misgivings, and real and false knowledge concerning it. Asa Briggs in *Victorian People: A Reassessment of Persons and Themes: 1851–67* (1955, 1965) addresses this problem as it relates to the generation before Gissing wrote:

> The nineteenth century can be understood only when we realize that many of the roads back to it are blocked and that the historical landscape we hope to explore looks at first glance like a *terra incognita*. We can only understand Victorian England by examining particular segments of it. [15–16].

Thirty-five years later John Sutherland states in a foreword to *Rereading Victorian Fiction* (2000):

> We have to accept we are where we are and Victorian Fiction is where it is, and that the gulf between us and it is widening. We shall never, however hard we try, understand the Victorians as well as they understood themselves (and their books). But we read, and reread and, as G.M Young once put it, if we do it well enough we can, again, "hear the Victorians" [xii].

Much can be known and recovered about late nineteenth century England, but the feeling of living it as one lives through one's own time is largely lost except through the culture imagined in Gissing's and other writers' literary works. In a February 3, 1882, letter to his sister Ellen, Gissing writes:

> I have vast faith in imaginative literature of all kinds. If the choice had to be made I had rather have a girl well acquainted with Dickens & George Eliot

> & Shelley & Browning than with all the science in all the text-books. These
> writers show you what is meant by life, & teach you to distinguish the good
> & the bad in it [Mattheisen, Young, and Coustillas 2: 72–73].

Through the creative act, Gissing does firsthand what modern critics and
readers struggle to accomplish, i.e., to imagine his world. And, his is only
one contemporary interpretation, and one in sharp conflict with those of
other writers. Historical analyses are valuable and provide insight into past
eras, but the imaginative constructions and reconstructions of poets, novelists, and dramatists give one a greater lived feel of the past. Far from Michael
Collie's assertion in *The Alien Art: A Critical Study of George Gissing's Novels*
(1978, 1979) that Gissing is "unimaginative" (19), his work is probably better understood by approaching him through Asa Briggs' statement in *Victorian Cities* (1963, 1968):

> What may be called the "image" of the particular city depended, therefore,
> not only upon the facts but upon the imaginative power with which people
> arranged the facts in a pattern [87].

Gissing did pay close attention to his society and went to great pains to
authenticate what he believed to be present conditions. But to say that this
realist approach lacks imagination is to misapply the term *realism*. The concrete examples are only the surface; the novelist's use of them is what matters, and Gissing's well-documented artistic focus reveals his imagination at
work. In "The Place of Realism in Fiction," he writes, "There is no science
of fiction. However energetic and precise the novelist's preparation for his
book, all is but dead material until breathed upon by the 'shaping spirit of
imagination,' which is the soul of the individual artist" (Korg and Korg,
George Gissing on Fiction 85). Prose descriptions and extended essays such as
those in Charles Dickens' *Sketches by Boz* (1836–37) and Thomas Carlyle's
On Heroes, Hero-Worship and the Heroic in History (1841), respectively, might
be added to the kinds of works in which the imagination is dominant.
Attempts to understand the physical, institutional, intellectual, and emotional aspects of a social structure will, at least, partially succeed with the careful study of imaginative literature.

Several assumptions need explanation. One is that literature is different
from other kinds of writing when the imagination strongly infuses it. The
problematic questions that arise, e.g., what is literature, what is the imagination, and how does one determine the presence of a strong infusion of the
latter, rely on the passage of time to settle any arguments regarding them. A
general consensus forms, open to subsequent alteration, concerning the
answers. Few would deny that at some point in time certain writers demonstrate a strong element of the imagination in their literary work. Whether the
imagination is a discoverable quality in humans is not the issue. Over time

critics and readers have observed the different effects produced by an author's individual works and have employed the word *imagination* to indicate the source of these effects, especially when the works have been greatly admired for many decades. A second assumption is that there exists a reality not dependent on anyone's existence or control and that it exists through time. A corollary assumption is that mankind can interact with this reality through its senses and reason. Finally, analysis is necessary to understand, if not be moved by, this imaginative portrayal of culture through literature. To Sir Philip Sidney's argument in *An Apology for Poetry* (1595) that poetry's superiority to history and philosophy lies in its greater ability to move (143), one can add that poetry can also rival philosophy in the latter's ability to teach when analysis reveals the results of literature's imaginative power (143–44).

English Romantic poet-critics speak of the power of the imagination in new and dramatic ways. Although William Wordsworth only refers to the imagination a few times in "Preface to *Lyrical Ballads*" (1802), *The Prelude* (1850) dramatically changes the emphasis. He calls the imagination the "glorious faculty" (Bk. 14, line 89). And in his "Preface," his discussion of the way in which he composed his poetry strongly suggests that the imagination infuses the poems throughout the whole process. Samuel Taylor Coleridge, Wordsworth's friend and colleague, lays the foundation for the Romantics' emphasis on the imagination. In *Biographia Literaria* (1817), he discusses the imagination by first dividing it into two categories, the primary and secondary imagination. Coleridge defines them:

> The primary IMAGINATION I hold to be the living Power and prime Agent of all human Perception, and as a repetition in the finite mind of the eternal act of creation in the infinite I AM. The secondary Imagination I consider as an echo of the former, co-existing with the conscious will, yet still as identical with the primary in the *kind* of its agency, and differing only in *degree*, and in the *mode* of its operation. It dissolves, diffuses, dissipates, in order to recreate; or where this process is rendered impossible, yet still at all events it struggles to idealize and to unify. It is essentially *vital*, even as all objects (*as* objects) are essentially fixed and dead [321–22].

In a Nov. 22, 1817, letter to Benjamin Bailey, John Keats combines into one term the powers of the imagination:

> I am certain of nothing but of the holiness of the Heart's affections and the truth of the Imagination — What the imagination seizes as Beauty must be truth — whether it existed before or not — for I have the same Idea of all our Passions as of Love they are all in their sublime, creative of essential Beauty [Abrams and Greenblatt 334].

He continues, "The Imagination may be compared to Adam's dream — he awoke and found it truth" (334). Keats observes of Shakespeare, a month later in a letter to his brothers George and Thomas Keats:

> At once it struck me, what quality went to form a Man of Achievement especially in Literature & which Shakespeare possessed so enormously — *Negative Capability*, that is when man is capable of being in uncertainties, Mysteries, doubts, without any irritable reaching after fact & reason [Abrams and Greenblatt 336].

Finally, Percy Bysshe Shelley's "A Defence of Poetry" (1821, 1840) is a paean to the imagination and the poetic faculty. The former he refers to at one point as the "imperial faculty" (341) and begins the essay by defining the imagination as man's fundamental creative force (339). Poetry is the medium through which the imagination preeminently works (341). This concentration of insights into the nature of the imagination by four of the five major English Romantic poets remains as a permanent contribution to an understanding of its role in literature.

The history of the social/cultural criticism of literature is a mixed one. It ranges from Roland Escarpit's study of the book as object to the more theoretical Marxist critiques of Georg Lukacs, Lucien Goldmann, and Terry Eagleton. Other methods such as feminist, Afrocentrist, psychological, and myth criticism blend ideological and thematic elements that attempt to understand human complexity through imaginative literature. Few of them have absorbed from New Criticism that the text is an effective place to begin and that superimposing as little as possible on the text will allow one to gain a better understanding of it. No criticism operates without preconceptions, but the general framework discussed above will permit the greatest access to a social structure analysis. For example, Fredric Jameson's chapter on Gissing in *The Political Unconscious* (1981) devotes a little more than twenty percent of its pages to the discussion of *ressentiment* in fiction. However, Jameson is aware of Gissing's value as a novelist. He describes him as "an incomparable writer whose unique novels have only begun to be rediscovered in the present decade" (186) and acknowledges the difficulty of recovering the past. In discussing the "theme of the alienated intellectual," Jameson states:

> As with some of the earlier materials of the present chapter, indeed, I will argue that this particular "theme" and the characters who seem to dramatize it are themselves simply so many allusions to a more basic ideological "sign" which would have been grasped instinctively by any contemporary reader but from which we are culturally and historically somewhat distanced [200].

Yet, even as he ties this theme to the idea of *ressentiment*, he only briefly explores its presence in *Demos: A Story of English Socialism* (1886) while alluding to twelve other writers and thinkers, some more than once to make his broader case. In Jameson's chapter, one expects less theory and more close examination of Gissing's use of the idea of resentment in his novels. As an exercise, post-modernism might leave a helpful residue, but it will hardly deflect the course of interpretation. For, every age will engage in an effort to understand, to make sense of imaginative literature through a thematic analysis of its texts. Harold Bloom's *The Western Canon* (1994) is one of the most important reminders of this ongoing practice. Bloom's dismissal of Western literature's disparagers helps to redirect criticism to its great classical sources and to reveal the obvious, that imaginative literature has in the past and continues in the present to engage the human condition. His assertion of Shakespeare's preeminence is not an ending point; rather, it is a tenable position that later critics will accept or not.

George Orwell and Raymond Williams are two critics with the clearest conception of Gissing's sense of nineteenth-century culture. Orwell, possibly from his own experience as a novelist, generalizes astutely from Gissing's fiction:

> Behind his rage and querulousness there lay a perception that the horrors of life in late–Victorian England were largely unnecessary. The grime, the stupidity, the ugliness, the sex-starvation, the furtive debauchery, the vulgarity, the bad manners, the censoriousness — these things were unnecessary, since the puritanism of which they were a relic no longer upheld the structure of society ["George Gissing" 51].

Containing echoes of Gissing's life as well, these words indicate Orwell's perception of the novelist's overall viewpoint as well as particular areas of society that Gissing covers. Gissing returns time and again to the above themes. From Carrie Mitchell in *Workers in the Dawn* to Daniel Otway in *The Crown of Life* (1899), Gissing dramatizes the underside of life. Of course, Orwell's is not a complete list of subjects in his fiction, but they often predominate, frequently driving out other concerns. In another essay, Orwell remarks, "All books worth reading 'date,' and George Gissing, perhaps the best novelist England has produced, is tied more tightly than most writers to a particular place and time" ("'Not Enough Money'" 1). Gissing's sharp focus on his time gives one a powerful sense of that world, even now only partially recoverable. Orwell's merit is to recognize Gissing's close portrait of his "place and time" as an ongoing literary practice. Reviewers from the beginning have recognized this quality in his work.

Raymond Williams begins the chapter on Gissing in *Culture and Society* (1958) by focusing on the author's connection to his times:

> The interest of Gissing in the present context lies in two aspects of his work: his analysis of literature as a trade, which makes *New Grub Street* a minor classic; and his social observations and attitudes, in such novels as *The Nether World* and *Demos*, which provide evidence of a significant and continuing process [172–73].

After quoting Jasper Milvain's favorable contrast between himself and Edwin Reardon as writers in *New Grub Street*, Williams states, "And Gissing sees to it that these observations by Milvain, at the outset of his career, are amply justified by the action" (173). In effect, Gissing incorporates his ideas, feelings, and reactions to the world around him into his fiction, creating one of his most important novels in the process. Williams' discussion of certain of Gissing's characters' "negative identification" (175–76) with the poor, growing out of a disillusion with them and the possibility of social reform, is somewhat beside the point. Williams typifies this disillusion as a "document of a particular category of feeling" (175) or "documents, not of a discovered reality, but of their [rebels' and outcasts'] own emotional pressures and recoils" (177). However, it is through a combination of powerful emotion and sustained thought that the imagination presumably operates, a process that includes both the negative identification and, according to Williams, the more instructive example, its breakdown (178). Nonetheless, Williams notes, "After *New Grub Street*, Gissing returns to his proper study, that of the condition of exile and loneliness" (178–79), but the importance of these two latter themes lies not so much in their relevance to Gissing's life as to their places in the culture. His dramatization of these ideas both before and after 1891 is crucial to acquiring a lived feeling of his world.

This work will analyze Gissing's many ideas on nineteenth-century culture. They will appear in various combinations and with varied emphases from one novel to another. Some ideas will reveal themselves as more important, overall, than others by their repeated inclusion in his fiction. From these, by the significance of their use, one should distinguish a core of themes in his work. This core, or social dynamic, should signify the ultimate embodiment of Gissing's cultural vision. Determining this social dynamic is no easy matter since each novel has a different group of ideas that Gissing employs to tell the story. Over time, the themes change, in retrospect revealing groups of novels that thematically cohere. Some novels that connect in this way appear consecutively, or nearly so, and others generally have widely spaced periods of publication. In the first type, novels concerning urban poverty come in the 1880s. *Workers in the Dawn*, *The Unclassed* (1884, 1895), *Demos*, *Thyrza*, and *The Nether World* (1889) are examples. Each of these novels, of course, has a wider significance than the life and conditions of the poor. In *Workers in the Dawn*, Gissing raises the question of what the wealthy or moderately wealthy should do with their money. Do they have an obligation to help the poor and alleviate their conditions? *The Unclassed* treats the theme of prostitution in a social rather than simply a moral context. This ambiguous moral position caused the publisher George Bentley of Smith & Elder to decline the novel in 1883 (Mattheisen, Young, and Coustillas 2:189) while apparently still thinking of publishing Gissing's previously written novel, *Mrs. Grundy's Enemies*, a work that never appeared and is now lost. Novels dealing with an expanding lower-middle class are also of this first kind, for example, *In the Year of Jubilee* (1894), *The Paying Guest*, and *The Town Traveller* (1898). *Demos*, with the post-legacy Mutimer household, prefigures this type in a limited way, but Luckworth Crewe and Beatrice French from *In the Year of Jubilee* are more authentic representatives of a changing economic and social climate. Miriam Baske in *The Emancipated* (1890), emerging from her confined dissenting background of strict chapel going and thinking, might also fit this type though hers is a cultural rather than economic emancipation.

Isabel Clarendon (1886), *New Grub Street*, *Born in Exile* (1892), and *The Private Papers of Henry Ryecroft* (1903) are examples of Gissing's reexamination of themes throughout his career. *Isabel Clarendon*, a lesser work, introduces the troubled writer and intellectual in the character of Bernard Kingcote and the overworked writer and family man Thomas Meres, foreshadowing Edwin Reardon, Alfred Yule, and Sykes in *New Grub Street* and Henry Ryecroft in *The Private Papers of Henry Ryecroft*. Five years later, Gissing published his most important work; *New Grub Street* is the classic portrait of the artist rendered silent in a hostile environment. *Born in Exile*, appearing after *Denzil Quarrier* in 1892, while not featuring a troubled artist, once more takes up a related Gissing theme, the educated young man who has no means of connecting to a society that would value his gifts. In *The Haunted Study: A Social History of the English Novel 1875–1914* (1989), Peter Keating generally describes the young men's experiences as "the class-based torments experienced by Gissing's male characters" (168). Eleven years later, Gissing published *The Private Papers of Henry Ryecroft* in the year of his death. This autobiographical novel returns to many of the themes of *New Grub Street* and uses some of the same incidents. Both works are to some extent autobiographical, but Gissing somehow maintains a distance from the events, which allows him to make artistic use of them. While *Our Friend the Charlatan* also introduces a protagonist with insufficient means to make and keep himself known, the tone and direction of the novel are completely different from that of *Born in Exile* and the other works in this group. Dyce Lashmar makes a virtue of his near poverty. Lashmar reminds one of Oscar Wilde's Algernon Moncrieff in *The Importance of Being Earnest* (1895) whom his aunt Lady Bracknell says has only his debts to recommend him.

Any novelist presents a welter of themes that shift and overlap through a body of work, and Gissing's twenty-three novels are no exception. One could decide on a social dynamic for each novel and then choosing common themes, select the core ideas for his fiction. However, this rather mechanical process will not work. The titles of the various chapters in this book do not necessarily add up to a social dynamic for Gissing's fiction either. Rather, they are ways in, and through their analyses one should sense what is vital for the author. This sounds more intuitive than analytical and possibly the combination of ways of knowing will yield the most systematic understanding of Gissing's work. Continued discussion and analysis, even a dose of the critical imagination, if this is not an oxymoronic liberty, lead one to a certainty, however temporary. Matthew Arnold argues in "The Function of Criticism at the Present Time" (1865) that the critic can also participate in the "creative activity" (Richter 398). But with a social dynamic, one that almost settles and sorts itself, Gissing's imaginative portrait of nineteenth-century culture takes on a solidity and penetration that enables the seeker after that lost world to grasp a sense of it, the lived feel of it. Early twenty-first century readers have little hope of more than that, but it is worth the effort to allow Gissing and other creative writers to show the present day what they, at least partially, knew about their world. Through the imagination, one bridges that perhaps ultimately unbridgeable gap between past and present.

PART ONE

The Social Imagination

2

The Triumph of Mediocrity: Gissing's New Grub Street

Individual freedom and the struggle for existence leading to the survival of the fittest are two important ideas in social Darwinism. In combination, they theoretically lead to progress but in reality are largely incompatible. George Gissing, in whose novels John Goode says a social Darwinist "vocabulary is not uncommon" (*Ideology* 63), dramatizes the incompatibility of these two ideas in *New Grub Street*. Although in a Jan. 19, 187 [9], letter to his brother Algernon George said of Herbert Spencer, "He is perhaps our greatest living philosopher" (Mattheisen, Young, and Coustillas 1:142), the lives of Gissing's characters ironically portray the failure, rather than the achievement, of Spencer's ideas. In *New Grub Street*, Gissing shows that the struggle for existence does not lead to progress, especially in the lives of creative artists, but rather to a leveling process in which the independent artist is defeated and the mediocre triumphs. As John Peck states, "What [*New Grub Street*] begins to seem is a work primarily concerned with the questions of the relationship between man and his whole environment, a work about man and the modern city" (153). And in that environment, the one who adapts best lives to define the relationship.

Edwin Reardon and Jasper Milvain represent the independent, creative artist and the facile adapter, respectively. Oswald H. Davis describes their situation as "the tug of war between ideals and commerce represented respectively by Reardon and Milvain" (87). But before examining the conflict between the ideas Reardon and Milvain stand for, it might be instructive to look at Alfred Yule who illustrates a middle position between the two men and who illuminates Reardon's failure as well as Milvain's success. Yule, a hardworking literary journalist barely sustaining himself in the struggle for existence, a precariousness symbolized by his failing eyesight, covets the editorship of the "The Study" (*New Grub Street* 96–97). What signals Yule's lack of adaptability are the reasons for which he wants the position. Unlike Milvain, who looks to what sells, Yule wants the power to settle old scores the editorship will bring (97). He looks inwardly and desires to fulfill his own needs; he has no sense of a plan to create a journal that will respond to the market (96–97). Adaptation to market requirements would be anathema to Yule. As the narrator says of Yule's varied literary productions:

> He took his efforts *au grand sérieux*; thought he was producing works of art; pursued his ambition in a spirit of fierce conscientiousness. In spite of all, he remained only a journeyman [96].

At home, Yule is increasingly isolated in his study from family and friends after he fails to secure the editorship, and his prospects for a real literary success dim. Peck observes the "contrast between light and dark" (148) with regard to Reardon, but it is possible also to contrast the dark moodiness of Yule's character with the light, realistic but optimistic nature of Milvain's and align Yule with the greater darkness that overtakes Reardon in death.

Marian Yule, Yule's daughter and indispensable researcher, also occupies the middle ground between the independent, creative artist and the skillful adapter. However, she is closer in spirit to Reardon than Milvain, and her comparative failure in the end as she becomes a librarian in a provincial city deserted by Milvain in favor of Amy, formerly Reardon's wife, underscores Gissing's sense of the danger the artist faces. Marian does research and writing for her father and toward the end of the novel submits work in her own name (*New Grub Street* 505, 506), but prefers a different life:

> She kept asking herself what was the use and purpose of such a life as she was condemned to lead.... She herself would throw away her pen with joy but for the need of earning money [106–07].

However, she does her work honestly, and if no genius, she exhibits no personal animosity as her father lacks the desire to manipulate the public taste in Milvain's fashion. When Milvain expresses such sentiments, Marian feels annoyance and cannot or will not take him seriously. Her sense of integrity endangers her in Gissing's sharp delineation of a world in which only the adapter prospers. Possibly Milvain's feeling that Marian is "'dangerous'" (45) when he first meets her is a reflection not only that she will deter him from achieving his goals but that she also morally surpasses him. The incident in which Jasper and Marian wait for the train to pass under a bridge on which they are standing reinforces Gissing's main divisions between the artist and the adapter. To Milvain, the power of the train "'makes me feel eager to go back and plunge into the fight again'" (33). Marian responds, "'Upon me it has just the opposite effect'" (33). If Marian tends more to Reardon's than Milvain's response to the struggle that life necessitates, it is not hard to imagine the greater effect this struggle has on the artistic consciousness.

Leo Henkin in *Darwinism in the English Novel: 1860–1910: The Impact of Evolution on Victorian Fiction* (1963), writing of men like Milvain and Reardon, clearly portrays Gissing's view of the difficulties faced by the independent artist in the struggle for existence:

> *New Grub Street* paints the struggle both among books and among men in the literary world of Gissing's day. Natural selection plays the role of villain; for the adaptation of writers to their environment and to prevailing conditions is the basis of the action.... Those authors who can change their writings to suit the fickle public taste for the new will survive and live.... Others, those poor souls with ideals who have set themselves rigid rules of composition, can exist only so long as the public favors their particular brand of literature [230].

Milvain skillfully blends intelligence and will, meeting Henkin's criteria for a successful career. Reardon, however, lacks the necessary force to survive in the literary world. Goode remarks:

> [T]he distance between Dickens and Gissing is marked by Darwin. The struggle for success and recognition, the pleas of private benevolence, the belief in reform, give way to the struggle for survival, the sense of a world in which oppression is systematic and inescapable [*Ideology* 26].

In the end, Reardon stops writing and returns to a position at a hospital; he does not die from outright starvation but rather from a congestion in the lungs (*New Grub Street* 446).

At the beginning of *New Grub Street*, Reardon, a failing novelist, looks back to a happier time with Amy. The novel also begins at a crucial time in the lives of nearly every one of the major characters and ends with the death of Reardon and the marriage of Amy to Jasper Milvain. Reardon's struggles are continuous, but the necessity of grinding out another novel to support his family has defeated him. He tells his wife:

> "My will seems to be fatally weakened. I can't see my way to the end of anything; if I get hold of an idea which seems good, all the sap has gone out of it before I have got it into working shape" [*New Grub Street* 49].

A few pages later the narrator comments on Reardon:

> He was the kind of man who cannot struggle against adverse conditions, but

whom prosperity warms to the exercise of his powers. Anything like the
cares of responsibility would sooner or later harass him into unproductive-
ness [63].

Reardon's struggles, because of his own personality, increasingly narrow his
chances to succeed further as a writer. He cannot adapt to the prevailing conditions of the literary market. Although initially successful (61–63), not even
Amy and his child can motivate him to write once the pressure to produce
novels becomes a dominant emotional focus. As Milvain observes, only "'favorable circumstances'" and the liberty to write a "'fairly good book'" every two
years would free Reardon to be creative (6).

Reardon's early literary successes before marrying Amy appear to belie
the idea that only with a secure income would he be able to write. Through
two legacies (*New Grub Street* 57, 62), a device that Gissing uses elsewhere
in the novel, Reardon first moves to London and on the occasion of the second legacy leaves a fairly simple job at a London hospital to write full time.
When he takes the job at the hospital, the £200 from the first legacy is nearly
exhausted, and Reardon is in a "state of semi-starvation" (61). For the work
at the hospital, Reardon receives a pound a week (61). On this money he
"found that the impulse to literary production awoke in him more strongly
than ever" (61); however, the income is very modest and his job no sinecure.
Although Milvain makes his statement after Reardon's marriage, the question
still arises as to why he is able to write without a secure income. First, the
writing of Reardon's first two novels is entirely unrelated to his survival. Second, he then has no one else depending on him. The £400 legacy he receives
on the death of his grandfather encourages him to leave his hospital job. For
his third and fourth novels, Reardon receives £50 and £100 (63), respectively.
Money has definitely freed his creative powers. It is possible that Reardon,
alone and with no sense of struggle, could have continued to support himself from his writing. However, this is a transitional stage that, given his need
for love and affection, could not last. Ten weeks after meeting Amy Yule, Reardon marries her (64), and not long after this his true struggles begin. He cannot, owing to his social position and Amy's attitude toward the proprieties,
take another clerical job. He must succeed as a novelist, and this necessity
dries up his creative powers and leaves the abject figure encountered earlier.
Now, one realizes the significance of Milvain's statement that only "'favourable
circumstances'" (6) would free his creative powers in any long range way.
Neither the earlier legacies nor his job could have given him the necessary
security, since sooner or later Reardon's growth and development as a man
would have forced him into the step he actually takes, i.e., marriage, and
without a private income the struggle for survival would be too much for him.

Bernard Bergonzi in *The Turn of a Century* (1973) questions whether

Reardon could survive as an artist even with a secure income. Though the thrust of Gissing's novel supports an interpretation of environmental pressures leading to failure, Bergonzi's view that Reardon is constitutionally incapable of succeeding needs addressing:

> In such a world, where literature has become a commodity and its production a mechanical business, one may either accept the prevalent standards and try to succeed by them, which is the role freely adopted by Jasper Milvain, or one can vainly struggle against them in the interests of a nobler ideal of literature, as does Edwin Reardon. But Edwin's struggle is undermined, not merely by his weak and faltering temperament, but by a radical skepticism about values of any kind, which, as an up-to-date positivist of the eighties, he is unable to repress [53].

Certainly, Reardon at times appears to want to fail and thus to confirm Bergonzi's emphasis on the psychological as the primary locus of Reardon's defeat, but Gissing throughout the novel carefully constructs external reasons, e.g., lack of money and changing taste, for Reardon's predicament. What Bergonzi adds to an understanding of the novel and what deepens an appreciation of Gissing's craft is not so much Reardon's predisposition to failure as an inability to overcome difficulties. However, Jacob Korg locates the difficulty in the environment, "Industrial civilization rejects the art he [Reardon] offers it, and since he cannot manufacture a product adapted to the demands of the literary market, it calmly eliminates him" ("Spiritual" 248). Gissing starts with a temperamentally weak character and places him in a world where the necessity to struggle for success is paramount. Reardon, relieved of the prop that Milvain states will save him, is free to succumb; no heroic struggles emerge as he takes the path easiest for him. Thus, the harsh environment is structurally guaranteed to win as Gissing is transformed from a weak success to a certain failure. As John Halperin observes:

> The clash between art and materialism-between the creative man wanting to do something worthwhile and the circumstances of his life which force him to be mediocre or die — is at the center of *New Grub Street* [*Gissing* 148].

Reardon, writing in this climate of despair, cannot undo himself and thus cannot live.

Both Reardon and Harold Biffen, with the possible exception of Milvain Reardon's sole literary friend, display a self-destructive pride and independence that prevent them from seeking anyone's help at the most needed moments. When Milvain attempts to promote Reardon's next to last novel, the latter refuses his aid on artistic grounds even though it would have been financially remunerative to accept (*New Grub Street* 162). And Biffen, who in the past has borrowed from his brother, finally refuses to do so again (491), and his consequent, extreme poverty, coupled later with his frustrated passion for Amy, by then Reardon's widow, drives him to suicide (493). It is unlikely that if he had £400 a year he would kill himself. In *The Common Writer: Life in Nineteenth-Century Grub Street* (1985), Nigel Cross somberly appraises Biffen:

> The one character in *New Grub Street* who possesses unshakeable literary integrity is Harold Biffen, whose novel *Mr. Bailey, Grocer*, dealing with "absolute realism in the sphere of the ignobly decent," is the ultimate in unmarketable fiction [235].

Earlier, Reardon addresses Biffen after the latter's novel appears: "'I have a superstitious faith in "Mr. Bailey." If he leads you to triumph, don't altogether forget me.'" Biffen's reply appears to underscore the failure of both men's lives: "'Don't talk nonsense'"(436). Just as Amy's presence and pressure cannot help Reardon, neither does the friendship between Reardon and Biffen enable them to prosper in an alien world. They are examples of Michael Collie's fundamental observation: "That Gissing saw social disintegration in contemporary, evolutionary terms is quite clear (*Alien Art* 159). Reardon and Biffen cannot fight a power greater than themselves that destroys more than just themselves. André Guillaume, although he minimizes their struggles, fairly accurately sums up the situation of Reardon, Alfred Yule, Marian Yule, and Biffen: "There is no literary darwinism about them, as they in no wise exemplify the survival of the fittest, but passively live out the life of the oppressed and weak" ("Jamesian Pattern,1984," 33). Certainly, neither man, given their temperaments, can be one of those few benefactors of mankind Gissing envisions in his *Commonplace Book*: "The progress of the masses is by no means due to general effort among them, but to the hard struggle against universal sluggishness of a very few energetic men, - mostly in the enlightened class" (53). However much needed, these few "enlightened" ones who might reverse the disintegration hardly ever appear in Gissing's fiction. As he states in *Notes on Social Democracy*, "[T]hey [the masses] must be, in every sense of the word, educated to progress" (14). But, in a letter on March 5, 1891, to Eduard Bertz a few months after finishing *New Grub Street*, Gissing stated that he did not expect to live to see any "spiritual growth" that may result from material progress (Mattheisen, Young, and Coustillas 4:276).

In contrast to Reardon, Jasper Milvain adapts ideally to the literary market. His advice to his sisters, Dora and Maud, to begin an authorial career reveals his sharp awareness of future trends:

> "I maintain that we people of brains are justified in supplying the mob with the food it likes. We are not geniuses, and if we sit down in a spirit of long-eared gravity we shall produce only commonplace stuff. Let us use our wits to earn money, and make the best we can of our lives. If only I had the skill, I would produce novels out-trashing the trashiest that ever sold fifty thou-

sand copies.... For my own part, I shan't be able to address the bulkiest mul-
titude.... I shall write for the upper middle-class of intellect, the people who
like to feel that what they are reading has some special cleverness, but who
can't distinguish between stones and paste" [*New Grub Street* 13–14].

Milvain, conscious of his own limitations and the world in which he must
exist and rejecting any claim to the role of an independent, creative artist,
has no illusions as to what is needed in the literary marketplace. Toward the
end of the book, Jasper discusses with Dora the future of Harold Biffen's
"realistic" novel and comments on the work of Reardon's friend, 'The struggle for existence among books is nowadays as severe as among men'" (456).
Milvain, in clear social Darwinist language, skillfully connects the literary
world with the larger world; he is to succeed in both. J. P. Michaux, in examining the significance of names in *New Grub Street*, notes the first syllable of
Milvain's name:

> [A] mill can also be a pugilistic encounter, and there is no doubt that here
> again is underlined the Darwinian theory of adaptability of the survival of
> the fittest: Milvain loses no opportunity and he sacrifices Marian's love to
> reach his goal ["Names, 1981" 205–06].

Robert L. Selig maintains that Milvain suffers, like Reardon and Biffen, from
"a similar alienation, a debilitating isolation from full human contact" ("Valley, 1981," 171). But, Milvain's "alienation" leaves him with Amy and the monetary and sexual comforts, among others, that she brings, thus an alienation
only from what the more genuine artist would seek but not what society
would admire and reward. Adrian Poole in *Gissing in Context* (1975), commenting on *New Grub Street* and in words that clearly apply to Milvain, goes
even further than Selig's idea of alienation: "There is a strong evolutionary
thesis underlying the narrative, according to which physical victory and moral
degeneration are interconnected" (146). At the end of the novel, "Jasper [lies]
back in dreamy bliss" (515) listening to Amy play and sing, creating an image
almost of decadence when one remembers the lives of those lost or discarded,
e.g., Reardon, Reardon and Amy's child Willie, Biffen, and Marian.

Additional characters further elaborate Gissing's despairing portrait of
the creative artist. Whelpdale and his wife, the practical Dora Milvain, succeed in the literary world. While Reardon declines artistically, Whelpdale initially flounders, trying one direction after another from novelist (*New Grub
Street* 148) to literary adviser (165), before succeeding in such a way that not
only reinforces the image of Milvain's success and methods but comes dan-
gerously close to caricaturing them. However, the danger is avoided in the
most convincing manner. Whelpdale changes the name of a magazine from
"Chat" to "Chit-Chat" and is immediately successful (478–79). The half-
literate reading public has its supreme vehicle with articles designed exclu-

sively for its taste and abilities. If there is a center of mediocrity in the literary world, Whelpdale triumphantly occupies it. In contrast, Milvain's views verge on the highbrow but only in contrast, if one remembers Milvain's statements on the writer's calling. Dora's success with children's stories (458) is also less subservient to the lowest taste than Whelpdale's, but it is plainly commercial in origin (269). Whelpdale's cheerful vulgarity is his one redeeming feature; he acknowledges his aims without hypocrisy (459–60).

Gissing's position in "The Hope of Pessimism" is that resignation and withdrawal from the world's strife are the only answers; the competition for existence, no matter what it may bring, is not worth the consequent travail (96–97). However, characters such as Milvain happily work to achieve what the world considers success with scarcely a doubt as to the terms exacted for it. Possibly the independent artist can maintain his position only by a stance such as Ryecroft's, who, looking back on his literary life, states:

> Hateful as is the struggle for life in every form, this rough-and-tumble of the literary arena seems to me sordid and degrading beyond all others. Oh, your prices per thousand words! ... And oh, the black despair that awaits those down trodden in the fray [*The Private Papers of Henry Ryecroft* 52].

Ryecroft, a blend of Reardon and Milvain, "withered by his struggle within the pattern of modern civilization" (Cope, 1957, 133), survives only by leaving the arena with a legacy (*Ryecroft* 99). Reardon, left in the literary battle, cannot adapt and is dragged down from his state of precarious emotional and material independence. Freedom, if the struggle for survival is too great and the person too weak, is freedom only to fail.

3

Deception, Violence, and the Criminal Act

Given the subject matter of George Gissing's novels, it is surprising that crime and violence do not occupy a larger place in his fiction than they do. *Workers in the Dawn*, his first novel, pictures in part the degraded life of London's poorest classes among whom the delicate child Arthur Golding finds himself at his father's death after running away from the Rev. Edward Norman's country home and returning to the city. And yet, the poverty and the portrait of a world seemingly corrupt and violent at its foundations serve more as backdrops than present, inescapable conditions. One reads of these circumstances, if not as mere afterthoughts, at least not as so finally determinable of human aspirations even when Golding and Helen Norman, the two principal characters, observe them directly. In later novels, violence is largely mass violence (*Demos*, *The Nether World*, *In the Year of Jubilee*) and can be avoided, at least by the middle class, through a careful arrangement of their lives. In *George Gissing* (1995), Robert L. Selig describes the masses in *The Nether World*: "the workers choose despicable entertainments: bread and circuses at the Crystal Palace, barrelfuls of beer, and fights among the mob" (35). However, in Gissing's fiction, in addition to several shootings and assaults, suicide, prostitution, fraud, and theft appear more prominently, the cases of suicide an ironic echo of the futility that invests some of his characters' lives. With Godwin Peak in *Born in Exile* and Dyce Lashmar in *Our Friend the Charlatan*, Gissing delineates, as noted in Chapter One, two striking portraits of men who believe themselves cut off, although Lashmar does not feel alienated, from a society they have a right to join. They operate through deceit and deception, illegally or bordering on illegality, to break through society's limitations on their desires for advancement. In *The Haunted Study: A Social History of the English Novel 1875–1914*, Peter Keating remarks:

> The uncertainty that [James and Conrad] now constantly expressed about the motivation of their own characters' actions was shared by many other authors; by Gissing, for example, in the moral ambivalence that is a central theme of novels like *Born in Exile* and *Our Friend the Charlatan*, and by many writers of the new subgenres [396].

Thus, Gissing's portrayal of crime in late Victorian England ironically minimizes physical violence and emphasizes illegal or near-illegal acts in which trickery rather than seizure plays the principal role.

Gissing's novels generally eschew explicit violence in a potentially violent world. While he writes in an August 5, 1900, letter to Eduard Bertz, "I have grown to abhor Zola's grossness" (Mattheisen, Young, and Coustillas 8:74), *Workers in the Dawn* parallels the metaphorical violence of *L'Assommoir* (1877) and *Nana* (1880) with its emphasis on the negative effects of alcohol, greed, and prostitution. The corrupting conditions of the lives of some, if not all, of the poor strip them of their humanity and reduce them to a kind of predatory voraciousness. Some can rise above the poverty around them, but for every Samuel Tollady and Will Noble, Arthur's guardian and friend, respectively, Gissing shows a John Pether who functions almost as a barometer of society's inhumanity to man. Henry Ryecroft in *The Private Papers of Henry Ryecroft* resembles Pether, minus the rage, in that he goes almost reeling into his retirement from society's symbolic pummeling of his spirit. Ryecroft has before him a quiet rural existence but no chance of recovery. No more does Pether who dies in misery of spirit. And yet, there are some acts of violence in *Workers in the Dawn*. While armed with the moral purity of her acts and vision, Helen Norman can walk the poorer quarters of London unaccompanied, but Carrie Mitchell's lifestyle as a prostitute endangers her as she suffers the hard life of the streets. However, Gissing does not limit actual violence to the lower classes in this novel. Maud Gresham Waghorn, daughter of the painter Gilbert Gresham, also suffers abuse, in this case from her husband, John Waghorn. In neither instance is there recourse to the law. Maud's superior social position does allow her to redress the imbalance between herself and her husband; Carrie, on the other hand, suffers from the abuse, trapped by her alcoholism.

The Whirlpool (1897) exhibits one of the few examples of a killing in Gissing's work. One year after the publication of the novel, Gissing, in his *Charles Dickens: A Critical Study* (1898), states his dislike for the theme of murder. Discussing *The Mystery of Edwin Drood* (1870), he writes:

> One cannot help wishing that Dickens had chosen another subject — one in

which there was neither mystery nor murder, both so irresistibly attractive to him, yet so far from being the true material of his art. Surely it is unfortunate that the last work of a great writer should have for its theme nothing more human than a trivial mystery woven about a vulgar deed of blood [56].

In *The Whirlpool*, Hugh Carnaby accidentally kills Cyrus Redgrave when he thinks that his wife Sybil is having an affair with him. The situation is ludicrous and parallels Alma Rolfe's ineffectual efforts in the same novel to establish a career as a violinist. Carnaby serves two years in prison, another oddity in Gissing's fiction.

Demos presents a special case of the role of violence in the novels. First, inter-class tensions create a sense of possible violence and conflict. This is initially a somewhat paradoxical example since the classes generally live separate lives. With the Walthams, Eldons, and the Rev. Wyvern on one hand and the Mutimers and many of their working-class friends on the other, Gissing initiates social forces that fatally interact, clashing, intermingling, glancing off, and ultimately falling back into the original groupings as if by a natural process. Of course, all is not harmony in either the lower or upper class in the novel. The Mutimers represent the principal lower-class focus with Emma Vine and her sister Jane and Richard Mutimer's friends and associates, especially Daniel Dabbs, also important. Richard Mutimer is the central lower-class figure in the novel. His sister Alice and his brother Harry are necessary appendages that provide the color and limitations of the world from which Richard attempts to escape. Mrs. Mutimer acts as a class force that cannot be moved from her home and circumstances. After Richard builds his house in New Wanley, she eventually returns to her former environment in London. Alice, a pretty, vulgar girl, cannot be restrained by Richard, titular head of the family, and makes a bad marriage to Willis Rodman, a shady character who sometimes beats her. Harry is weak and veers into petty crime with Rodman. While Richard has no quarrel early on with his mother, he fails in his attempt to instill his socialist principles into either Alice or Harry. They resist all his efforts to look beyond their immediate desires. Prior to his inheritance, Richard is a union leader who organizes the workers with a genuine sense that he does good — hence his attraction for Emma Vine. Emma is an anomaly, a naturally refined woman who owes her refinement to no class. Richard's rejection of her for the upper middle-class Adela Waltham says nothing against Emma but reveals the steady corruption of Richard's purpose. Adela's feelings of revulsion toward him finally indicate Richard's failure as a man.

The marriages of Alice Mutimer and Willis Rodman and Adela Waltham and Richard Mutimer release the forces of violence, physical and verbal, respectively. Richard warns Alice about Rodman's character, and after their marriage, Rodman suppresses Alice, robbing her of her sense of life and vitality. The beatings she suffers underscore the degradation and lifelessness to which he reduces her. Richard's potential for violence, clearly class-based, shows itself when he is forced to give up what he thought he had lawfully inherited. Adela's private evaluations of him gain substance from her class background, though her marriage to him in the first place makes her denunciations somewhat suspect. However, disgusted by him, Adela is superior to his rages, and only his death at the hands of a mob relieves her of her marriage burden. Adela's subsequent marriage to Hubert Eldon, the man she originally planned to marry but rejected, lays the ground for a last, symbolic act of violence. Hubert is discovered to be the rightful heir to Wanley. Richard had built a factory and houses for the workers, calling his creation New Wanley. But Hubert, supported by his confidant the Rev. Wyvern and surveying what he feels is the devastation of a beautiful valley, plans to dig it up entirely and restore the land to its natural state. This he does, and no traces exist of New Wanley as he later shows the results of his actions to Adela.

Noteworthy are the acts of violence aimed at oneself. While Gissing depicts many characters who patiently bear their sufferings and live out exemplary lives, Arthur Golding in *Workers in the Dawn*, Lilian Northway Quarrier in *Denzil Quarrier*, and Harold Biffen in *New Grub Street* commit suicide after failing to gain a loved one or, in the case of Lilian, feeling a burden to a loved one. None of the novels is a successful love story, with the possible exception of the early parts of *Denzil Quarrier*. For Golding and Biffen, their inability to achieve a lasting romantic connection occurs at the end of so many hopeless struggles that other reasons might well serve for their deaths. Golding falls in love with Helen Norman who lives with her guardian Gilbert Gresham. Through no fault of Helen's or Arthur's, they become estranged. Subsequently, Arthur meets Carrie Mitchell, and they marry. After many bitter experiences with Carrie's drunkenness and her relationship with her prostitute friends, they separate though Arthur continues to give her money. When Arthur receives a legacy from the Rev. Norman, Helen's father, he begins to paint in earnest and again renews his contact with Helen. Later, she learns of his marriage to Carrie and ends their relationship. This and her death profoundly affect Arthur. Many incidents lead to Arthur's suicide, but one senses that his dramatic leap over Niagara Falls at the end of the novel is nearly inevitable. This act parallels his father's death through drink, surely as clear an act of suicide as his son's. Golding's merging auditorily and physically with the watery maelstrom underscores his desire to be overwhelmed and to obliterate himself in the process of dying.

Lilian Northway Quarrier also takes her life, as she feels it closing in and shutting off possible avenues of escape to a sense of vitality and hope. This will be examined more extensively in Chapter 10. She, however, has an observer and would-be savior in the feminist Mrs. Wade who, admittedly with mixed emotions but with no real attempt to save her, watches her drown. John Halperin says of Lilian, "She is a sort of female Arthur Golding, tied to a lower-class spouse while courting a middle-class lover. Arthur, of course, is saved from immorality by Helen Norman's rectitude — but his end is the same as Lilian's" (*Gissing* 170). While not as physically isolated as Arthur at the end, she is socially and emotionally shut off from aid. After earlier telling Quarrier of her marriage to Arthur James Northway (*Denzil Quarrier* 106), Lilian and Quarrier eventually pretend to marry in Paris (111, 125). Eustace Glazzard's subsequent threat to reveal her supposed bigamy frightens her more for Quarrier's sake than her own. However, he refuses to let that interrupt their life together. This puts an emotional burden on Lilian, one that she can only lift by sacrificing herself. Her suicide differs from that of Golding's or Biffen's in that she believes her act aids someone besides her. Thinking little of herself, she does not realize the loss that Quarrier will feel. He is independently wealthy and could easily sacrifice his political career, retiring into private life with the woman he loves. This aspect of Lilian's suicide, so different in another way from Golding's and Biffen's who have no one that cares for them intimately, connects her to those who commit acts of violence toward others. Lilian violates the trust of Quarrier as effectively as Waghorn in *Workers in the Dawn* and Mutimer in *Demos* do those with whom they are involved.

However much he might have wished it, Harold Biffen cannot connect with anyone in any meaningful way after Reardon's death. John Goode remarks that "Biffen will die, ultimately, of loneliness" (*Ideology* 140). Impecunious, proud, and sensitive, Biffen is destined to fail, even more so than Reardon, whose illness at the end causes his death and prevents a reconciliation with Amy. Biffen visits Amy a few times after Reardon's death — she always represented to him the ideal woman — but at his second call he realizes that she receives him with a questioning courtesy. Once his body is found in Putney Heath, where he achieves a final isolation, Biffen is reduced to no more than a sympathetic comment between Amy and Jasper Milvain, her future husband. Gissing may have felt this to be a proper end to those who persist in taking pupils, writing novels, and studying Latin and Greek, ominously suggestive of his own life, but the very image of Biffen's death is destructive of the social fabric. The heath is ostensibly a place of rest and recreation, a place to relieve the stresses of modern life, not a place to emphasize one's inability to bear them anymore. This is not to blame the victim but rather to examine Gissing's use of this action. He seems subtly to suggest that the attainment of some of the best qualities in human life, e.g., love, kindness, tolerance, support for others, learning, hard work, will not suffice to live in a world that not only breaks people but prevents them from knowing one another. If there is no sense of lamentation in Biffen's portrait, he is a lamentable figure, a failure in an unknowing and largely uncaring society.

Prostitution and theft are two other criminal categories that reflect Gissing's use of the self and others as targets. Gissing's inward and outward focuses, the individual consciousness and the social structure, intermingle and give depth to his fiction. The first two novels, *Workers in the Dawn* and *The Unclassed*, use the idea of prostitution in strikingly different ways. While it might be difficult to see Carrie Mitchell as more than a reflection of Nell, Gissing's first wife, she has a sufficiently dramatized life to argue for a separate consideration. Arthur Golding meets Carrie in a lodging house kept by Carrie's aunt. When Mrs. Pettindund discovers that her niece is pregnant, she forces her onto the street. Carrie's middle-class lover ("'A.W.,'" 2:56), of course, does not marry her, the child dies, and only Arthur's timely rescue saves her life. At this point, Carrie has not become a prostitute, but she later meets women, especially Polly Hemp, who are. Once the conventional seduction and abandonment are past and Arthur has found Carrie and then marries her, Carrie's unconventional route to a life on the streets begins. Arthur tries to educate her, but the beautiful but barely literate Carrie, possessed of a vulgar nature, fundamentally resists his efforts to lift her up to another level of existence. It is important to realize that Carrie's long final descent into the underworld begins from a position of safety after the earlier danger has receded. Many a Victorian heroine has gone from a sheltered life into one of danger and poverty, but Carrie has survived. Gissing's focus is on temperament even more than on character, though the latter is the final area in which Carrie fails. However, she does not have the temperament to read and study; she cannot live a quiet, respectable life; and these attitudes have not been encouraged by her first dangerous experience of being alone with a child and with no way to support herself. It is not that the prostitute and alcoholic come out in Carrie but that she is impatient of any outward restraint and too morally weak to impose necessary restraints on herself. Gissing may have seen this as a class characteristic, but one might equally portray her as an individual who fails because of her own nature. In contrast, Ida Starr in *The Unclassed* does recover and largely due to her own efforts to live a different life.

Gissing describes another interesting facet of Carrie's personality. She has a vestigial desire to change her ways and so returns to Arthur on more than one occasion. Each time he nurses her back to health, and for a while she is quiet and sober, but the old restlessness returns, and she secretly begins to drink and visit her disreputable friends. The possibility of reform exists, but the probability that she will alter her life is remote. At this point, the Carrie, degraded both physically and emotionally, who reveals to Helen Norman through Lucy Venning the truth of her marriage to Arthur (*Workers in the Dawn* 2.354–55), lies in the future. Gissing describes her on her early returns to Arthur as still possessing beauty and the necessary sentiment to appeal to him. However, her inner and outer lives do not then match. Later, they do, and Gissing's portrait of her is one that shows her as irredeemably fallen. This certainly suggests religious overtones that are absent from the agnostic Gissing's intellectual framework but not absent from a morality without God felt by Helen Norman and Arthur Golding. So much conventional abhorrence of lower-class attitudes and practices is mixed up with Gissing's supposed moral positions that one cannot always clearly distinguish one from the other.

What is striking in Golding's recoil from the lost Carrie is the reversal of gender roles. Frequently in Victorian fiction, the woman appears by nature morally superior to the man. Gissing will occasionally write of female purity as if it were somehow removed from its biological and social influences. Everard Barfoot, however, speaks to Rhoda Nunn in *The Odd Women* in a different vein. She generally agrees with him that women, in their present condition, are not deserving of much respect, but she does not go so far as to say that they are by nature prone to immorality. Both she and Mary Barfoot, Everard's cousin, are arguments for a womanhood superior to the male, one who can live on a higher moral plane. And, Everard's choice of Agnes Brissenden seems to imply a loftier female version than the general run of modern women whom he knows or observes. As Gissing makes clear, it is the man, afflicted with sexual desire in his youth, who bears the greater moral burden. Helen Norman breaks off her relationship with Arthur Golding though she loves him. Would the same situation occur in reverse or would Golding act as the eponymous Denzil Quarrier does when he overlooks Lilian's marriage because he still wants her? Finding nothing for which to live after Helen's death, Golding commits suicide. Lilian drowns herself with Quarrier still alive and in love with her. Carrie's prostitution effaces her from Golding's life in deeper and more profound ways than simple moral repugnance would allow.

It is no wonder that *The Unclassed* shocked the Victorian reading public. A principal character as a prostitute is strong enough but having her mother one as well transgresses the limits of a Mudie-influenced middle class. While the heroine, Ida Starr, has abandoned her erstwhile profession, a necessary move, she demands the reader's interest and sympathy by virtue of her position in the novel. She is no anti-heroine; she operates, with Osmond Waymark, as the focus of the moral and emotional interest in the work. Except for the naturalistic detail, Emile Zola's *Nana* is far more in keeping with conventional moral attitudes of the late-nineteenth century; disease and a horrible death seem the inevitable outcome to her life. This juxtaposition allows one to recover Gissing's radical position in *The Unclassed*. Ida's shift from prostitute to one who benefits the poor and works for her living in morally acceptable ways lies at the source of the social and moral heresy she represents. Ida as a suicide or Ida as one who shuts herself away from the gaze of the moral, forever to be shunned, is a more expected image. She not only does not do that; she has the temerity to live as the moral equal to those who have not sunk to her former level. Gissing seems to imply that she bears no moral stain. Dickens's portrait of Martha in *David Copperfield* (1850) prior to her salvation through marriage to a farm laborer after her emigration to Australia illustrates his unerring insight into the Victorian moral position on prostitution (Ch. 63, 862). When David and Mr. Peggotty talk with her in London as they attempt to find Emily, Peggotty's niece, she acts as, and they initially, if involuntarily, respond to her as, a leper. The scene is at night on a riverbank, symbolic of her probable launching point when life overcomes her; she appears withdrawn, cut off (Ch. 47, 677–80). Ida, far from a minor, shadowy figure, could not be more diametrically opposed to the pre-reclaimed Martha. Pierre Coustillas writes, "When in *The Unclassed* (1884) he took up the subject of fallen girls and their possible reclamation, he again gave way to his youthful illusions" ("Gissing's Feminine Portraiture," 93, 1963). Yet, Ida speaks and acts with little authorial special pleading, giving the reader few options but to accept or reject her depiction. Ida's lack of sufficient penitence, her ultimate vindication against Harriet Casti's false charge of theft, her inheritance equally with Osmond Waymark, and their eventual marriage place her in a socially safe position. John Sloan states:

> Ida's shame does not derive from the experiences of her past life — her inner self has, after all, remained inviolate. It derives from the disaccord between her inner sense of worth and society's judgement. It is a social injury that demands society's absolution [*Cultural,* 35]

Lady Ogram's social elevation in *Our Friend the Charlatan*, in which she rises from the working classes to become a successful actress and then marry well, is not as thorough-going a change as Ida's.

Theft is probably the simplest form of criminal behavior in Gissing's fiction, but it occurs frequently. For all the graphic pictures of human suffering, he seldom turns to actual crime either to dramatize his characters' plights or to employ them as a means of changing their material circumstances. Gissing might react to their vulgarity with unconcealed dislike, but he does not over-represent their criminal acts. In fact, in the novels of the 1880s, it is not solely the working class but the lower-middle class as well that steals. In *The Unclassed*, Harriet Casti's false charge of theft against Ida Starr is no clear-cut class attack since Harriet is married to the poet Julian Casti and Ida is loved by the novelist Osmond Waymark. The two men move slightly upward in class by their intellectual pursuits, and Ida also changes class through the alterations in her life. In *Demos*, Richard Mutimer is a more ideologically drawn figure. A working-class leader, he inherits money and marries the middle-class Adela Waltham. When an earlier will is found that disinherits him, he wishes to destroy it, but Adela persuades him not to and in the process comes to see him as beneath her. This illegal delay in bringing forth the will grows, for Adela, from the baseness and vulgarity in his character. In this instance, Gissing seems to portray Mutimer's act as a natural response to temptation by someone at his class level. Of course, Emma Vine and her sister, working-class women, argue against this type-casting. Bob Hewett, in *The Nether World*, counterfeits, at one time a capital offense; he is another lower-class man who turns to crime when opportunities present themselves. However, in *A Life's Morning* (1888), James Hood, Emily's father, a faithful clerk to the wealthy Richard Dagworthy, steals money from Dagworthy to replace his hat when his own is lost through a railway carriage window. Hood is a respectable, lower-middle class family man, and in his case, Gissing has located the cause for his criminal act in larger social forces than merely class. This social determinism, situated everywhere and nowhere, that requires a man to wear a hat out of doors, is beyond anyone's control and is as omnipresent as the wind.

In the Year of Jubilee's Nancy Lord knowingly deceives the Barmbys, executors of her father's will, by secretly marrying Lionel Tarrant and later living on her illegally obtained inheritance. This bald statement of the fact, employing the plot cliché of a will, does not reveal Gissing's subversive position *vis-à-vis* her crime. He, of course, adds a child to the mix and Tarrant's unconventional desire to live apart from his wife while concealing the marriage. Possibly, Tarrant's decision is not so unusual except for the fact that he continues the conjugal pattern of separate living after the truth of their relationship surfaces. What is subversive of the spirit of the law and middle-class morality is Nancy and Lionel's assertion of private versus public good. First, the generational conflict between Nancy and her father reveals a weakened patriarchal authority. Stephen Lord literally cannot control his daughter. She and to a lesser extent her brother Horace represent a new generation, with sufficient money for leisure replacing the hard necessity of earning it. Their various reactions to their father take place against the background of a home in which they could live if obedient. Even in disobedience, they are not absolutely forced to change their ways. A second, rather crowded background to Nancy's willful acts involves several diverse characters. Jessica Morgan, Nancy's friend and confidante, who betrays her to the Barmbys, the younger of whom wishes to marry Nancy, is a conflicted example of Gissing's belief in improved education for women leavened with a doubt as to their ability

to master really difficult subjects. Possibly, Gissing himself never satisfactorily worked out his position on this subject. While Jessica Morgan is a distinct character and while her type of limited intellectual capacities is liable
to appear in both women and men, she reflects the worst kind of intellectual
ambition, i.e., that mixed with vanity and supported by weak gifts. Two other
background characters to Nancy's position are Arthur and Ada Peachey. Situated on the same class level as Nancy, their situation signifies to Gissing
more nightmare than reality. Echoes of Edith Underwood, Gissing's second
wife, sound throughout Ada's portrait; her uncontrollable outbursts drive the
innocent Arthur to distraction.

Gissing, in an often casual way, includes deceit and deception in his
novels. And, he does this with little sense of moral fervor. In fact, moral cru-
sading was apparently furthest from Gissing's mind in his fictional explorations of late-nineteenth-century society. Two novels especially show
Gissing's diverse attitude toward the themes of deceit and deception: *Born in
Exile* and *Our Friend the Charlatan*. The latter novel, probably only equaled
by *The Town Traveller* and *The Paying Guest* in its exuberant embrace of life,
has its roots in the picaresque tradition. Dyce Lashmar, the protagonist, goes
from one desperate situation to another and usually recovers his energy and
spirit regardless of embarrassing exposures and failures. Except possibly for
Jasper Milvain and Whelpdale in *New Grub Street*, Lashmar is the antithesis
of the usual alienated and despairing Gissing hero. Given a compelling vision,
some recover from misfortune as does Piers Otway in *The Crown of Life*. By
his very strangeness, one could well argue that Lashmar owes his existence
more to a literary tradition than Gissing's fictionalization of some aspect of
his own world. Passing off a socio-biological theory as his own, Lashmar
drops it with insouciance when exposed as a plagiarist. Rejected by one
woman, May Tomalin, he turns to another for the second time, Constance
Bride, only to be spurned once more. From that state, he falls, disgruntled,
into the arms of Iris Woolstan who has admired him all along. Only a
magnificently experienced ego would allow one to suffer humiliation, and
suffer it knowingly, but still revive with an intact self. Sloan observes, "For
Gissing's charlatans the inner and the outer worlds are always separate. Indeed,
it is their very capacity to separate them which guarantees their survival in
an individualistic age still bound to moral formulae" (*Cultural* 21). Gissing's
success in this novel lies, in part, in his uncommon examination of the life
of an uncommon fraud.

Juxtaposing Lashmar with Godwin Peak in *Born in Exile*, one immediately notices the difference in tone. Jacob Korg states:

> Unlike Godwin Peak, Lashmar is a wholehearted opportunist, incapable of
> moral conflict or remorse. *Our Friend the Charlatan* does not address itself to

a moral problem, as *Born in Exile* did, but is concerned with the simpler satisfaction of showing a villain defeated by his own schemes [*George Gissing* 237].

Driven by his own family and social complaints, Peak's is a darker portrait, one compelled by a bitter awareness of the gulf between the classes and the isolation of the man of brains but no means in such a world. Gillian Tindall argues, "The loss of personal integrity is nowhere so completely illustrated as in *Born in Exile*" (*The Born Exile* 137). Disgusted with the masses and desiring a relationship with a cultured, refined woman of the middle class, Peak lies about his religious beliefs. It is a harsh irony for one of Gissing's temperament to portray religion as the place that surrounds a man's sexual desires. Not just outward piety but real belief, a belief on which one rests hopes for this world and the next, are the initial foundations for Sidwell Warricombe's life. Also, she despises radicalism and stands in her quiet way for the old traditions, although talk with Peak expands her views. She desires nothing more than to live in her Devonshire home and see and experience all that she has seen and experienced before. Sidwell's binary female opposite is Marcella Moxey, in love with Godwin Peak but unable to attract him. Peak and she see society in the same way, as a force that needs overturning and redirecting, but he also wants desperately to exorcise all aspects of his former poverty and lower-class origins. To him, Marcella is sexually unattractive; he can find no way through the mind to value her. This situation resembles Halperin's observation of Osmond Waymark in *The Unclassed*:

> Waymark's sexual fantasy is the same as Golding's in *Workers in the Dawn*: to be married to a respectable woman (Maud Enderby, the successor of Helen Norman) while sleeping with a decidedly less respectable one (Ida Starr, an ex-prostitute, a Carrie Mitchell with self-respect) [*Gissing* 53].

The difference between Peak and Waymark is that Peak has now focused his desire on the respectable woman; she excites him in a more comprehensive way than Maud does Waymark.

Gissing's inclusion of criminal behavior and deception in his fiction reflects the human condition. Lacking a sustained view of crime's danger to society, he nonetheless portrays its irremediable presence. His characters weave in and out of the threads of crime and violence that they encounter and that they, usually successfully, learn to untangle. Like the biblical poor, they seem to expect criminality to be with them always but not overpower their private hopes or public expectations.

4

New People: George Gissing's Rising Classes

Gissing, hater of the masses, could neither stop from writing about them nor marrying two of them. Forced to live among the London poor after returning from his American exile in 1877, Gissing shortly afterward began writing *Workers in the Dawn*, setting the novel in the East London slums. Four of his next six novels also deal with the working classes. With *Demos: A Story of English Socialism* and *The Nether World*, Gissing was to gain a reputation as a realistic portrayer of the poor. His grim and graphic descriptions worked against his financial success as a novelist. Notwithstanding Raymond Williams' assertion in *Culture and Society* that Gissing is the "spokesman" of "the despair born of social and political disillusion" (175), Gissing's working-class and lower-middle class characters are not easily kept down. In fact, whether in their numbers, and thus representing the mob, or their energy, the lower strata of society both make their presences felt and imagined and push themselves into the world of business. For every refined and gentle member of the working class such as Samuel Tollady and Lucy Venning in *Workers in the Dawn*, Emma Vine in *Demos*, and Sidney Kirkwood and Jane Snowdon in *The Nether World*, Gissing fills his novels with others ranging from the criminal to the entrepreneur whose chief assets are energy and imagination. Luckworth Crewe in *In the Year of Jubilee*, whom Robert L. Selig describes as "a shrewd but uncultivated advertising agent" (*George Gissing* 66), is a good example of the latter. Evenhandedly, Gissing includes women and men in both categories.

40

While from *The Emancipated* on Gissing focuses largely on the middle-class, working-class and lower-middle class characters and environments disturb the action. In *Born in Exile*, Godwin Peak withdraws from Whitelaw College when his uncle Nicholas Peak plans to open a café opposite the college entrance. And, in *The Paying Guest*, Louise Derrick, the daughter of a successful lower-middle class entrepreneur, nearly breaks up the Mumford suburban household with her intemperate ways. Thus, Gissing's force from below threatens to reshape British society in its own image regardless of the interests or desires of the higher social classes.

Gissing draws contrasting portraits of working-class despair and rage and working-class energy and vitality, with the preponderance going to the latter. Not all of these are admirable figures since occasionally their efforts go to satisfy only themselves. No one could deny that Clem Peckover in *The Nether World* is a dominant figure in her sphere, limited only by her mother's superior knowledge of ways to harm others, especially her servant, Jane Snowdon. Clem puts into effect her mother's suggestions on ways to make Jane's life miserable; only the former's narrow range prevents her from being a wider social menace. But, she elaborates on her mother's none-too-loving intentions toward Jane. Clem finds satisfaction in harming the young girl whom Sidney Kirkwood's kindness and her grandfather Michael Snowdon's return from abroad rescue from serious danger. Luckworth Crewe from *In the Year of Jubilee*, an up-and-coming man, has a more extensive view on how to employ his energies. Crewe works "in advertising," though that phrase possibly implies more today than would be meant in the nineteenth century. Crewe has a sense of being in a new kind of business or at least a sense of looking at it more expansively than is generally done. Not well educated, having no superior class connections in the way that Lionel Tarrant, of the same novel, has, Crewe relies on his energy and hard-headed assessment of business propositions. He associates himself with Beatrice French in a dress-manufacturing operation but is very direct in what he will or will not accept in their project. Beatrice, more like the working-class man on the make that Crewe represents than the lower-middle class pretensions from which she escapes, nevertheless falls back on a presumed class difference in an ineffectual attempt to control Crewe. Crewe's dilemma, not one that affects his work, is that only a woman of a higher class will suit him. Nancy Lord, who does nothing, is his choice rather than Beatrice. However, Crewe is both aggressive and visionary in his attempts to attract Nancy who is instead drawn to Lionel, someone of a slightly higher class position than she. Crewe "tempts" Nancy from atop the Monument, asserting that he will make his name down there. If disappointed in his desire for Nancy, Crewe's energy and drive encompass her and her interests.

Not principally interested as a novelist in characters such as Crewe and Beatrice, even portraying their modern ways as onslaughts against a cultured life, Gissing's fiction is, nonetheless, strongly dependent on their existence. From his early novels onward, he portrays figures who exist slightly outside the sphere of his primarily neurasthenic protagonists whose travails occupy so much of his fiction. Will Noble in *Workers in the Dawn*, Richard Mutimer in *Demos*, and Luke Ackroyd in *Thyrza* are active characters although, with the exception of Mutimer, not central to their novels. If these are energetic actors, they are not all going in the same direction. Noble is an incompletely drawn character whose actions, subsidiary to Golding's, recede in importance when Golding inherits money from the Rev. Norman, thus rejecting his socialist principles and working thenceforth as an artist. Mutimer, temporarily the beneficiary of his grandfather's will, is a working man active in his union. However, the money changes the direction of his life, and although he sees himself as the benefactor of his fellow workers in the construction of the works at New Wanley, he also rejects his patient, loving fiancée, Emma Vine, for the middle class Adela Waltham who unaccountably marries him. Adela loses none of her presumed superiority by marrying a man she does not love and whom she actively comes to dislike. Adela's safety lies in her class position that allows her to recover from a serious moral error in marrying Mutimer and still be the longed-for choice of the middle class Hubert Eldon. (See Chapter 3.) Luke Ackroyd can be described as the third man out in his attraction to Thyrza Trent, the working-class girl loved by Gilbert Grail and, for a time, the philanthropist Walter Egremont who enters their London environment as the uplifter of the poor. Grail has long cared for Thyrza and wants to marry her. He is her logical suitor, but Egremont's presence inadvertently turns her head. This melodramatic result is central to the novel. Ackroyd, Thyrza's working-class neighbor, wants her as well. Gissing so positions Ackroyd that for all his youthful energy he has no chance in gaining her love. However, Ackroyd marries Lydia, Thyrza's sister, who initially sympathizes with him over the treatment he receives from Thyrza. Ackroyd is limited by his place in the plot, but his portrait reflects Gissing's continuing awareness of those working-class figures, male and female, who possess honest energy.

The examples of working-class despair and rage, while possibly not as numerous as those reflecting energy and vitality, are nonetheless striking. Gissing draws, as it were, a bracket around those people from the lower class who are balked by society in nearly every aspect of their humanity. Society here stands for myriad processes and structures, many of them fleetingly understood, which hinder, constrain, and often kill those affected by them. In *Workers in the Dawn*, John Pether's family gradually dies around him. His ferocity in attacking society neither impedes its effects on his family nor gives him an increased understanding of his enemy. Samuel Tollady, his friend and Arthur Golding's substitute father, attempts to allay Pether's outbursts and lead him into some acceptance of that which he cannot prevent, but Pether rages until he dies. However, his many grievances do not lead him to harm anyone but himself. This implosion is a startling instance of the relatively small amount of political violence in the society even given the occasional mass eruptions. For Pether, the injustices are, paradoxically, personal rather than social. John Hewett in *The Nether World* represents this same paradox. Living in squalor in two upstairs rooms in Mrs. Peckover's house, the Hewetts barely make ends meet. Sidney Kirkwood finds it almost impossible to render aid to them because of Hewett's intense pride. Notwithstanding their poverty, they succor Jane Snowdon. Hewett's anger at these conditions makes it difficult for him to hold a job, yet he internalizes his rage and never sees possibilities for concerted action to change social conditions. Slimy, in *The Unclassed*, stands for this internalization more than any other Gissing character. Slimy robs Osmond Waymark who has become a rent collector for Abraham Woodstock, Ida Starr's grandfather. Slimy overpowers Waymark when he comes to collect the rent and leaves him bound in his room. He tells Waymark that he plans to use the money to drink himself to death. His miseries are so great that he cannot see any resolution save that of immediate obliteration. Woodstock is not an object on whom to seek vengeance nor is his representative Waymark. Slimy takes vengeance on society through himself. When Woodstock rescues Ida from her life of poverty (she lived better as a prostitute), Ida turns to philanthropic work among the poor who inhabit Woodstock's buildings. She principally helps the children and from that encourages Woodstock to repair his buildings. Slimy's death is not an unimportant aspect of this change.

Will Warburton, in the novel by that name (1905), may seem an odd choice when discussing the rising classes. After all, he is middle class, he partly owns a sugar refining business, and is sufficiently well educated to enjoy higher expressions of culture than those below him on the class scale. Admittedly, this is entirely relational, higher and lower being those perceived and acknowledged to be so. Gissing's complex psychological and social frameworks do not prevent him from acting on the relational nature of cultural attainment, though he and some of his creations might resent that their absolute level of learning and cultural appreciation is higher than any social recognition will ever acknowledge, much higher, in fact, than that of those who give and receive such recognition. Paradoxically, Warburton's membership in the rising social classes rests on his first falling in class, in going behind the counter in the retail end of the grocery trade. In his falling, Warburton maintains his own understanding of the world and is able to know the hypocrites who "abandon" him in his misfortune and refuse anymore to acknowledge him socially. His appreciation and understanding of the world enable him to recognize the pettiness and shallowness of such people and not just resent them as those who would hold him back if he were truly rising up. Mingling with a slightly lower social class than before, Warburton strengthens possibilities for those who move to his level from below. In his acceptance of his new situation and with the love and encouragement of Bertha Cross, who shares many traits and some experiences, Warburton anchors any class movement made.

If Warburton is not initially part of the rising classes, he has at least risen and fallen back. His importance thus lies in his acquired knowledge of the world and the way it works. Gissing divides characters over this issue into two groups. On Warburton's side there are also two parts with Mr. Allchin, Mrs. Hopper, and Mr. Potts in the first part. The second half connected to Warburton consists of Jane Warburton, Warburton's sister, and Bertha Cross, his fiancée. Those in the second group are Rosamund Elvan, Norbert Franks, Godfrey Sherwood, and Ted Strangwyn. The first group is generally more ethical, loyal, and productive than the second group. On Warburton's side, Jane Warburton, a horticulturist, and Bertha Cross, a book illustrator, are closer to him educationally and culturally. Mrs. Hopper was Warburton's housekeeper in his economically better days. Mr. Potts owns a stationery shop, and Warburton helps him change homes at the end of the novel. Mr. Allchin, an unsuccessful if hard-working shopkeeper, quits and goes to work for Warburton. Through his energy and steadfastness, he benefits from his association with Warburton. Each one of these five characters demonstrates energy and perseverance. Warburton participates in Mr. Allchin's and Mr. Potts' life improvements through his entry into the lower-middle class occupation of retail grocer. And, along with Jane and Bertha, he supports the value of honest, productive work for all.

Rosamund Elvan and Norbert Franks abandon Warburton once his money is misappropriated by his business partner Godfrey Sherwood. Strangwyn wasted Sherwood's wrongfully acquired funds in an unwise business investment. None of these four inspires admiration. In *Workers in the Dawn*, Gilbert Gresham, a popular portrait painter, tutors Arthur Golding in the art of painting. Gresham is shown as someone careless of the welfare of those around him, a somewhat cynical society figure who happens to have a craft that confers respectability. However, his daughter Maud reflects his attitude that very little matters, especially earnest endeavor in any field of life. Helen Norman, who does care about herself in ways that reveal a moral earnestness, lives with him and Maud until she comes of age. Notwithstanding his friendliness when Warburton is a successful sugar refiner, i.e., he does not then stand behind a counter and serve customers, Franks' actions resemble Gresham's superficiality and contrast unfavorably with Warburton's. Warburton and the members of his group reveal a fundamental depth of character that is lacking in Elvan, Franks, Sherwood, and Strangwyn. Society accepts the latter and disdains the former, but that unmerited disdain allows those who are productively engaged in life to supplant them in significance.

The workings of tradition when the generality of people live within their socially, politically, and religiously defined spheres apparently exclude the idea of rising classes. For not only those in power but also those from the lower strata of society have difficulty in thinking outside their given places. Not that any society is totally free from innovation, and the assiduous scholar will find the slow beginnings of later significant transformations even in ancient Egypt, for millennia one of the more stable social systems. Gissing's portrait of late-nineteenth-century British society argues for some remnants of tradition affecting the people even when change evinces itself in a broad range of social categories. The first two sections of this chapter show the presence of change but set the changes within a functioning class system. However, Gissing also develops the idea of a classless intellectual or artist that somehow survives and thrives. The world of the bohemian first appears when some characters not only exist outside the class structure but have no aspirations to enter it. However, Gissing portrays a more fundamental, even inevitable figure in the classless intellectual who lacks the trappings of rebellion. *The Crown of Life* includes, in addition to Jerome Otway, Piers' father, two other characters who exemplify this social type, i.e., Miss Bonnicastle, a commercial artist specializing in advertising, and Kite, an artist. Gissing develops Miss Bonnicastle as someone who is practical, independent, and cheerful. She focuses on her work and has no time for pretense. Olga Hannaford, daughter of the inventor Lee Hannaford, engages herself to Kite but has almost no sense of her own identity. Even her mother, in choosing Daniel Otway, Piers' ne'er-do-well brother, as a lover near the end of the novel, demonstrates a greater sense of self-knowledge by choosing a life she desires even though Otway's unsavory reputation militates against the match. Olga, fearful of how she and Kite will live, breaks their engagement and marries Florio, a man acquainted with the principals in this instance. Olga's shallow character disgusts Miss Bonnicastle who takes Kite in out of kindness. Neither Miss Bonnicastle nor Kite evinces a need to advance in the class system. A new world of opportunity offers them a chance to arrange their lives in ways that suit themselves, paying little attention to class inhibitions. They appear to have cleared away the need for any approval stemming from that aspect of the social structure.

Born in Exile's Godwin Peak, paradoxically, is another example of the classless intellectual who at first requires little from traditional society. After leaving Whitelaw College, Peak becomes a successful, if occasional, journalist, developing his own independent views on the place of religion in society. Peak earns his living in industrial chemistry and associates with friends in London who share a generally critical attitude toward the dominant society. He befriends John Edward Earwaker, a journalist, and Marcella Moxey, a studious young woman who lives with her brother Christian. Marcella loves Godwin, but he does not return her affection. However, after her accidental death, she has left him £800 per annum. Along with Janet Moxey, a doctor and distant relative whom Christian later marries, Godwin lives in a world that alters in its very processes traditional observances. Of course, this picture leaves out the Warricombes, especially Sidwell. Though her brother Buckland, Godwin's former Whitelaw classmate, will expose Godwin's pretended religious conversion, Sidwell and the world of culture and refinement she represents, a siren song issuing from her comfortable, sheltered life upend's his ambitions, both intellectual and practical. Prior to knowing her, Godwin writes an article attacking religion and the church. Her life centers not only on her family and friends in Exeter but also on her religious faith. Godwin is someone alien to her world. After his exposure, Godwin cannot continue with his plan. Sidwell has come to love him, but he no longer has the confidence to respond. Class subdues him even while he has half-liberated her from her brother's desire to close ranks against him. Godwin loses sight of the chance to value ideas and work and reject social privilege. Even Marcella's legacy does not lift him from his failure, not only with Sidwell, but with his idea of himself.

In *New Grub Street*, Edwin Reardon wants not so much to join Amy Yule's world as have her join and enrich his. And, the enrichment is personal rather than strictly class related. Of course, Amy comes from a cultured middle-class environment, but she represents enrichment to his emotional life more than any other consideration. Reardon and Peak contrast much as Amy and Sidwell do. Through work and family legacies, Reardon has managed to achieve some modest fame as a writer before he meets Amy. To have Amy as a wife seems, in prospect, to offer bliss, but she is both ambitious and class conscious, resembling the somewhat freer Jasper Milvain whom ambition, as he cheerfully acknowledges, drives. Like Edwin, Sidwell seeks her own life and mind once Godwin awakens her, but he fails to match her open, honest questioning, a position that resists family pressures on her to reject him. Edwin's decision to take the hospital job after he cannot continue to write reflects a deep awareness of what he must do to survive as a person. Amy asserts class as the deciding factor in refusing to accompany him into a lower-middle class lifestyle. As a classless intellectual, Reardon has the ingredients to create a viable life, but his initial refusal to share Amy's £10,000 inheritance from her father's brother and his final illness prevent any resolution to his dilemma.

Harold Biffen, Whelpdale, Alfred Yule, and Marian Yule, his daughter, represent other possibilities for the classless intellectual in *New Grub Street*. Although Alfred married a lower-class woman and feels that someone of a higher class would have helped rather than impeded his career, as he occasionally reminds her, he and Marian have forged a professional life, however, dissatisfying to both, to a large extent independent of the class system. For Alfred, his success does not depend on whom he knows except as it relates to literature and literary journalism. His ambition through most of the novel is to be given the editorship of another literary magazine. However, the general opinion, represented to Marian by her fiancé Jasper Milvain, an up-and-coming young man in the world of literary journalism, is that her father does not have the right touch to achieve editorial success. Magazine and journal owners do not worry about his wife's background; they wonder whether he will make money out of the venture. Disappointments come to him from practical and literary standards, not those based on class. Even his daughter realizes that her father would fail and refuses to give him the £5,000 she hopes to gain from her uncle's will. Jasper, much to her great sorrow, maneuvers her into breaking their engagement when the amount she will receive drops to £1,500. After Edwin Reardon's death, Jasper marries Amy and her money because he believes her beauty and personable nature, combined with her wealth, will lead to his literary success. It is not Amy's middle-class position that opens doors, though to an extent she is a product of her upbringing, but rather Jasper's ambition, hard work, and confidence that, with luck and money, success will come. John Goode states, "He will succeed because, in the first place, he offers a rational account of his own working life ... and secondly because he has adapting energies" (*Ideology* 109). Marian supports her family with a job as a librarian in a provincial town and income from her legacy after her father's blindness ends his literary career, but class does not determine the outcome of their lives. Jasper genuinely cares for Marian and, if she had received the original amount promised, would have married her and doubtless would have prospered then as well.

Several other characters in *New Grub Street* fit into the category of the classless intellectual. Dora and Maud Milvain, Jasper's sisters, admittedly, have few intellectual pretensions, but when Jasper urges them to try to write children's stories for the religious press, they make the attempt and succeed. Necessity spurs them on since their mother's annuity ends with her death, and neither wishes to continue in their former work with Dora as a day governess and Maud a music teacher. They move to London with Jasper's support and encouragement and there befriend Marian Yule, an event that, especially for Dora, turns out well. They continue as middle-class young ladies, but gain some initial independence through following Jasper's advice. Jasper's success comes from his own mind and his diligent application to writing. Although his middle-class background and education make him presentable, he generates the direction and outcome of his life. No one has expectations for him that would be assumed in a middle-class setting where family and friends combine to push one on in life. It is true that his mother loaned him money and his sisters hoped for his success, except when Maud begrudged him the money, but they could not advance his career in any other way. Of the two sisters, Maud's path is more traditional when she marries a wealthy man whom she apparently does not love. However, Dora eventually marries the then-successful Whelpdale, a man who has indeed been buffeted by life. Before his sudden, dazzling success in becoming the editor of a paper whose name he suggested should change from *Chat* to *Chit-Chat*, noted earlier in Chapter 2, Whelpdale was one of life's experimenters both in love and writing. He fell in and out of love, proposed to and was rejected by several women, and tried countless ways to succeed as a writer. He wrote novels, taught people how to write them, and eked out a living as a journalist. He was working at *Chat* when he had his flash of inspiration. Through Jasper, he meets and falls in love with Dora and with her support begins his life as an editor and, surprisingly, succeeds. Whelpdale, like Jasper, Alfred Yule, and Marian Yule, has no class support system, but he can fit into respectable society once he has the income. Harold Biffen is a profoundly different story of the classless intellectual who has no chance of success.

At an early point in the novel, Biffen and Reardon meet Sykes, a true representative of the eighteenth-century Grub Street world. Sykes is what many of them fear becoming. Surviving as a writer who can produce something on most subjects, Sykes cannot market himself. With nothing to fall back on besides his writing, Sykes toils almost in desperation to stay alive. Writing holds no pleasure or satisfaction for him except as a means to his daily bread. Prior to his marriage to Amy, Reardon solved his writing problem, as noted above, by working as a clerk in a hospital, a job to which he desires to return. When he asks his friend Albert Carter for his old job back, Gissing gets it and eventually receives an even better opportunity from Carter as the director of a boy's home. However, Amy sees this as a loss in class and refuses to rejoin him. Biffen writes as diligently as anyone in the novel while he earns his living tutoring. Some of his pupils hope to pass exams and qualify for better jobs in the civil service. Biffen hints to Reardon that few will succeed since they have so little educational foundation on which to build. Biffen holds out little hope for himself. Well educated, he cannot find a foothold by which to advance materially. Although Reardon encourages him to work on his novel, *Mr. Bailey, Grocer,* mainly because Biffen is determined to finish it, Reardon does not believe that it will be successful, and he is correct since Biffen only makes £10 from it. Biffen's suicide is only confirmation that some will fail while others rise.

Although Gissing draws few hopeful portraits of those who socially and economically rise, his novels, paradoxically, occasionally depict just those possibilities. His presentation of the difficulties that lie in anyone's path in a society that hinders advancement underscores that one can achieve something if one struggles hard enough. Even Biffen's pupils, endeavoring to learn how to write and to acquire a modicum of knowledge, represent a real path since the exams are there to take if one has the requisite knowledge and skills to pass them. Probably the least hopeful of men this side of suicide, Gissing, if only reluctantly, dramatizes examples of people struggling and improving their lives against all odds. This narrative theme provides a fitting epitaph to his own life.

5

The Loss of Innocence: Progress, Science, and Technology

The idea of human perfectibility, suggestive of Christian salvation in humanistic form, pervades the works of Jeremy Bentham and the early nineteenth-century British Utilitarians. Contrasted with the end of the century, the early years, paradoxically so conflicted at home and abroad by the Napoleonic wars and the consequent repression, reflect a vitality in most areas of the humanities. While the Romantic poets cover a wide spectrum of opinion concerning human growth and reform, Bentham attempts to develop a social, moral, and political philosophy that would lead to human advancement. Social organization, rather than any form of conversion theory and practice, underlies Bentham's ideas. Yet, from early in the nineteenth century, Thomas Malthus raises questions about the efficacy of technological expansion and improvement to solve the age-old problems of hunger and disease. By mid century, novelists, poets, essayists, and social reformers dramatize the negative effects of industrialization. Raymond Williams states that George Gissing's "*Demos* (1886) and *The Nether World* (1889) ... stand in the direct line of succession from the 'industrial novels' of the 1840s" (*Culture and Society* 174). Gissing's 1880 novel *Workers in the Dawn*, noted by Robert L. Selig as a work "grounded in a harsh material existence" (*George Gissing* 21), also continues this tradition, leavened with a dislike for the London masses amounting at times to a profound antipathy. In *The Nether World* and even as late as *In the Year of Jubilee*, group images of the people tend to be negative, their manners and behavior often little short of brutish. Jacob Korg describes the latter work as "sprawling story about marriage problems and the corruption of values in industrial society" (*George Gissing* 195). Gissing's urban portraits in his early novels make it hard to believe that any positive social change occurred during the century, but statistically, living conditions, e.g., urban sanitation, medical health, and increased educational opportunities, were better. In Gissing's fiction, the modern city represents a vast cacophony of people and technology that erodes the quality of life and threatens to over-whelm whatever peace and beauty of nature remain.

While it may seem logical to end rather than begin by examining Gissing's dire views on modern society, knowing the reality and extent of his pessimism about change, progress, and the value of human hope short of death determines the boundaries within which analysis of his fiction is profitable. The important question is, does Gissing think the best thing for humans to do is give up and wait for the end, whatever that may be? Faced with this question about his fiction, one must say no. Regardless of his criticism of modern culture, Gissing is no bleak fatalist. However, his fictive world produces serious, complex interruptions of any idea of a movement toward human happiness greater than transient relief. This paradoxical position implies a recurring hope, however faint, that he continually challenges. If hope can survive, it will have to earn its place. In this way, Gissing does not have to believe that life can be improved for the lowest classes or those who cannot fit into their "rightful" places in the middle class. He has only to accept the inevitable, the logic of circumstances that leaves some in possession of their lives. Will Warburton, in the novel of the same name (1905), finds himself defrauded and de-classed but nevertheless recovers his equanimity and a sense of balance toward the past and an acceptance of the present. (See Chapter 4.) Korg states, "At the end of the novel Warburton is moving away from his upper-class friends, and there is the clear suggestion (somewhat surprising in Gissing) that he is well rid of them" (*George Gissing* 255). The future lies unknown. One wishes to label this as un–Gissing-like, but it merely transcends or shifts aside ideology. Similarly, in *The Private Papers of Henry Ryecroft*, Gissing gives Ryecroft a legacy and peace for several years and then lets him die. Ryecroft appears to find himself blessed in his escape from the drudgeries of the writing life for even that short time. Not only the content but also the title of Gissing's essay "The Hope of Pessimism" begins to assume a sense of clarity. A real, if chastened, idea of hope results from an acknowledgment of Gissing's bare vision of human life.

Although it may not be progress, Gissing does not portray any Luddite leftovers acting on the edges of labor unrest. This is a significant change from the early part of the nineteenth century when breaking the looms offered a possible surcease from an advancing industrialization. Accommodation and incorporation are surely the watchwords in the 1880s and 1890s. In fact, Gissing dramatizes no serious threat to the industrial world. Its wealth permeates the society and preempts, if not silences, alternative discussions of social change. Tom Cobb in *The Paying Guest* moves into the realm of the needed expert who, if not the manager, is vital to his firm's success. The lower class and the lower-middle class are not only the operators of the machinery, as happened during and after the Luddite outbreaks, but they also become its technicians and engineers. Gissing makes Cobb a generic electrical worker, though Mrs. Mumford thinks of him as "the electrical engineer, or whatever he was" (39) who functions more importantly as a symbol than a specific instance of expertise. Mr. Higgins, Louise Derrick's lower middle-class stepfather, is "rich" (14), with a business address in Fenchurch St., the City, and thus connected with the growing wealth of the country. Although he pays for Louise's sojourn with the Mumfords, the action centers on Louise Derrick's fruitless attempts to flee her class and/or Tom Cobb's ardor. Gissing matter-of-factly gives Cobb "the girl," success for the modern man without surprise at the outcome.

A fundamental consideration on the subject of progress is whether it is inevitable. Is the nineteenth century shift or change under the pressure of scientific and technological innovation bettering society? Ideas on free will and determinism come to mind, and if the latter rules, would man have any say in the event, whether the result is considered good or bad? Richard Mutimer's inheritance in *Demos* transforms Wanley into New Wanley, and the discovery of an earlier will just as surely shifts it back. Is Hubert Eldon, the later beneficiary, any more in control of the destruction of the works at New Wanley than Mutimer is in their creation? Gissing's use of the hackneyed device of a will to move the plot may have more significance than is usually the case since its importance lies not so much in its effects on Eldon's financial prospects but rather on the effects on technology's inevitable march to social dominance. Gissing appears to reverse the century's determining forces and suspend technology from its position of mastery. Dickens' images of technological harm in *Hard Times*' (1854) Coketown with its air and water pollution, and the general adaptation of that city, in its pervasive drabness, to the factory, train, and scientific educational methods lie upended in Wanley Valley's newly recreated, pristine environment. Gissing makes Eldon most enthusiastic in his planned, complete eradication of the mines and the works. He tells Adela:

> "I shall sweep away every trace of the mines and the works and the houses, and do my utmost to restore the valley to its former state.... For my own part, in this little corner, at all events, the ruin shall be delayed. In this mat-

ter I will give my instincts free play. Of New Wanley not one brick shall remain on another. I will close the mines, and grass shall again grow over them; I will replant the orchards and mark out the fields as they were before" [338].

John Halperin comments on this process: "At the end of *Demos*, when Mutimer is disinherited and Eldon comes back to power, New Wanley is joyously destroyed" (*Gissing* 82). The narrator describes the aesthetic pleasure in the natural beauty as Eldon gazes at the prospect with the Rev. Wyvern. Society's inevitable expansion on every scientific and technological front to the betterment of living standards, especially for the poor, is temporarily halted. The narrator observes:

> Hubert Eldon has been as good as his word. In all the valley no trace is left of what was called New Wanley. Once more we can climb to the top of Stanbury Hill and enjoy the sense of remoteness and security when we see that dark patch on the horizon, the cloud that hangs over Belwick [462].

This representative incident of the disruptive force of science and technology, its dramatic power lying in the paradoxical calm of the prospect, rises in its increasing suggestiveness.

To return to *Hard Times*, Sleary's statement about the circus's necessary role in society emphasizes another anti-progressive position that helps to illuminate the social alterations in *Demos*. First, the traditional, unchanging aspect of a circus is important to note. It is a world set apart that shows and reshows the same or similar acts and that one can see from childhood to adulthood and find in it little difference. Second, Sleary stresses the circus's purpose when he says that people must be amused. In the Preface to *The Picture of Dorian Gray* (1891), Oscar Wilde later writes, "All art is quite useless" (17). The shock of the unusual makes Wilde's statement memorable, but the subtlety of Sleary's words are more profound. William Wordsworth's assertion in "Preface to *Lyrical Ballads*" that pleasure is the chief end of poetry (311) is a possible source for the statements by Dickens' Sleary and Wilde. For them, art speaks to human feelings and emotions; it does not create social processes, technological or otherwise, though it does have the moral power to shape the society in which they operate. Wordsworth, Dickens' Sleary, and Wilde present essentially static images. These images are repeatable and full of meaning but do not move from one state of affairs to the next in a sense that the word *progress* would suggest. And, *Demos's* Eldon functions in this tradition. To give pleasure in art, amusement at the circus, or the chance to appreciate an unchanged, however ironically presented, natural beauty is not to deny the possibility of progress or even that science and technology could participate in it. However, by Gissing's placing in *Demos* the static, recurrent experience on the site of the formerly dynamic, progressive one built by a working-class man become wealthy, and Eldon's announced intention to keep it as it was, the author values the aesthetic over the socially progressive act. Sleary travels from one city to the other putting on the same show; Hugh and Adela will view the same prospect many times; pleasure, at the expense of Coketown and New Wanley, respectively, temporarily rules.

Gissing infuses his novels with objects, processes, and the products of modern science and technology. Unlike Upton Sinclair's open investigation of the excesses of industrialization in *The Jungle* (1906) and *Oil* (1927), Theodore Dreiser's picture of Chicago in *Sister Carrie* (1900), and Frank Norris's novel about the expansion of the railroad in *Octopus* (1901), none of Gissing's novels so openly engage the subject of industrialization but rather provide the physical results of science and technology as background and connection. In *The Social Context of Modern English Literature* (1971), Malcolm Bradbury provides a sense of this atmosphere:

> With the application of technology to communications, the nation as a whole was shrinking, while the individual environment was becoming wider: the railways, from 1860 the tramways, the postal and telegraphic services, the spread of gas and electric light, the wide-circulation and national newspaper broke into separated communities, enfranchising them but producing greater social and political complexity. The need for abstract, impersonal social arrangements increased, and local and national government alike had to commit themselves to civic arrangements, services, sanitation, health matters [45–46].

The emphasis in *New Grub Street* on the train that thunders under the bridge on which Jasper Milvain and Marian Yule stand is not so much as an industrial product with all the suggested effects of the factory system but rather as a contemporary symbol of force and energy. (See Chapter 2.)

The moon rising from the fog and mist in the last book of Wordsworth's *The Prelude* and the frozen northern wastes that Dr. Frankenstein gazes on in Mary Shelley's work (1818) function similarly as symbols. To the young Jasper and Marian, looking to the future and interested in one another, the train symbolizes their different expectations from life. Wordsworth and Shelley, as seems appropriate for the Romantic period, incorporate natural images into their characters' hopes and frustrations, images that provide them with understanding and from which they can obtain emotional and intellectual sustenance.

In *New Grub Street* and *In the Year of Jubilee*, Gissing also employs the London Underground, the telegraph, and electric lighting. In *The Odd Women*, the recently invented typewriter figures in the plot as a means to achieve female emancipation in a male-dominated world. Rhoda Nunn says:

> "My first engagement here was as shorthand writer to the secretary of a company. But he soon wanted some one who could use a typewriter. That was a

suggestion. I went to learn typewriting, and the lady who taught me asked me in the end to stay with her as an assistant. This is her house, and here I live with her" [23–24].

Gissing uses some of these technological products in a positive way and some in a negative one but does not generally invest the product with the negative or positive qualities. The smoke and dirt from the Underground, not electrified until the early 1900s (Saint and Darley, *The Chronicles of London* 223), counterbalance the ease and speed with which one moves around the city. In a striking scene between Jessica Morgan and Samuel Barmby in *In the Year of Jubilee*, Gissing describes the Underground with echoes of Homer's, Virgil's, and Dante's images of the underworld (259). The news that Reardon receives in London of his son Willy's illness in Brighton is not made worse by the telegraph's quick transmission of it (*New Grub Street* 439) nor does the train that rushes him to Brighton, as sick as he is, convey negative overtones. Marian Yule, in the same novel, complains of the harsh effect on her eyes of the British Museum Library's electric lighting, but the problem may lie as much in Marian's physical and emotional condition as in this new means of illumination:

> But then flashed forth the sputtering whiteness of the electric light, and its ceaseless hum was henceforth a new source of headache. It reminded her how little work she had done to-day; she must, she must force herself to think of the task in hand. A machine has no business to refuse its duty. But the pages were blue and green and yellow before her eyes; the uncertainty of the light was intolerable. Right or wrong she would go home, and hide herself, and let her heart unburden itself of tears [108].

Other than Rhoda Nunn's estimation that "'It takes a good six months' work to learn for any profitable use'" (*The Odd Women* 39), acquiring efficiency on the typewriter is an opportunity that women can take to achieve independence.

Shelley's *Frankenstein* taps into the fear of disruption that science and technology create. It is not so much fear of any specific disruption but of the state or condition of disruption. True, Shelley explores the application of electricity to the generation of life, a fundamental displacement of the God-like role to the insistence by one human that he must know if he can create life: Do his scientific ideas have merit? However, any dramatic example would suffice since an underlying theme of Shelley's work is that a new world is coming, one that human beings will fashion and in which they will turn intractable natural processes and functions into obedient servants. The scientific and technological advances of the nineteenth and twentieth centuries fall far short of this goal, but they do produce inroads into nature's ineluctable laws. A sense of an oncoming force pervades Gissing's fiction. The city of London seeps into the suburbs; the masses of people swarm throughout the city; the buildings stretch endlessly and dismally on some streets; the noise of the city penetrates every recess. Earlier literature, to go no further back than Wordsworth's "Lines Composed a Few Miles above Tintern Abbey" (1798) and Books First and Seventh of *The Prelude*, has produced images of a London that parallel these, but science and technology sustain the greater momentum of later nineteenth-century occurrences. Processes and products, ideas and things proliferate under a more dynamic system in the last several decades. The word "dynamic" might have positive overtones, but it could merely mean activity, kinetic energy. The sense of decline in *The Nether World* does not cancel the above images. In fact, one could well speak of an irreversible, dynamic decline that afflicts the lower classes in all their swarming numbers. However, Gissing does not depict a compression that is prelude to a revolutionary explosion. In *In the Year of Jubilee*, Nancy Lord and Luckworth Crewe witness the police and the masses "in brief conflict" (64) on Jubilee Day, but the people are more stirred by drink than ideas. One might well ask what good is science and technological change if not to improve humanity's lot? Disruptive change that narrows options is not sufficient.

Gissing's emphasis on the social effects of science and technology distances the reader from the factory and the laboratory. While he employs no affective images of machinery as Dickens does in *Hard Times* such as the machine as lumbering elephant or in *The Old Curiosity Shop* (1841) as Little Nell and her grandfather escape from Quilp through an industrial landscape of glowing fires, the ominous spread of London portends a new world spawned by technology that increases wealth as it sometimes debases society. Admittedly nostalgic, Gissing's fiction displays a desire for something more than the world not only fast approaching but already mutating under the new order's hegemony.

6

The Failed Triangle: Marriage, Family, and Children

In George Gissing's fiction, marriage occurs and children are born, but only the first idea plays a significant role. Using the city as his principal venue, Arthur Golding in *Workers in the Dawn* is an important exception. It is, in part, a coming-of-age novel like Charles Dickens' *David Copperfield*, William Makepeace Thackeray's *Vanity Fair* (1848), and Samuel Butler's *The Way of All Flesh* (1903). Though these three works reflect different childhood experiences, they trace their protagonists' lives from early youth onward, attempting to show cause and effect relationships and making it important to know the child as well as the adult. But, Gissing quickly drops this focus even though Ida Starr, Maud Enderby, and Harriet Smales in *The Unclassed* appear as children. He only sketches in their early lives, however important the incidents. *Demos: A Story of English Socialism, Isabel Clarendon, Thyrza*, and, to a lesser extent, *The Nether World* push children further into the background of their respective stories. The young now are generally in their mid teens to early twenties. If mentioned, children represent noise and disruption and heavy responsibility, inevitable by-products of marriage. John and Margaret Hewlett in *The Nether World* have young children, one an infant, but John's grown children, Bob and Clara, share the family focus on their difficulties in moving into full independence as adults. The younger children in the novel fill space and require care, but none has the importance of the thirteen-year-old Jane Snowdon who is on the point of becoming a woman. In *The Eman-*

cipated, very young children do not exist, and Edwin and Amy Reardon's Willie in *New Grub Street* is only a name; Gissing gives him prominence when father and son die close in time. Earlier patterns continue in *Born in Exile* and *In the Year of Jubilee*. It is not until *The Whirlpool* that a young child, Hugh Rolfe, appears again as a significant character but then largely to define the relationship between Harvey and Almah Rolfe and reveal Almah's inadequacies as a mother. In the remaining twelve novels, children disappear almost entirely with the exception of Leonard Woolstan in *Our Friend the Charlatan*, Dyce Lashmar's pupil.

While children are biological products and with family would seem to demand some attention in any writer's work described as realistic, Gissing increasingly focuses on marriage, culminating in his paean to the institution in *The Crown of Life*. Admittedly, few novels have as unalloyed focus on marriage, with Piers Otway's becoming quite lyrical on its imagined pleasures when joined with love. This novel introduces a generational element into the subject since Jerome Otway, Piers' radical father, employs the phrase "the crown of life" in one of his early poems. From *Workers in the Dawn* until *The Crown of Life*, Gissing represents marriage in a variety of ways; for marriage can be bad, e.g., Arthur Golding and Carrie Mitchell's in *Workers in the Dawn* and Julian Casti and Harriet Smales's in *The Unclassed*, or indifferent, e.g., Maud Gresham and John Waghorn's in *Workers in the Dawn* and Dyce Lashmar and Iris Woolstan's in *Our Friend the Charlatan*, with the indifference in the latter lying solely on Lashmar's part. Family, obviously linking marriage and children, plays a problematic role in Gissing's novels. With the emphasis on the emotional lives of the characters and the good, bad, or indifferent marriages they contract, family is a present if shadowy idea, something created by nature and the state. While loving families occur, almost no character has the idea of family as a driving need. Families exist and Gissing records them but for the most part shunts them aside. The triangle of marriage, family, and children is broken in Gissing's fiction, and from his first novel to his last, he creates no dynamic that heals it.

The Nether World, Gissing's seventh published novel, marks a watershed in his fiction. Gissing writes on March 16, 1890, to Algernon that "Little by little, the subjects of my books will probably change a good deal; in fact, the process has already begun, as you will see in 'The Emancipated'" (Mattheisen, Young, and Coustillas 4.202). Four of his first seven novels, portray working-class life extensively, and three, *The Unclassed*, *Isabel Clarendon*, and *A Life's Morning*, explore lower-middle class to middle-class existence. Children, when they appear, figure in the four working-class novels, and even *The Unclassed* places the few principal children in economically restricted environments. One, Ida Starr, grows up to surmount her mother's life and her own as prostitutes to become the benefactor of the children from her grandfather's East London slum housing. Poverty, sometimes hopeless futures, and a perilous survival characterize childhood in the working class. From these conditions, one understands Sidney Kirkwood's sense of hopelessness in *The Nether World* regarding the people among whom he lives and of whom he represents, along with characters from other novels, e.g. Will Noble from *Workers in the Dawn*, Emma Vine from *Demos*, and Gilbert Grail and Thyrza from *Thyrza*, the best example of his class. Pennyloaf Candy is a special case regarding childhood in *The Nether World*. When she first appears, she works as a maker of shirts for export and is seventeen years old (72). How has she survived her family's difficulties? Her mother is an alcoholic and her father has just recently left home after a quarrel with the mother. Pennyloaf seems in poor health. Gissing has caught her as she emerges from childhood into an adult life of grinding poverty and long hours of work. And, hers is not the worst case in the London slums. It is against the image of this pale survivor that one must see the lives of most working-class children, unnamed, shadowy background figures who suggest worse conditions even than those depicted.

Although Gissing shifts his focus from the working class and their children after *The Nether World*, *The Town Traveller* (1898) does echo the plight of children in *The Nether World* in the case of Moggie, the general in Mrs. Bubbs' boarding house. Nine years after the former novel, Gissing's working-class portraits and interests are pale copies of his earlier diatribes against the poor and their miserable circumstances. In *The Nether World*, Mrs. Peckover's house is a grimmer place than Mrs. Bubbs' establishment. Not only Jane Snowdon's unhappy life as Mrs. Peckover's servant and her daughter Clem's target of abuse, but the Hewetts' precarious existence with numerous children and a sickly wife demonstrate this. The novel's tone is far heavier than that of *The Town Traveller* with Sidney Kirkwood's despondent outlook in marked contrast to Mr. Gammon's belief that energy and will are sufficient to make it in the traveling salesman trade. However, Moggie raises other questions. A child-woman, she slaves in Mrs. Bubb's house, though she is not ill-treated. Yet, one wonders where she came from, what her younger childhood was like, and what her prospects are. Gissing includes her because she was probably an indispensable element in late nineteenth-century boarding houses, underpaid and overworked but necessary if neither the landlady nor her children want, or in the case of the latter, are made to assume the burdens. Arguably, she works at Mrs. Bubb's by chance rather than somewhere more similar to the regions of Whitecross Street that Gissing depicts in *Workers in the Dawn*. Nothing about Moggie separates her from that world or offers a defense against her slipping into it. An isolated example of lost children from his later fiction, it only emphasizes that Gissing has shifted his interests and not that society has changed its practices. Gissing is not a writer whose imagination penetrates easily into the world of childhood. He does not see children as children, bringing out their individual consciousnesses. And, for those whom he does depict as children, they usually have other than strictly working-class connections. One could make a good case that Gissing portrays Arthur Golding's inner world. Especially after he flees the comfortable confines of the Rev. Norman's home, Arthur's viewpoint dominates his immediate surroundings. But one generally has a sense that Gissing is seeing through their childhood to a later period when their sensibilities will register on those around them. Gissing provides a few set pieces of childhood suffering until Arthur lands safely in Samuel Tollady's home. It is the adult or near-adult experiences of desire, loneliness, and ambition that interest him.

Gissing seldom portrays a happy, harmonious family even if love is present. The Warricombes in *Born in Exile* come close to this ideal, but different generational needs make it impossible for its members to live in complete accord. Sidwell Warricombe is the epitome of a loving daughter who has no fundamental disagreement with anyone in her family, including her father and brother, Buckland. But, when Godwin Peak insinuates himself into her family and she grows to love him, not even Buckland's revelations concerning Peak's supposed call to the ministry, a stratagem he devised solely to make himself appealing to Sidwell, can make her reject him completely. Clearly, Gissing shows only moments or periods of harmony that time and experience will stress and either destroy or redefine. In *The Paying Guest*, Clarence and Emmeline Mumford seem happy with their one child and suburban home. Like most novels, the beginning is the starting point for something, and Louise Derrick, with her lower-middle class manners, provides the catalyst for a near-dismemberment of the Mumfords' marriage. Louise goes to the Mumfords to rise above her class origins. However wealthy her step-father Mr. Higgins might have become, neither he nor Louise's mother can shake off their essential vulgarity. They and Louise's step-sister Cissy pull Louise back into their dramas and shatter the Mumfords' home life. The pretext for what appears in Gissing to be an inevitable shift from harmony to disharmony is Louise's desire to change classes. Thus, behind the simple story of Louise and the Mumfords lies the idea of class division.

Being of the same class does not guarantee family harmony. In fact, the arguments and misunderstandings can be as sharp as those deriving from class differences. Alfred Yule in *New Grub Street* clearly illustrates this. Alfred does not get along with his elder brother John. The latter despises the craft of writing and thinks little of those who choose it as a career. Since Alfred is a professional writer, there is no possibility of agreement between them. The other brother Edmund is dead. John Yule carries his prejudices beyond the grave by leaving nothing to his brother and to Marian, Alfred's daughter, only half of what he gave to his other niece Amy Reardon. Disappointed for much of his career, Alfred, who married a working-class woman, assumes a tyrannical position towards Marian and his wife. His attitude to his wife derives from her lower-class upbringing but not that regarding his daughter. Marian is completely unlike her mother but to no avail submits to her father's whims. In *The Morality of Marriage and Other Essays on the Status and Destiny of Woman* (1897), Mona Caird's essay on "The Emancipation of the Family" seems to speak directly to the Yule family crisis:

> If we could only realise how fundamental, in our traditions, is the old patriarchal feeling, we should then more clearly see that marriage, with its one-sided obligations, is not a thought-out rational system of sex relationship, but a lineal descendant of barbarian usages, cruel and absurd, even when the warlike condition of society gave them some colour of reason, revolting now to all ideas of human justice and of dignity [57–58].

Marian's eventual rebellion against her father's unreasonable moods brings a greater isolation for her, broken only when he learns of her bequest and hopes to use it to revive his career. Her refusal completes the family break-up even though they continue to live together. Analyzing Alfred's relations with his original family and his married family, it seems clear that personality predisposes one to conflict, and class differences are an easy path to engagement in it.

Alfred Yule is one of only a few characters who can be seen in family settings with more than one class represented. His is not, of course, the only exogamous marriage. However, lower-class, lower-middle-class, and middle-class families exhibit a wide range of harmonies and disharmonies. In *Workers in the Dawn*, the Rev. Orlando Whiffle's family represents a happy if chaotic establishment with only Augustus Whiffle, their son, creating disappointment. The Rev. Edward Norman and his daughter Helen live in peace with one another. Carrie Mitchell's aunt and daughters, though loud and vulgar, coexist with Carrie, but they quarrel seriously with her and throw her out of the house when she becomes pregnant. Finally, Gilbert Gresham and his daughter Maud live on mutually acceptable terms with no severe conflicts. Each one of these families exists within its own class, but resembles one another in generally finding a way to tolerate individual personalities. Equally, the Peacheys and the Lords in *In the Year of Jubilee*, both lower-middle class, live in sharp disagreement with one another if not the same degree of uproar. Arthur Peachey is eventually driven from his home by his shrewish wife Ada and the loud and vulgar Fanny, his sister-in-law. Beatrice, the other sister-in-law, is more self-contained and ambitious to succeed as a businesswoman. When the family breaks up, no one remains in contact with the others, and

Arthur has even secreted his child from the vulgarities of Ada. Stephen Lord is suspicious of the direction in which he sees both Nancy and Horace going in their lives. He dies a bitter man, and his will puts monetary restrictions on Nancy's freedom to marry. Finally, as a representative lower-class family, the Hewetts in *The Nether World* suffer from John's irascibility at work and his inability to hold jobs, but at home he looks after his family and only quarrels with his two older children, Bob and Clara, when they resist his desire to control them. Clara runs away and becomes an actress, leaving that profession when a rival throws acid in her face. John seeks her out and brings her back home. Bob, however, marries, beats his wife, and becomes a criminal.

One peculiarity of Gissing's family portraits is the happiness of some of the broken or partial families, those with only one parent present or a child and another relative. In these cases, Gissing seems to set up contrasts with the norm in order to suggest other possibilities. Behind this might lie the idea that life can go on, even when the expected grouping of mother, father, and children is absent. Though sometimes futilely, family members stand against the world and support one another in desperate circumstances in a callous environment. In *Workers in the Dawn*, Arthur Golding, Sr., and his young son are reduced to living in the vilest possible lodgings. Golding is an educated man; he attended university with the Rev. Norman, but drink and dissipation have ruined him while not forfeiting his son's love. Arthur clings to his father even after death and runs away from the Normans' household to return to the exact spot where his father died and which for Arthur contains his memory. The boy starts from that spot to move up in the world, sleeping on the bare floor of their former room that the landlady so "kindly" lets him use for the night. Aside from the lower-class families in the novel, this first family sets the tone for families in the work. And, the home to which the Rev. Norman takes him is also a partial one since Norman's wife and Helen's mother is dead. Helen and her father have a real closeness and vie with the Whiffles as images of happiness. While the Whiffle household contains the Rev. Whiffle, Mrs. Whiffle, and the children, their happiness is presented with some negatives, e.g., the large number of children, the noise and disorder, and young Augustus's increasing rebelliousness.

Aside from the odious Dr. Tootle and his family in *The Unclassed*, the novel contains relatively few whole families. All the major characters come from partial families, families that form and re-form throughout the novel. One of the most striking of these is Lotty Starr and her daughter Ida, the heroine of the novel. When Lotty defies her father Abraham Woodstock and marries Ida's father, now dead, Abraham disowns her. Unable to find any other way to support herself and Ida and repulsed more than once by her father, Lotty becomes a prostitute. One of Ida's first conflicts involves throwing a slate at Harriet Casti when she suggests that Ida's mother is leading an immoral life. Thrown out of school, Ida fiercely supports the mother she loves even when Lotty sends Ida down to stay with the landlady while she entertains customers in their room. Ida also becomes a prostitute and remains one until she meets Osmond Waymark, the male protagonist and potentially her husband. Regardless of her unpromising beginnings, Ida never turns on her mother nor does she reject her memory. Gissing clearly shows the love that they bore one another, a love that compares in intensity to that between Arthur Golding and his father. Maud Enderby, Harriet Casti, and Julian Casti also come from partial families. In Maud's case, her father becomes an embezzler, her mother commits suicide, and Maud goes to live with her aunt, Theresa Bygrave, a devoutly religious woman who either destroys Maud's ability to live a fuller life or confirms in her a predilection for strict religious observance. Harriet, Ida's antagonist throughout the work, lives unhappily with her father until she marries Julian Casti. She has a morbidly suspicious personality and effectively destroys the weak poet. Ida reconciles with her grandfather and becomes an heiress at his death. One could argue that these characters come from unrepresentative family structures. The families are all lower-middle class or middle class and generally have some financial resources. However, Gissing presents marriage as an unstable social institution in this novel, a condition that begins in *Workers in the Dawn* and that recurs in his later fiction. Humanity's ability to survive without whole families and the precariousness of that situation balance one another but with somewhat ominous overtones for social stability.

Three pairs of novels give additional examples of partial or broken families. First, *Demos* and *In the Year of Jubilee* represent a repressive model. The Mutimer family includes only the mother and her three grown children. However, Richard has assumed the role of the father and dominates his sister and brother. Neither Alice nor Harry is happy with their brother's exercise of patriarchal authority, and they both break away with unhappy results. In *In the Year of Jubilee*, discussed above in terms of a family in disagreement, Nancy and Horace lack a mother and suffer from the father's autocratic rule. Second, *The Nether World* and *The Crown of Life* offer examples of chaotic broken families. In the former novel, Mrs. Peckover and her daughter Clem make a viable if disturbing family. They quarrel and celebrate with a violent intemperance. In addition, they happily, even savagely mistreat the young Jane Snowdon, their servant. In *The Crown of Life*, Piers and his two brothers, Daniel and Alexander, have almost no contact with their father Jerome. All the brothers are grown, but through their father's money to Piers, Daniel and Alexander invade his life, borrowing money that they never repay and that he can ill afford to lose. The father presently lives with his third wife and never married Piers' mother. In the final group, *The Town Traveler* and *Our Friend the Charlatan* show especially positive examples of partial families. Mrs. Louisa Clover and her daughter Minnie portray an almost idyllic mother-daughter relationship in the first novel. The father is alive but does not live with them. He is part of an overly complicated sub-plot and is both a lord and a bigamist, neither of which has much significance due to the manner in which these details are revealed and concealed. The nearly impoverished Lord Dymchurch in the second novel tenderly cares for his sisters. As the head of the household in a remote Norfolk village, he is their sole support. These three types of partial families reveal the subtleties of Gissing's creative exploration of late-Victorian family life.

In the lone splendor of the Devon countryside, Henry Ryecroft in *The Private Papers of Henry Ryecroft* provides Gissing's most eloquent alternative to the institutions of marriage, family, and childhood. Along with the silent Mrs. M., restricted to a letter and not even a last name, Ryecroft lives out his final years with only the sounds of nature occasionally interrupted by the visits of his one friend. Mrs. M., reminiscent of Mary Woodruff of *In the Year of Jubilee*, ministers to him in an atmosphere of mutually accepted quiet. Ryecroft's married daughter is referred to but never seen, and he makes no visits to her. Contrasted with the previous examples and with additional ones from his novels and short stories, Ryecroft's essential need for respite from his strenuous literary career and the noise and dirt of London argues for separation and isolation as the only states of existence commensurate with happiness. Harold Biffen in *New Grub Street* is the most striking example of an opposite tendency. Living a lonely life in London except for his friendship with Edwin Reardon and his contact with his pupils, Biffen could only choose death when Amy Reardon, Edwin's widow, rejects him as a possible suitor. To an extent, his existence parallels Ryecroft's. A legacy rescues Ryecroft from his Grub Street drudgery, but Biffen's only resource would be his brother who apparently does not begrudge him financial aid. However, Biffen finds his isolated life unbearable after Amy's clear indication that she does not care to see him again. His retreat to the countryside is Putney Heath where he commits suicide. Ryecroft's solution to life's difficulties is only one example to be contrasted with many others, but its place near the end of Gissing's career is a striking one. Ryecroft's hope for a few more years of enjoyment cannot be a universal solution to the complexities and tragedies people struggle with and endure, but it is a strongly felt and embraced choice.

In addition to the ideas of class, family harmony or disharmony, and partial or broken families, Gissing dramatizes the fragility of family life. Chance, if not fate, lies at the core of this latter idea, robbing characters of any control over their destinies. In *The Emancipated*, Mrs. Denyer and her daughters, Barbara, Madeline, and Zillah, live at an Italian boarding house. They await word from the husband as to where they will settle and on what they will live. While Mrs. Denyer's improvidence does not help matters, Mr. Denyer is forever attempting one unsuccessful business venture after another. He is in need of money and takes too many risks. When circumstances become too precarious, they fortunately have recourse to the husband's sister Dora in Southampton. In the same novel, Ross Mallard is Cecily Doran's guardian but lets Mrs. Edith Lessingham, Cecily's aunt, direct her education. Mrs. Lessingham believes in learning by experience and allows Cecily more freedom than a middle-class girl would have normally been given. With Mallard essentially absent from her life and Mrs. Lessingham's loose supervision, she and Reuben Elgar, Miriam Baske's brother, have little more than their own desires to guide them. He pressures her to elope with him, and she consents. Of course, part of the fragility of this family is its very loose structure. Mallard is not even related to Cecily and was only made her guardian because of his close relationship to her father. It takes little to break this socially advanced family since they have almost no underpinnings to ameliorate rash actions. While the Denyers' family fragility lies as much in character as circumstance, the Maddens in *The Odd Women* are the victims of a completely unforeseen action. Called out on a case one night, Dr. Elkanah Madden dies when he is thrown from his carriage. He spoke earlier that day to Alice, his oldest daughter, about his decision to buy life insurance so that his three remaining daughters would not have financial difficulties in the event of his premature death. Pure chance thus robs the women of a father and separates Alice and Virginia from Monica who goes to work in a London draper's shop. The two older women, essentially unemployable, survive on a meager income and maintain a tenuous relationship with Monica.

While circumstance and chance disrupt the fragile balance of some families, acts of will also produce the same result. Alma Rolfe in *The Whirlpool* insists on pursuing a musical career although she begins to suspect the limitations of her talent. Harvey Rolfe ultimately refrains from any attempt to control her and watches while she goes on to destroy any chance of happiness they might have had. This is not an example of the Victorian male attempting to stifle female independence. Gissing stresses her willfulness in pursuing unrealizable aims. Her actions have distinct overtones of her father Bennet Frothingham's illegal activities. After being discovered as an embezzler, he killed himself. Alma appears to inherit his willful disregard of the consequences of his dealings. Mrs. Eldon in *Demos* disapproves of her son Hubert's romantic adventures, and when he returns home after being shot in a duel, she refuses to welcome him or attempt a reconciliation. He was equally willful in his previous actions, but she spurns him, her only living son. Hubert Eldon was not dissolute, just mistaken in where he placed his affections, but his mother's moral pride has no room for youthful error. His later actions in restoring Wanley Valley to its original condition and marrying the now-widowed Adela Waltham Mutimer help to change her mind. Finally, Lady Ogram in *Our Fried the Charlatan* has both the image and the quality of the supreme autocrat as she destroys her newly found relationship with her niece May Tomalin. Admittedly, May, in collusion with the ever-scheming Dyce Lashmar, gives her sufficient provocation. But, as Gissing carefully draws her portrait, stubborn willfulness is a major component of her character. Only Constance Bride and, briefly, Lashmar himself have managed to influence her during the novel's events, but she must have her way in all things. Dying, she dispossesses May when she learns that Lashmar plans to marry her and not Constance as Lady Ogram had ordered. Clearly, Lady Ogram is one who believes, if not my way, then no way. Such absolute destruction of a fragile family structure fits her character, and her knowledge that she is dying while she carries this out completes her portrait.

Some characters' emotional and mental states also undermine their families' cohesion. Edwin Reardon in *New Grub Street* is a prime example of this condition. Reardon feels the pressure of his having to produce a novel every year, and his creative abilities wane. He cannot follow Jasper Milvain's advice to let him promote his work, especially his latest novel, and when the certain success comes, relax and know that his worries are over. Amy also urges him to follow that path, stating that it does not matter if the novel is a work of art; it is good enough for the public. This is sound advice for Milvain himself; he indeed is in the process of implementing it, but for Gissing, it is impossible. He cannot assume the public role that Milvain says would enhance his prospects. Reardon would rather write nothing than produce rubbish, even well-paid rubbish. When Amy upbraids him over his attitude and asks what they will live on, Reardon responds that it is just this lack of sympathy, different from their earlier married life, that undermines his ability to write (50, 52, 56). His wife and child's dependence on his artistic output freezes his imagination, and he winds up unable to write anything. He takes a job as a clerk in a hospital, and Amy is not only humiliated by his move but leaves him, taking their son Willie and returning to her mother's home. Although they have no children, Harriet Casti in *The Unclassed* drives her husband Julian to distraction with her unwarranted jealousy. Julian is a poet, and she ultimately destroys his peace of mind. Her mental unbalance leads to Julian's death. Not in good health, he cannot work out any way to live with her or overcome his feelings of guilt at the idea of leaving her. Reardon's and Harriet's mental and emotional conditions irreparably damage their families.

Gissing's ideas on marriage, like those on childhood and family, reveal his multifaceted understanding of human relationships. In *"The Vice of Wedlock": The Theme of Marriage in George Gissing's Novels*, Christina Sjöholm writes:

> Marriage is a recurrent theme in Gissing's novels from the very first. It is therefore possible to follow the process of development of this theme over nearly two decades: at first underdeveloped, sometimes autobiographically coloured, or caricatured, it matured to the penetrating portrayals of the complex marital relationships in the novels of the 1890s [10].

The idea of marriage comes to the fore in the middle-class novels of the 1890s, but the picture of marriage throughout his fiction provides insight into his views on the institution from many perspectives, e.g., class, education, wealth, experience, age, and gender. Looking at marriage over time provides greater depth to any analysis of Gissing's work, since the examples he uses, almost without thought, hidden as it were in the background, reveal his unconscious attitudes. One must be careful when stating that he writes without thought, but it is possible for a writer to use some character or group of characters to support the main story without considering every aspect of the characters' lives. A rich thematic background thus develops, reflecting the author's imaginative engagement with his or her story.

Gissing employs missed or near marriages throughout his fiction and uses this idea to further his plots. In *Workers in the Dawn*, Arthur Golding and Helen Norman come close but do not marry. The marriages of Arthur and Carrie Mitchell and Maud Gresham and John Waghorn take place, foredoomed due to the participants' incompatibilities. The ease with which the two marriages occur and the insurmountable difficulties that prevent Arthur and Helen from marrying reflect a basic aspect of Gissing's philosophy of life, i.e., happiness is hard to achieve and is fleeting when two people do experience it. If a happy marriage does develop, it is frequently only after great struggle and privation. Ida Starr and Osmond Waymark in *The Unclassed* exemplify this. From the moment they meet, Ida and Osmond endure many unhappy experiences before they can accept what lies before them. Ida is a prostitute who determines to change her life, and Osmond is in love with Maud Enderby, whose other-worldly perspective prevents her from responding to him as a woman. Thus, Waymark operates between the two women, failing to convince Maud to marry him and almost losing Ida because of his inability to accept her past and appreciate her. In one sense, Ida teaches Osmond to value her through her good work with poor children after she goes to live with her grandfather, Abraham Woodstock. Ida is willing to wait until Osmond awakens from his self-absorption to realize that what he truly wants is what she has become. (See Chapter 12.) These three missed marriages, one only temporarily so, resemble Adela Waltham and Hubert Eldon's failure to wed early in *Demos*. As Gissing has structured the novel, they seem ideally suited for one another, but Hubert's youthful escapade, resulting in his being wounded in a duel over a woman he comes to despise, prevents Adela from seeing him for the man he has become. On his return to Wanley, the scandal over his actions and his mother's rejection of him strongly influence Adela's opinion. However, unlike Helen Norman, circumstances and hard experience as a consequence of her marriage to Richard Mutimer give Adela another chance, and she and Hubert renew their relationship.

The missed or near marriages in *The Unclassed* and *Demos* that turn to reconciliation are a novelistic convention generally more common in Victorian fiction than the tragic separation and lonely deaths of Arthur and Helen in *Workers in the Dawn*. However, Gissing tends more to the tragic than the happy ending. His very next two novels, *Isabel Clarendon* and *Thyrza* reflect this pattern. In the case of Bernard Kingcote and Isabel Clarendon, it might be too strong to call their reluctance to wed tragic. Both are old enough to be cautious about changing their lives. Isabel is a widow, and Kingcote has never been married, but calculation replaces sentiment, not a scheming calculation but one that foresees the vicissitudes of life and doubts whether he or she is capable of handling them. In *Thyrza*, however, Thyrza Trent dies of a broken heart. In another near marriage in the novel involving her, she has called off her wedding to Gilbert Grail almost at the altar. Through her love for Walter Egremont, Thryza rejects the faithful Grail and changes her life to make herself worthy of Walter. At the suggestion of Mrs. Ormonde, Thyrza and Walter agree to wait two years before they marry. Mrs. Ormonde hopes that Egremont will see the foolhardiness of an exogamous marriage even though Thyrza makes enormous efforts to raise herself to Walter's class level and develop her talents as a singer. Contrary to the difference between Harvey and Alma Rolfe in *The Whirlpool* over her desire to pursue a career as a violinist, Thyrza's professional attainments do not lead to a rupture with Walter. Rather, deceived by Mrs. Ormonde, Walter thinks that Thyrza equitably accepts the status quo between them. He has changed, but she has not, and the loss of his love leads melodramatically to her death.

Unlike the disruptions or delays in marital plans discussed above, *Our Friend the Charlatan* introduces a farcical touch in the triangle between Constance Bride, May Tomalin, and Dyce Lashmar. This novel presents a satiric portrait of human desires and vanities, drawing on that sense of irony that Gissing claims is in much of his fiction. Discussed earlier under the idea of family, Constance, May, and Dyce jockey for position relative to one another and Lady Ogram ("Lady Ogre"?). Constance wants Dyce, Dyce wants May and the money she will inherit, and May wants Dyce and her aunt's money and social contacts. Although their actions grow out of their personalities, one senses Gissing's social manipulation of these fictive archetypes. All three are dealt with in such a way that resembles a weighing up of their faults. The needy but foolish Iris Woolstan marries Dyce; Lady Ogram dismisses May but rewards Constance with funds to continue one of Lady Ogram's charities. *Our Friend the Charlatan*, in addition to its tone of satiric irony, suggests a diminishing interest in the subject of marriage. This contrasts strongly to the passion in the near marriages in *The Nether World* and *Born in Exile* published twelve and nine years, respectively, before *Our Friend the Charlatan*. Sidney Kirkwood, honest and well meaning, cancels his vows to Jane Snowdon to marry Clara Hewett in *The Nether World* after an acting rival throws acid in Clara's face. Even considering Kirkwood's plausible rationalizations, this represents an act of moral weakness and one that condemns Jane and himself to unhappy lives. Jane and Sidney prepare for their marriage over a long period. Sidney watches her grow from a young teenager to an adult while they learn to love one another. Sidney reels from his constant observations of the unhappiness of those he encounters. They include the Hewett family and the lonely Jane, misused by Clem Peckover and Mrs. Peckover, who hungers for Sidney's occasional kind words. In *Born in Exile*, the improbable occurs, and Sidwell Warricombe grows to love Godwin Peak. Even after she learns of his deception, she goes to see him, but his sense of shame and moral weakness prevent him from frankly facing her with his love.

The disrupted marriage plans in *The Nether World* and *Born in Exile* harm those involved. No real good results in the changes in the protagonists' lives, even in the case of Sidwell Warricombe. It is no light matter to engage the affections of someone like her. And, although it might be argued that Gissing develops their romance ironically, Godwin Peak truly desires what Sidwell represents in her class position and cultural refinement. He even grows to love her. However, Gissing is at his most ambiguous, ambivalent, and ironic in the emotional complications surrounding Rhoda Nunn's and Everard Barfoot's disrupted intentions to marry in *The Odd Women*. This is a positive instance of a marital disruption. Given their equal mixture of strong desire and the need to manipulate each other, Rhoda and Everard have lived out their dramas from the safe bastions of achieved opinions, opinions derived from experience of who they are and what they want from life. At one and the same time tempted to change their statuses and intent on maintaining their positions, emotionally and intellectually, they have little chance of coming together. This may reflect Elaine Showalter's position regarding Gissing that "he was always profoundly skeptical about the possibility of fulfilling permanent relationships between men and women" (30). Assessing the ways in which Gissing draws their characters and develops their brief romance, one may be right in stating that he had no intention to explore how they could overcome the many obstacles between them but rather a desire to show that, no matter the emotional and physical attraction, two people thus constituted will not succeed in finding a way to forget their differences and remember their possibilities. If this is so, their imagined point of conflict, i.e., Rhoda's demand that Everard explain his conduct regarding Monica Madden Widdowson and his refusal to do so, supports Gissing's ironic narrative stance. What seems on the surface an insoluble dilemma need not be so save for the preponderance of will over desire in both their characters. (See Chapter 10.) Given this, they part, satisfied at having fought to a draw. Gissing, with his examples of those who should not marry or at least not marry those they do, ends Rhoda and Everard's relationship on a positive note when they coolly meet after Everard has married the even-tempered Agnes Brissenden and Rhoda has rededicated herself to helping the odd women.

The interactions of the themes of marriage, family, and children challenge Gissing's imaginative exploration of late-Victorian culture. However, he rises to the challenge, seeming to relish the near impossibility of reconciling the human dilemmas revealed. His many cancellations and/or revisions of works in progress, even completed works, testify to this mindset. Not many of his novels end with the bleak results of *Workers in the Dawn*, a bleakness reinforced by the paradoxical engagement of Maud Waghorn and a Russian prince.

7

Politics, Work, and Business

As stated in a previous chapter, most of George Gissing's early novels focus all or in part on the English working class. He reveals a largely unsentimental view of its living conditions, family experiences, and working environment. *Demos: A Story of English Socialism* and *The Nether World*, the first a story of class upheaval and social change and the second one of stasis and the narrowing of possibilities for workers, present Gissing's visions of the deep forces molding the masses and thus the political direction of the nation. Jacob Korg writes of *Demos*, "Its thesis is that the poverty of the poor debases them beyond remedy and makes them incapable of the self-rule that democratic socialism proposes to grant them" (*George Gissing* 84). Later novels such as *Denzil Quarrier* and *Our Friend the Charlatan* dramatize aspects of political contests. Alongside and sometimes coupled with the political dimension of his fiction, Gissing examines work done in many forms. *Workers in the Dawn* deals largely with middle-class figures, but through its protagonists Arthur Golding and Helen Norman, the novel dips in and out of the lower-class. Similarly, *The Unclassed* follows Osmond Waymark's involvement with lower class life. If not always the actual work performed, Gissing does portray the lives of workers struggling with social and economic forces, and not those solely from the working class. He expands the idea of work in *Thyrza* and *New Grub Street* to include a wide range of characters pressed by material demands to find ways to stay alive. Business gradually rises to prominence in Gissing's fiction as he describes it from multiple viewpoints in *Born in Exile*, *The Odd Women*, *In the Year of Jubilee*, and *The Crown of Life*, culminating

71

with *Will Warburton*, a novel whose hero "drops" from his position as a sugar refiner to one as a grocer. Gissing intertwines politics, work, and business to create a dynamic social picture, one with no stable boundaries either in terms of class or human aspirations.

First, Gissing's political focus reveals a private dynamic that pulls public political actions and interests into its sphere. Fear of the mob operates in his fiction, especially from a class-based perspective. The cultured onlooker observes the lower class at play and is repulsed by it. Masses of people and the free flow of alcohol, even when the mob is generally good humored, suggest a latent, ugly outbreak always potentially there as in novels such as *The Nether World* and *In the Year of Jubilee*. In the former, Sidney Kirkwood is a craftsman and a person with a natural refinement. This is not to suggest that he is a polished gentlemen but rather that he possesses essential traits of a gentleman, minus wealth and higher class status, that enable him to understand and help others and that provide him with an expansive view of people's lives, placing him in their circumstances. A basic honesty and loyalty to oneself and others, traits also possessed by Kirkwood, are part of the portrait of a gentleman of whatever class. Through the perspective of Kirkwood and Nancy Lord from *In the Year of Jubilee*, Gissing shows the power of numbers by means of which people become a mob. In Kirkwood's and Lord's eyes, the mob during a bank holiday and the queen's Jubilee, respectively, are on the move though in no immediate political direction. The strong inference drawn from these two episodes is that when they find both a leader and a direction their power will clearly manifest itself.

Gissing never writes a novel in which a successful political leader rises from the lower class. However, he very early portrays two strong political figures in *Workers in the Dawn*'s Will Noble and *Demos*'s Richard Mutimer. Noble, Arthur Golding's friend and, for a while, inspiration, is not a conventional political leader, but his efforts to understand the political, social, and economic forces operating in the larger society and develop ways to counter their harmful effects on the working class underlie the political direction of his character. Golding, the novel's chief protagonist, shifts, much to Noble's disappointment, to a private life once he decides to use for himself the legacy from the Rev. Norman's will. In sharp contrast to the public direction of Noble's efforts, Golding works to become an artist, a course that his guide and benefactor Samuel Tollady encourages. John Pether and Mark Challenger, Tollady's friends, display a corrosive bitterness against the upper classes due to their families' sufferings. Pether especially rages, to no effect, and stands as a possible warning to Golding against social and political agitation as vehicles for change. Like Voltaire's Candide, Golding tends his garden. To choose an example closer to his own time, Gissing has Golding follow Thomas Carlyle's advice in *Sartor Resartus* (1836, 1838) to turn to the work nearest to hand and do it as well as possible (188). From the moment he realizes the legacy's possibilities for himself, happiness will no longer have a public but a private goal.

It would be wrong to say that Richard Mutimer inherits both wealth and a vision of how to employ it from his grandfather's will. He is already a skilled engineer and an accomplished agitator for workers' rights. The money allows him to launch an Owenite scheme to transform Wanley Valley into a workers' paradise. Only Mutimer's too-ambitious personality prevents his complete success before the will is overthrown by an even later one. Mutimer's socialist and writer friend Westlake can point the way to success, but he cannot lead from within a movement that he only observes from a higher class position. And, Mutimer's abandonment of his fiancée, the patient Emma Vine, alienates his socialist comrades. Mutimer, in the few years he has to implement his ideas, does not aspire to political office, but it is the type of opportunity in England open to the newly wealthy after the electoral reforms in the later nineteenth century. Not surprisingly, money also leads to political influence in Gissing's fiction.

In *Our Friend the Charlatan*, Lady Ogram, a former actress who married money and has become a social tyrant, attempts to launch Dyce Lashmar on a political career. Attracted to Lashmar's plagiarized social and political philosophy, she attempts to force him on Hollingford's electors. In *Denzil Quarrier*, Quarrier also has a secret, though not of his making, which derails his political career. These two novels have the most direct political connection and reinforce Gissing's idea that the personal controls the public in human affairs. Quarrier and Lashmar begin from the same class level. The Reverend Philip Lashmar lives under straitened financial circumstances. Much like Jasper Milvain in *New Grub Street*, whose mother has financial difficulty in helping to further his journalistic career, Lashmar's father must also cut back on his support for Dyce. Unlike Milvain, Lashmar has little success to show for the allowance given him. However, both men tell their respective parents that they can survive without it. One would like to think that Lashmar's subsequent falsities and treacheries result from his fear of poverty, but this is not the case. Lashmar is a man who always looks out for the main chance, a confidence man to the core. Robert Selig observes, "the satire exposes him as a mere lazy dilettante. In place of work or strain, this Oxford-trained hero prefers cash donations from women" (*George Gissing* 90). Without as many disguises as Herman Melville's protagonist in *The Confidence-Man: His Masquerade* (1857), he has as many faces. At one time simultaneously making love to the plain Constance Bride and the pretty May Tomalin while maintaining contact with the infatuated Iris Woolstan whom he eventually marries, Lashmar also attempts to deceive Lady Ogram who acts quickly once the moral Lord Dymchurch reveals Lashmar's falsehoods regarding his promise to marry Constance and foreswear her niece May. The collapse of Lashmar's public career has no impact on his politics, since personal ambition in what looked like a promising area was his sole motivation. After his exposure, Lashmar once again brazenly approaches Constance Bride as a lover only to be brushed aside. Lashmar's failure as a politician emphasizes Gissing's position that larger issues must wait on smaller ones. Parliament and its election contests and government with its many ministries lie in the background, assumed by the generally stable society depicted, but in the foreground, personal dilemmas demand the attention even of those turning their attention to public issues.

The earlier novel *Denzil Quarrier* exemplifies this private dominance over a public call to duty. The degree and sincerity of this call are always suspect in Gissing, and especially in this novel that Selig ambivalently characterizes as "a potboiler, though the materials might have made for a serious narrative" (*George Gissing* 75). However, it is the weight of the novel's focus on individual lives and not some larger didactic purpose that calls in question any person's capacity to think much beyond the self. In fact, Gissing does not condemn those whose self-interest motivates them. From first to last, Quarrier acts from his own desires in offering himself as a Liberal parliamentary candidate for Polterham. Even his intention finally to withdraw his candidacy arises from a wish to spare his "wife" Lilian from being revealed as a bigamist. Samuel Quarrier, Denzil's uncle, opposes his election and does so because of their political differences; the uncle is a conservative, but the most important aspect is that he has maintained his political position in Polterham for years. Samuel does not wrestle with policy differences and then, deciding what is best for Polterham and the country, oppose his nephew. From a more suspect position, Eustace Glazzard, Denzil and Lilian's presumed friend, betrays them for personal reasons. Glazzard secretly wishes to run for parliament, and a deep resentment of his friend's successes in life leads him to seek out Northway, Lilian's legal husband, and expose his friends. The feminist Mrs. Wade also reveals the private source of her actions. Infatuated with Denzil Quarrier and wanting him for herself, she does not interfere with Lilian's decision to commit suicide. In fact, she stands and watches the desperate woman drown herself. Finally, Northway, probably the least admirable character in the novel, weakly accepts Eustace Glazzard's money and reveals his earlier marriage to Lilian. (See Chapter 10.)

Just as the examination of the political forces at work in Gissing's fiction reveals the many conflicting currents, so also the idea of work leads one deeper into the thematic swirl. This latter phrase is a suggestive correction to any desire to tidy up his novels and establish final meanings for them. As Gissing trusts his imaginative grasp in his fiction, he introduces more and greater complexities than he could have expected before starting any particular novel. One should add, before he finally decides, at any given time, which one he will write and send to a publisher. While it is true that his many fits and starts, sometimes destroying completed or nearly completed novels, could be seen as the actions of an incoherent thinker, one could also see these as the struggles to find the exactly right theme to explore and the exactly right way to explore it. *Workers in the Dawn* is the most appropriate novel through which to analyze the idea of work and not just for its title. Negative images dominate the idea of work in Gissing's fiction even if there are some positive ones scattered throughout the canon. Adrian Poole comments on the novel's opening scene in Whitecross Street during market night:

> The degradation of the setting and the human beings in it is virtually total. Such slender compensations for the drudgery of their daily work as are provided by the weekly release may lead to even deeper misery and subjection [*Gissing in Context* 60].

The Goldings, father and son, supply striking examples of the above situation. the Rev. Norman witnesses the nearly complete inability of his college friend Arthur Golding, Sr., to prosper in life. After many past efforts to connect with the world and support himself and his family, the elder Golding succumbs to drink, leaving the sorrowful Arthur to his friend's care. Fortunate in having the Rev. Norman as his first guardian, Arthur once again avoids disaster when Samuel Tollady informally adopts him. However, Arthur does not find sufficient meaning in life as a printer or painter. Work can neither save him nor Helen Norman, the Rev. Norman's daughter. Both, suffering the losses of their parents, have money and friends on which to rely but cannot achieve happiness through work or personal relationships.

Work absorbs much of the energy of the novel. Except for John Waghorn and Augustus Whiffle, none of the male characters, besides Arthur Golding after he receives his legacy, have means to survive other than by work. Not that Gissing presents many middle-class males as living on the edge, but even the relatively wealthy society painter Gilbert Gresham works at his profession. The Rev. Orlando Whiffle, Augustus's father and Edward Norman's financially strapped curate, must cope with the needs of a large family on an inadequate salary. He and the Rev. Edgar Heatherley, the pastor of a working-class London parish, through whom Helen Norman serves the poor after inheriting her father's money and moving to London, have an assured income but one contingent only on their continuing service to the Church of England. For people on a lower-class level, beginning with those who grudgingly help the child Arthur after he flees pennilessly to London, no guarantees exist, regardless of the effort expended over many years, to support themselves. The state has no concern with their condition, beyond the often-rejected aid that comes through the poor laws, unless they break the law. Carrie Mitchell, expelled from her Aunt Pettindund's house when she reveals her pregnancy, faces the street as her first and last alternative. Friends, in her case the now-grown Arthur, remain her only hope. However, other friends that she meets before and after she marries Arthur encourage her to drink heavily and prostitute herself. Prior to her pregnancy, the meager wages she receives for long hours as a hatmaker underscore the negative aspects of work.

The often ineffectual ability of work to provide any protection against life's contingencies appears strongly in the case of *The Odd Women*'s Monica Madden and her older sisters, Alice and Virginia. Michael Collie states:

> When he described the efforts Rhoda and Mary make to teach interested and willing girls the shorthand, book-keeping, commercial correspondence that will allow them to live, that will allow them to escape the slavery of other types of employment, Gissing as usual shows that he has taken the trouble to know what he is writing about [*Alien Art* 150].

Given Gissing's frequently realistic picture of his culture, the Madden sisters' plight is not an unusual one. Although Monica has a chance to escape the "slavery" through learning what Rhoda and Mary offer, neither she nor her sisters are successful in their attempts to achieve a healthy independence. However, the first threat to their survival comes with their father Dr. Elkanah Madden's death the very day before he is to insure his life and thus protect his remaining children. This melodramatic incident shatters their sense of safety and breaks up their home. Barely surviving on a small legacy and work as governess and lady's companion, Alice and Virginia know that their prospects will only narrow with age. Monica, however, is pretty, and the sisters pin their hopes on her marrying well. She takes a job in a London draper's establishment, Messrs. Scotcher and Co. (27). The owner regiments the lives of the young women who work and live in the dormitory, giving them little freedom of movement. In addition to the restrictions, the women work long hours standing behind counters. For the women, the place furnishes the bare necessities of life while generating dreams of escape. In a well-orchestrated duet of frustrated desire, Monica meets Edmund Widdowson, a retired clerk, and they marry. For her, this act offers a false sense of liberation since she moves from the shop's control to Widdowson's. The shadow of work hangs over Monica's and Edmund's lives; both fled gladly from the ordeal of labor with no sufficient purpose. Monica dies soon after giving birth to a son. Gissing seems to argue that work and Widdowson kill her. Alice and Virginia Madden raise the child, with Widdowson's financial help, though he apparently doubts that he is the father. While the sisters' revived hope for a meaningful end for which to work, i.e., raising Monica's child and starting a school for children (385), has positive overtones, Monica's death robs it of some value.

Mary Barfoot and Rhoda Nunn modify this picture of pointless work destroying lives, but only slightly. Together, they run a business training respectable young women for office work. Near the end of the nineteenth century, changing attitudes toward women and the invention of the typewriter helped open this field to them. The paradox lies in the fact of the cumbersome nature of the early typewriters. Rhoda tells Everard Barfoot, Mary's cousin, that it takes six months to become proficient in its use (*The Odd Women* 39). The grudging admission of women to work at jobs previously reserved for men will expand when class barriers are lowered. Mary and Rhoda agree to dismiss a woman of whom they have moral suspicions. The tension they reveal in removing this danger underscores the need to guard against male prejudice toward women advancing in a wide range of occupations. Olive Chancellor in Henry James' *The Bostonians* (1886) and Vivvie Warren in George Bernard Shaw's *Mrs. Warren's Profession* (1895) exhibit two methods of countering any retrograde action on the part of men. Both women cut themselves off from any romantic involvement for the sake of the feminist cause and a career in accounting, respectively. Rhoda dallies with the possibility of marriage or an affair with Everard Barfoot only to reject him for her career and her loyalty to Mary. The irony is that Mary feels an attraction to Everard as well, but he appears unaware of it. While Barfoot has no connection to their business, the emotions he arouses in the two women come close to severing their relationship and diverting them from their ultimate goal to help unmarried, and possibly unmarriageable, women establish themselves in the business world.

The world of business emerges slowly in Gissing's fiction and undergoes multiple transformations before reaching its thematic apotheosis in *The Crown of Life* and *Will Warburton*. During this process, some professions are included in the essentially moral uplift that business involvement gives to certain characters. Gissing, as it were, rings all the changes on the theme of business, from the base to the honorable. Before Samuel Tollady, the charitable bookseller and printer in *Workers in the Dawn*, meets and saves Arthur Golding, the latter comes as a child under the control of some despicable characters. Several mistreat him as they enlist him in their very small business pursuits. Tollady, however, aids those less fortunate than himself, but at this stage in using businesses and businessmen, Gissing shows Tollady's ruin by the grasping John Waghorn. Not for Gissing the likes of Dickens' Cherryble brothers in *Nicholas Nickleby* (1839) who both give to others and survive the giving intact. In *The Unclassed*, Abraham Woodstock, who rejected his daughter and only reluctantly accepts his granddaughter, Ida Starr, is morally redeemed by her and

Osmond Waymark. Woodstock's wealth and potential for good do not appear on their own but are liberated by others. Bernard Kingcote in *Isabel Clarendon* weakly declines to become involved with Isabel, and Godwin Peak in *Born in Exile* cravenly flees from the courageous Sidwell Warricombe who goes to see him after her brother's exposure of Peak's scheme. Each retreats into business, Kingcote as a bookseller in a provincial town and Peak as a chemical engineer. The first major shift to business as a transformative endeavor occurs in *The Odd Women* in which Mary Barfoot and Rhoda Nunn train young, respectable women for business work and support themselves in the process. As Tollady relieved distress from the proceeds of his business so Barfoot and Nunn work for female emancipation, saving some women not only from Alice and Virginia Madden's unrewarding work but the equally deadening employment at which Monica Madden labors in the London draper's shop.

Before *The Odd Women*, Gissing uses business as theme and setting but seldom focuses on it in a positive way. The comical Nicholas Peak, who sets up his café outside the gates of Whitelaw College in *Born in Exile* and sets his nephew Godwin fleeing in horror to escape identification with him, is but the most obvious image of business as a form of social degradation. *In the Year of Jubilee*, paradoxically, continues what *The Odd Women* has begun. The Barmbys, father and son, former partners to Stephen Lord, and Lord himself, mortally ill, who takes his loyal housekeeper Mary Woodruff as a confidante, are more than just types. Through their actions and desires, Gissing deepens them, making them essential to the plot while limiting their appearances in the novel. Stephen Lord wishes to control his children while alive and through his will after his death. They exist as a family in uneasy friction with Horace Lord rebelling against and disappointing his father's hopes that he would settle into a business career. Lord is suspicious of his daughter Nancy because she is a woman. His worries prove all too true when Lionel Tarrant seduces and secretly marries her before her father's death (111). Nancy keeps the marriage secret since according to the terms of Lord's will she cannot inherit her portion of the estate if she marries before she is twenty-six. Samuel Barmby, the good-natured if somewhat pompous son of Lord's business partner, is appointed Lord's executor. He grows to love Nancy, and while she does not respond romantically, she conceals her marriage to Tarrant. Eventually, she reveals what she has done, and though disappointed, Barmby colludes in hiding her illegal right to inherit. Stephen Lord and Samuel Barmby are not seen so much as businessmen in action as complex human beings who play small but important roles in the narrative.

With Beatrice French and Luckworth Crewe, Gissing continues the theme of the businessman and businesswoman as full human beings. At first,

Beatrice appears as the sister of Ada and Fanny. Ada is the slatternly wife of the long-suffering Arthur Peachey. Ill-tempered and quarrelsome, Ada makes his life unbearable. Fanny, regardless of her poor life choices, cannot be persuaded to act sensibly. She runs off to Brussels with a man who eventually abandons her. To the lower middle-class family, this is unacceptable. While Beatrice is also willful, she conducts herself in a way that leads to an independent life. She disdains the actions of both sisters, an attitude that does her credit. She sets herself up in business by establishing a dress company that appeals to women who want a semblance of the fashionable. As John Carey observes in *The Intellectuals and the Masses: Pride and Prejudice among the Literary Intelligentsia, 1880–1939* (1992), "Beatrice alone [of the three sisters] displays any ability" (98). Beatrice meets Luckworth Crewe, and they join forces in business. Nancy Lord has rejected Crewe as a suitor, and Fanny French dismisses Horace Lord, Nancy's brother, because he represents a too-safe life. Horace eventually marries her, but neither long survives the event. Crewe has fastened on advertisement as a new medium that will revolutionize business. He dominates Beatrice after her failed attempt to control him. However, Crewe presents himself as a hard-headed businessman who knows, absolutely, the way to success. Gillian Tindall states, "Like a number of other characters in the later books, Crewe has a respect for money which outweighs his respect for other things" (258). Unlike her sisters' dealings with men, Beatrice gives way to Crewe's superior assurance and business acumen. Although they represent a minor part of the plot, Gissing adroitly portrays Crewe's rise from a class position slightly lower than Beatrice's. From the top of the Monument, Nancy rejects Crewe's offer of the fruits of the world of business spread out below them, but this leaves her with Tarrant and the emotional dead end of their marriage. Nancy cannot see beyond her seemingly higher-class status to what Crewe means by his offer, in effect a world in which achievement, rather than attitude, counts above all.

The Town Traveller, *The Crown of Life* , and *Will Warburton: A Romance of Real Life* end Gissing's late but absorbing dramatization of the world of business. The protagonists of the three novels, i.e., Mr. Gammon, Piers Otway, and Will Warburton, respectively, exhibit the dynamism, even the salvation, that business opportunities reflect and offer. Mr. Gammon, that cheerful town traveler or sales representative for any London company smart enough to hire him, sets a confident tone in the novel that he has a valuable skill and that there exist many companies who will employ him. He is a businessman in that he appears to act as an independent contractor. His working-class manner and leisure activities conceal the entrepreneur who moves from one situation to another as it suits him. His capital is his ability in his trade and the ease with which he deals with people. Otway, better educated, goes into business abroad. Although he makes a success, his principal aim is to marry Irene Derwent. Otway believes that the love of a beautiful and superior woman is the crown of life. Business thus becomes a means to an end, but its importance lies in the fact that business and not some more conventional sphere of activity is that means. Yet, the novel presents a harsh estimate of the effects of business. John Halperin remarks:

> The vulgarity of money-worship, the negation of culture, the unimportance of individual feelings are epitomized for Gissing, as for Dickens before him, in the horrors of modern commerce, which interests itself in "products" rather than individuals [*Gissing* 293].

Otway becomes a successful writer as well as businessman and lives down the taint of illegitimacy and his brothers' unsavory reputations. Both Gammon and Otway, though separated by the nature of their businesses and their level of culture, rely to a certain extent on their business accomplishments as a measure of who they are. While Gammon demonstrates his ability to act in the world of petty commerce, Otway restores his reputation and self respect through a successful career in international business. Sinclair Lewis's *Babbitt* (1922) and his broadly satiric portrait of the businessman lies some time in the future and reflects somewhat different circumstances.

Will Warburton, Gissing's last published novel, is an ironic high point for the role of business in Gissing's fiction. Initially, Gissing presents Warburton as a sugar refiner, a position that sets him higher than a retail grocer. But when Godfrey Sherwood misappropriates Warburton's share of their capital, Warburton goes behind the counter and advertises himself as Jollyman. Through hard work and the help of Mr. Allchin, the brother-in-law of his former housekeeper Mrs. Hopper, Warburton succeeds and earns the respect and love of Bertha Cross, a friend and an independent woman who stands by him when Norbert Franks and his wife Rosamund Elvan turn their backs as he falls economically into the lower-middle class. Bertha is a book illustrator who, like Warburton's sister Jane, a horticulturalist, works for her living. Early in the novel, Warburton states to Norbert Franks, "'To make money is a good and joyful thing as long one doesn't bleed the poor. So go ahead, my son, and luck be with you!'" (15). Warburton's attitude to honest work and his coming marriage to Bertha (331), all the while maintaining his interest in culture, contrast sharply to the pretentious Franks. Gissing depicts Warburton's initial ascendancy in business, but the subtitle of the work suggests Gissing's matter-of-fact acceptance of the romance of business with no sentimental design intended.

Politics, work, and business assuredly focus on practical affairs, but countless writers from Morley Roberts on speak of Gissing's impractical nature and his disparagement of the mundane aspects of how wealth is created. Negative portraits in each of the three thematic areas appear in his fiction; however, in the later novels, with the possible exception of *The Whirlpool*, he seems to speculate realistically on what happens in business operations, what a businessman or businesswoman does, and what an involvement in business changes or alters in one's possible relation to literature, art, or music in comparison to other interests and occupations. Politics and work receive the same unsparing examination in Gissing's novels and stories. Like any good artist, Gissing leaves his work to speak for itself.

8

Education Old and New

George Gissing's views on the role and place of education in nineteenth-century culture are replete with examples of conflict, loss, frustration, and false hopes. Publishing his first novel, *Workers in the Dawn*, a decade after the 1870 Education Act, Gissing portrays education for the masses with few positive values. Possessing on the whole a static view of society, he does not often portray the generative function of learning. If the economists can claim that a rising tide lifts all boats, educators have even more right to assert that the general spread of not only literacy but learning is essential to and aids all levels of social activity — economic, political, and cultural. Geniuses, apparently, do not multiply proportionately with an increase in education's availability, contrary to Thomas Gray's wistful expectations in "Elegy Written in a Country Churchyard" (1751); nevertheless, one can safely assume that twenty-first century industrial societies could not function with a populace that had no more schooling than its nineteenth-century counterparts. Contrary to his attitudes toward movement between the classes, Gissing begins as early as *Workers in the Dawn* to show some practical benefits of education even though, as Jacob Korg observes, Arthur Golding's "radical principles lead him to make an attempt to reform and educate [his wife Carrie Mitchell]" who "fails to respond and abandons him" (*George Gissing* 33). This practical aspect includes the betterment of working-class girls who will transfer what they have learned to their family lives. Helen Norman's star pupil, Lucy Venning, will be an immense improvement on women like Carrie Mitchell and her female relatives. The basic cultivation of Lucy's mind, with no false aspirations towards rising beyond her class level, will bring peace and harmony to any environment in which she presides as wife and mother. However, the deep pessimism reflected in "The Day of Silence" (1893) in which an entire working-class family die on the same day remains an important aspect of Gissing's social vision. Resistance to the broad benefits of learning is clearly part of his educational views. More positively, general cultural attainment is a worthy social goal, though his interest in this area is generally limited to those who already appreciate learning. Finally, education as liberation appears in several instances but not always coupled with worldly success. Gissing's complex view of education and learning undergoes many shifts throughout his writing career with the private area eclipsing the public in importance.

It is tempting to discuss education and class through a series of vignettes since the examples from Gissing's fiction are so varied. Women who are acquainted with literature and art as part of their upbringings generally appear with other cultural refinements and are sought after and valued. But women who acquire this background seldom hold their admirers after an initial attraction. In *Thyrza*, Thyrza Trent develops into a woman of culture and refinement, but after a separation of two years, and after she has supposedly met Walter Egremont's hopes and expectations, he no longer wants her. "The Sins of the Father," a crude melodramatic story in 1877 from Gissing's Chicago sojourn, uses a similar plot. Leonard Vincent's separation from Laura Lindon for two years while he teaches in New England cools his ardor even before his father falsely reports her death. What actually causes these changes? Gissing is largely silent, stating in both cases that his hero has altered. It is possible that these two instances, i.e, Thyrza and Laura, reflect a lack of belief in the possibility for real change and a suspicion that the cultural attainments were only a veneer. A different result occurs in *The Emancipated*. Miriam Baske is a severe member of a dissenting congregation who is living in Italy for her health after the death of her husband. The narrow, lower- middle-class chapel world reaches from the English Midlands to Italy and initially constricts her ability to see and understand the present and past of the country she temporarily inhabits. In one sense, it is the story of Pygmalion and Galatea, for Ross Mallard, a well-educated and cultured artist, finds her frozen in her beliefs and unable to let herself feel the southern influences. Slowly, and with great difficulty, Miriam responds to Mallard's tutelage; he refuses to accept that she will return to the world of chapel going in England with its heavy moral censures and convinces her that some inner conflict over this fate has led her to Italy. Painting, literature, classical ruins, and the beauty of the natural world are Mallard's allies in teaching or letting her teach herself what her real nature desires and that desiring and wanting things in this world are good in themselves. Jacob Korg states:

> Mallard, his talks about art, and a reading of Dante are the first influences that make her begin to see the sterility of her Evangelical beliefs. After opening her mind to Italy and visiting the Sistine Chapel and the Vatican with

Mallard, she can see no point whatever to her former church enthusiasm [*George Gissing* 139–40].

Some twenty-three years later, D.H. Lawrence in *Sons and Lovers* (1913) is to replay the same struggle, but Paul Morel fails to liberate Miriam Leivers. While Paul and Miriam are close in class, especially through Paul's mother, this does not prove an aid in opening her to a world of books and art. Unlike Miriam in *The Emancipated*, the voices that Lawrence's Miriam hears warning not to trust her feelings, not to trust the passions, overcome natural responses. Paul eventually turns away from her and Clara Dawes, a coworker at Jordan's with whom he has an affair. While Ross Mallard knows who he is and what he thinks, intellectually and emotionally, Paul is growing into his self-knowledge during most of the novel and cannot well educate anyone else.

Psychological, emotional, and intellectual refinement are depicted outside class limitations on a few occasions in Gissing's fiction. Hardly a character in his novels possesses these gifts to a greater extent than Samuel Tollady in *Workers in the Dawn*. Though he exhibits true human compassion in raising and loving Arthur Golding and caring for the irascible John Pether as well as performing numerous acts of charity in his community, Tollady lacks the social graces if not the instinct for them. He educates Arthur, a willing pupil, and has educated himself. He reminds one of Harvey Rolfe in *The Whirlpool* in his simple kindness and love for art and literature. Rolfe is of a higher class, but Gissing, in these two portraits, has vitiated class as a requirement for cultural attainments. The lower middle-class Harold Biffen in *New Grub Street* has primarily educated himself to a high degree and in the process has developed his true nature, resembling Tollady and Rolfe in the process. If one contrasts Tollady, Rolfe, and Biffen with Gilbert Gresham and John Waghorn from *Workers in the Dawn*, it is quite clear that the former group are the true gentlemen. And yet, both Gresham and Waghorn rank socially in the upper middle class. They may know some things, and in Waghorn's case it is very little, but their class level has not predisposed them to profit by this knowledge and thus become educated. Ironically, education has helped raise Marian Yule in *New Grub Street* above her lower-middle class roots, but has benefited Amy Reardon very little. She seems only superficially capable of learning and responding to any knowledge gained. While Amy's middle-class status has given her the outward semblance of being a lady, Marian has demonstrated her greater spiritual refinement. Thus for Gissing, class can matter when it comes to education, but one usually has to set aside social refinements in judging the true class level of his characters. And, this natural refinement frequently leads to the greatest benefit from education.

If being raised in a certain class level can help one to learn, but not always, and if the lack of that level can impede the learning process, but not in each instance, are there greater certainties about the practical benefits of education? Not often in Gissing's world. Discussing poverty in *A Life's Morning*, John Halperin writes, "[I]ndiscriminate education is rejected as a panacea" (*Gissing* 72). For every Harry Mutimer in *Demos*, one finds an Augustus Whiffle in *Workers in the Dawn*, one weak from the temptations of a working-class environment, the other a fool even with his university training. Even before his brother Richard inherits money, Harry evinces a fatal weakness of character, shared to a degree by his sister Alice. For the working class in Gissing, the restraints and controls of mental training are often missing. In "Devil's Advocate," Barbara Rawlinson states:

> The nineteenth-century poor remain victims of oppression because they lack the educational opportunity to improve their circumstances; in the case of women however, virtually all, regardless of class, are denied the right of educational equality and, in consequence, remain intellectually incapable of challenging the existing rule [3].

Life's severities replace the classroom, and if these and some firm home direction are lacking, then people can slip from any clear path that will bring them happiness. Harry and Alice experience the latter, and money from Richard makes little difference since neither character has any moral direction for his or her life. The Rev. Orlando Whiffle can certainly give no direction to his son Augustus. The chaotic picture that Gissing draws of the reverend's family and his somewhat distracted state of mind intensify in Augustus, especially when he tries bachelor life in London. The clear implication is that while Augustus may have been the target of books and ideas while in school, he successfully evades their positive effects. As with Gresham and Waghorn in the same novel, one must possess some moral character to benefit from education. It is clear that in Gissing's fiction women often get practical help from education. In addition to Lucy Venning and some other of Helen Norman's pupils in *Workers in the Dawn*, Ida Starr in *The Unclassed* is an admirable example of the will to learn, to better oneself through education. Forced from school because of her mother's prostitution, Ida later temporarily becomes a prostitute, but she never gives up on a better life. She knows that learning will help lead to this result, and she clings to this conviction in an almost superhuman fashion. Her strong moral fiber enables her to hold steady through all adversities even when falsely accused of theft by Harriet Casti. The latter, from a more stable family background, cannot profit from her chances, and nothing she gains through her formal education or life with her poet-husband Julian makes a dent in her ignorant willfulness. As with the younger Whiffle above, character helps determine who can learn, and the lack of character marks Gissing's fictional beings regardless of social class or their need for education's benefits. Gissing's subversive portrait of Ida Starr marks one of the reasons why his acceptance as a novelist was always so problematic. He selects moral character and a desire for learning and gives these attributes to a character distinctly outside the boundaries of respectable society. Of course, Ida is an aberration in his fiction since most of the women who benefit from education have more acceptable moral and class backgrounds than she.

Dora and Maud Milvain in *New Grub Street* are two representatives of the latter categories. They receive good educations at one of the new schools for young women. Gissing mentions this as a matter of course in the novel. Both they and their brother Jasper, similarly well educated, are in potentially precarious financial circumstances as their mother's annuity ends with her life. Dora is a visiting governess in the nearby town of Wattleborough, and Maud teaches music(10). Jasper has already embarked on a writing career, and once their mother dies, he encourages his sisters to come to London and pursue the same vocation. The practical benefits of their education, first in the work they perform in Wattleborough and second in London, might be conventional, middle-class examples in late nineteenth-century England. However, the actions they take are efficacious until marriage relieves them from the necessity of earning a living: Dora to the surprisingly successful Whelpdale, editor of a paper, and Maud to the wealthy, if dissolute, Dolomore. Marian Yule, the other chief female besides her cousin Amy Reardon, dislikes what she does with her excellent training, but when she takes a post as an assistant librarian in a provincial town (506) after years of drudgery for her father in the British Library, she apparently moves into more congenial work and becomes the primary support of her mother and her now-blind father. Amy, once Reardon dies, marries Jasper Milvain and achieves the goal for which her talents, education, and inclination have prepared her. Somewhat superficially interested in books and ideas, Amy's desire is to succeed in life. She is clever and socially astute, and given her background and the £10,000 she inherits, she is able to make use of her abilities. Being middle class and knowing how to act in society is not enough; some intellectual training and money enable her finally to marry a man who will succeed in the world's eyes and give her a position from which to help him and show her own nature.

If one resists learning or is intractable to its influences, at least two possible reasons explain this state. Either some experience prevents receptivity to ideas and knowledge or one has a native disposition that spurns anything gained through the printed word. Mr. Gammon in *The Town Traveller* is a perfect example of someone to whom formal learning is not an issue. One cannot even say that he rejects literature since the issue does not arise. Gissing never places knowledge from books as an obstacle that Gammon must overcome in order to succeed. One sees the distinction between a Gammon and someone who has a natural aversion to books and the process of learning when one contrasts Nancy Lord in *In the Year of Jubilee* and Louise Derrick in *The Paying Guest* to him. Nancy has a veneer of learning but gladly gives up any pretense at an interest in books when she falls in love with Lionel Tarrant. Possibly, the negative image of a female scholar in her erstwhile friend Jessica Morgan, whom Annette Federico calls Gissing's "portrayal of the frigid intellectual" (*Masculine Identity* 45), repels her. Gissing here certainly overloads his depiction of the inadequacy of certain (female?) minds to the tasks of scholarship. Seven years later, however, *Our Friend the Charlatan*'s Constance Bride is at the very least an intellectual match for Dyce Lashmar. Yet, Helen Norman in *Workers in the Dawn*, Gissing's first female intellectual, dies young, and besides her hard work with the East London poor and her disappointment in love, one senses a shadow of the idea that her theological and philosophical studies overtax her. Louise, the second example above of someone with a natural aversion to learning, has no place in her life for books. Even though it appears that her family circumstances would downplay any educational aspirations, her biological drive ultimately overcomes any pretensions to false class advancement when she chooses the electrical engineer Tom Cobb. Louise, in her victory over circumstances, could be seen as the antithesis of Helen Norman and Jessica Morgan if not of the practical Constance Bride. While Helen and Jessica fail to sustain lives in which books and ideas are important, Louise triumphs by rejecting any suggestion of their value. Constance's education is a prerequisite for her success with Lady Ogram, and she does not transfer her inheritance to Lashmar as Iris Woolstan later does. In Gissing's fictional world, books and ideas do not necessarily unsex one, but an education and a clear head give one an opportunity to think and act independently, traits that Gissing largely reserves for men.

Resistance to learning and the world of letters comes in different forms. On one side, Harriet Casti in *The Unclassed* refuses to have anything to do with literature and harasses her husband Julian because of his poetical activities. Harriet fears the influence of literature on their life together and therefore despises everything regarding it. On the other side, Marian Yule in *New Grub Street* feels a revulsion to adding further to the number of useless books already in existence. An unhappy denizen of the British Library in which she researches and writes for her father, Marian wants a life different from that of a literary drudge. As noted above, Gissing ironically makes her a librarian after Jasper Milvain goads the honorable Marian into canceling their engagement. Piers Otway in *The Crown of Life* temporarily abandons his studies when he falls in love with Irene Derwent. After she initially rejects his advances, Otway becomes a businessman and later turns to writing on Russian affairs, obliquely reflecting Gissing's early role as a correspondent to *Vyestnik Evropy* on English social and political affairs. Unlike Otway's partial rejection of learning for love, John Pether, Samuel Tollady's working-class friend in *Workers in the Dawn*, becomes incoherent with rage at the wrongs suffered by him and his class. Will Noble in the same novel believes that education will lift the masses, but Pether's mind, to use a mechanical metaphor suitable to this industrial age, seizes up and will not perform its human duties. One could well expect Ida Starr in *The Unclassed* to react similarly to her prostitute mother, but her particular combination of intellect and will enable her to understand and value learning.

Dora and Maud Milvain and Amy Reardon in *New Grub Street* probably present Gissing's most subtle resistance to learning. All three women receive a good education, especially for those who do not go to a university, but none appears to reverence literature in the way that Edwin Reardon and Harold Biffen do. Before coming to London to begin careers as writers at their brother Jasper's suggestion, Maud and Dora longed to escape from their music and governess work, respectively. However, their literary endeavors are not a source of great delight either, and both give up their efforts when they marry. Whelpdale, who eventually marries Dora, tries many stratagems to succeed in writing and achieves a secure living when appointed editor to *Chit-Chat,* which thrives principally through his suggested changes. Whelpdale stands alone in his almost fanatical zeal to join the writing world. Amy Reardon combines elements of Dora and Maud and of Whelpdale. In contrast to the former two, she has no real interest in literature except as a vehicle by means of which she can appear clever and current. But, she also senses the value that others put on intellectual labors and wants to be accepted as one who appreciates the most recent writing and literary intrigues. Thus, she triumphs when she marries Jasper and presides over their dinner table. Jasper becomes the editor of an important literary journal and has at best a cynical respect for the true artist represented by his dead friend Edwin Reardon. Reardon, Biffen, and even Alfred Yule, whose wounded pride and vanity swallow up his love for literature, are a dying race of those who love literature for its own sake.

The effect of general literary and artistic culture is an important theme in Gissing's fiction. This is a somewhat static idea because it implies no need for action on its possessor's part. He or she just *is* that way. Related to this is a necessary social standing and an instinctive knowledge of the manners that accompany it. In *Born in Exile*, Sidwell Warricombe, with perhaps a little more religious coloring than usual in a Gissing heroine, is such a figure. Her destiny is to live out all the implications of her position in society, all that her world has imbued her with for the little less than twenty years of her life. This does not imply that she is learned nor that she has an extensive cultural attainment. Rather, it implies that she has absorbed the culture available in her world and that she carries it well. Peak, far better educated, immediately knows that she has acquired an education that fits her for her place. Sidwell needs only to reflect her culture to be accepted and admired. Exeter may not be London, and in the city she may not be as striking, but none of that is necessary for her to experience and re-experience the core of her world. Peak instinctively recognizes her value and for a time deceives her, but her brother Buckland exposes the interloper. (See Chapter 10 for a more extensive discussion of this crisis.) Gissing occasionally views this ideal attainment from the point of view of a Peak, the outsider who wants in. For the outsider to long for this result, the woman he desires must remain whole in her perfection much as Irene Derwent also does in *The Crown of Life* for her class equal Piers Otway. For Peak, Sidwell has no flaw in her world, but he, an atheist and lower-middle class at best, must remake himself.

Godwin Peak uses deception to gain the world of general cultural attainment that Sidwell occupies from birth. But apart from rising in class, not an easy feat in Gissing's fictional world, can one move into the world of Sidwell and Irene in any other way? Gissing provides many examples of people holding onto the cultural level into which they are born, e.g., Mrs. John Yule, her son John, and daughter Amy in *New Grub Street*. Behind the façade of an achieved rank in society, however minor, Mrs. Yule struggles desperately on a limited income, but John and Amy have what they need to live in that world. John may have the least important aspects of culture, e.g., dress and manners, but, as stated above, Amy adds to that some knowledge of the world of books, art, and social and political ideas. Both she and John can move naturally in certain social circles. This is a true gift from Mrs. Yule and repays her sacrifices. In *A Life's Morning*, Emily Hood, Wilfrid Athel, and Richard Dagworthy might provide some insight into the question asked above. Only Athel is born into a world of general culture. Emily, the daughter of a clerk who works for Dagworthy, achieves an education and this, along with her natural refinement, attracts Athel. Dagworthy is the picture of the coarse businessman grown wealthy in the world's struggles. Emily, desiring Athel's cultural environment, is temporarily pulled back by her father's theft of money entrusted to him by Dagworthy. The latter uses this fact as a means to try to coerce Emily into a relationship. From this situation, one might well infer Gissing's skepticism on the ability to change one's past condition. Those who do so, like Alfred Yule's struggles to achieve success in the literary world in *New Grub Street*, often pay a terrible price. However, Emily appears to deserve someone like Athel, and Gissing describes her at the end as one who belongs, by her very nature, at his cultural and class level. The implication that it is her fate to be what she is, a positive outcome in her case, might be the source of Gissing's social vision, a carryover of that powerful idea from the classical past that he and some of his characters revere.

The play of the idea of education in Gissing's fiction shows an intuitive grasp of his society's dynamics. Born into the lower-middle class and educated for an academic career, Gissing was tossed out into the world by his youthful actions, experiencing the world's struggles and possibilities. From his experiences, he dramatizes the varied role of learning, revealing its unexpected facets but always keeping it as a central value in his world.

PART TWO

The Personal Imagination

9

Money as Language and Idea

The importance of money in Victorian Fiction can hardly be overestimated. From the 1830s to the end of the nineteenth century, money penetrates every aspect of the social structure and the very meaning of society. In *Masculine Identity in Hardy and Gissing*, Annette Federico writes, "The state of the economy and the political events of the 1880s and 1890s ... were frighteningly unstable, and in their public roles, men began to feel gradually overwhelmed, sucked into the whirlpool of financial risk and imperialist controversy" (18–19). Marriage, family, class, love, politics, education, work, the fine arts, literature, and, more generally, the very quality of life partially reveal themselves through the figurative power of money. Of Gissing, John Halperin observes:

> In the 1890s he was often ranked with Meredith and Hardy among the leading novelists of the time — yet he never earned much from his books.
> Because of his continual need for money he sold outright for ready cash the copyrights of many of his novels and rarely collected royalties under this arrangement [*Gissing* 2].

John Sloan, speaking more widely of writing in the nineteenth century, states, "The writer in effect lives out in his very labour a wider social conflict between the claims of free selfhood and the determinations of the market-place" (*Cultural* 86). Mr. Micawber's ironic adjuration to David in Charles Dickens' *David Copperfield* surely sets the decisive demarcation that money draws between happiness and misery:

> He solemnly conjured me, I remember, to take warning by his fate, and to observe that if a man had twenty pounds a year for his income, and spent

nineteen pounds nineteen shillings and sixpence, he would be happy, but
that if he spent twenty pounds one he would be miserable [173].

It is only when the full play of language and idea exists that money operates
in its manifold significances, testifying to its suggestive power. Gissing, writing at the end of the century, employs the ideas of love, art, and money in a
rich linguistic display that demonstrates money's essential, figurative role in
his fiction.

Juxtaposing Gissing's Arthur Golding from *Workers in the Dawn* with
Henry Ryecroft from *The Private Papers of Henry Ryecroft* resembles nothing
so much as an exercise in comparative literature, especially regarding their feelings and statements about money. For Golding, money is secondary to love
and the chance for happiness, while to Ryecroft, writing in an elegiac mode,
money has assumed mystical powers and hovers over and colors all that he
reveals about himself and his early struggles before the legacy, the fairy-tale-
like method of deliverance, descends and literally cuts him off from his previous life (*The Private Papers of Henry Ryecroft* xviii–xix, 99–100). In contrast,
Golding has some initial difficulty adjusting to the idea of the money left him
by his dead father's friend, the Reverend Edward Norman, father of Helen
Norman, the woman he loves but cannot have (*Workers in the Dawn* 1:240–44,
247–48). Money, affords Ryecroft a rich repose in the west of England which
he reveals in sensuous detail. His memoir is divided into the seasons and redo-
lent with a nature so long alien to his London existence. This sensuality suf-
fuses the book and exposes Ryecrofts longing for a few years in which to enjoy
nature's presence. Golding, cut off from Helen, first by her refusal to stay
with him once she learns he is married to, though separated from, Carrie
Mitchell, an alcoholic prostitute, and second by Helen's early death from disappointment and overwork, dramatically commits suicide by throwing himself over Niagara Falls (*Workers in the Dawn* 2: 436).

Golding's feelings for Helen resemble no one's more than Piers Otway's
love for Irene Derwent in Gissing's *The Crown of Life*. While the outcomes
of their love affairs are quite different, Golding would probably agree with
Otway that the crown of life is "the love of the ideal woman" (62). Harold
Biffen in *New Grub Street* repeatedly tells Edwin Reardon that he must reunite
with his estranged wife Amy, that the love of a woman such as she is not lightly
to be tossed aside or given up without a struggle (342–43, 368, 440–42).
Less weak than Golding in the pursuit of his ideal, Otway must first acquire
the money and position necessary to win Irene. Sufficient money, along with
the mature cultivation of his faculties, thus becomes a stream that eases his
way to Irene, lifting him over practical difficulties and bringing a calm steadi-
ness that creates a possibility for their union. (See Chapter 11 for a fuller discussion of this theme.) The application of this water metaphor also clarifies

Ryecroft's condition inasmuch as money has relieved him of his hard literary struggle, but Ryecroft does not continue his voyage beyond Devon once he gains the peace of his rural retreat. The stranded Edwin Reardon sees money's power to save one from misery and carry one into a better life but, like Golding's death at Niagara Falls, even when money becomes available, personal pressures and illness prevent him from fulfilling this envisioned hope. And, in *Workers in the Dawn*, Gissing also demonstrates, once one satisfies the needs of food, shelter, and clothing, money's profuse complexities. From the generosity of Samuel Tollady, the man who raised and sheltered the young Arthur, to Will Noble's projects to help the working man and woman to Helen's time, labor, and money to aid young working girls to the Christmas bacchanalia of Carrie's aunt's family and friends, money appears, paradoxically, to separate itself from ownership or control and spin off into the social world, somehow personified as both innocent and depraved. Jacob Korg, commenting on Helen Norman's sense of failure, states, "She finds that the poor do not respond to her kindness, that the money she gives them goes for drink, and her devotion and hard work produce no improvement" (*George Gissing* 36).

Although nearly every Gissing novel employs the language of money, *New Grub Street* represents its strongest use. Charles Dickens, one of the English novelists Gissing most admired, was a clear forerunner in incorporating money into the rhetorical and figurative structures of novels. Of course, in works such as *Nicholas Nickleby*, characters like the Cheeryble brothers paradoxically rob money of its importance by its abundance and freely given nature. The gain or loss of money in that novel has at times little urgency after the brothers appear in the lives of Nicholas, his sister, and their mother, and thus it loses in significance compared to its role in such works as *Oliver Twist* (1838), *Martin Chuzzlewit* (1844), *Bleak House* (1853), *Little Dorrit* (1857), or *Great Expectations* (1861). For Gissing, *New Grub Street* demonstrates the effect of money's thematic and linguistic saturation. Robert L. Selig notes, "Few other novels, in fact, devote so many passages to money" ("Valley" 170). And in *George Gissing*, Selig writes, "A single anti-idealistic principle runs throughout *New Grub Street*: in a society that values only money, neither love nor art can flourish without significant cash" (46). Nearly every character and event turn on the way that money describes, characterizes, or affects the momentum of the plot. Speaking generally of where the novel's writers live, John Goode remarks, "What is more important than the topographical region is the social zoning which commits the writer to living in a middle-class style on a working-class income" (*Ideology* 112). The intimate connection that Gissing makes between money and Harold Biffen's welfare presents money transformed into an organic substance, improving or lessening Biffen's physical condition by the amount he possesses. This organic image is strengthened when Reardon lies dying in Brighton, and Biffen, summoned by his friend, goes first to Amy as if invested with a new skin:

> She found him in the dining-room, and, even amid her distress, it was a satisfaction to her that he presented a far more conventional appearance than in the old days. All the garments he wore, even his hat, gloves, and boots, were new; a surprising state of things, explained by the fact of his commercial brother having sent him a present of ten pounds, a practical expression of sympathy with him in his recent calamity [*New Grub Street* 452].

Symbolically renewed by the fire that nearly destroyed the manuscript of his novel, *Mr. Bailey, Grocer*, Biffen appears, for him, resplendent; his brother's money thus becomes his new outward surface, giving him a presence that, as Amy observes, makes him socially more acceptable.

Edwin Reardon's situation prefigures this integration of money with all of life's activities and the necessity of its possession for any chance of happiness or success. In a crucial dialogue shortly after their introduction into the novel, Edwin and Amy speak of money or its lack in a series of metaphors reflecting an evolutionary momentum: money as holiday, business, security, art, fear, value, power, family and home, and social position (*New Grub Street* 50–55). Survival comes with money, and the novel's many allusions to Darwin, Spencer, and the struggle for existence emphasize this metaphorical portrait of money as sustenance (See Chapter 2.) Jasper Milvain, living on both an allowance from his mother and his hard-earned money, presents an image the reverse of Reardon's. Rachel Bowlby notes, in a metonymic figure, that Milvain's mental and physical efforts "will be wholly convertible into the 'value' of money" (*Just Looking* 109). As Milvain moves up in literary and social circles, his clothing reflects someone well adapted to succeed. Gissing notes his impeccable evening dress at the dinner that he and Amy, Reardon's former wife, give at the end of the novel (511). Just as Milvain has gained a surface polish so has he acquired both a decorative and socially valuable wife. Peter Keating states:

> The qualities Jasper Milvain looks for in a wife are unequivocal: she must possess money, good looks, and sufficient personality to help him advance his career. Reardon's widow Amy has all the necessary qualities, plus an appropriate touch of hard materialism [*Haunted Study* 202–03].

Gissing's descriptions of their material ascent support the image of harmony with one's environment. Michael Collie writes of Milvain:

> To be successful he needed money and that it made sense to marry for money, especially if that established a basis for understanding between husband and wife; and further that to marry for love, when everything about marriage was arbitrary and accidental, was the height of foolishness [*Alien Art* 119–20].

Reardon, in contrast, lacking the money necessary to clothe himself in ways that would image forth his cultural attainments, gradually has lost in the battle of life. Rushing to Brighton in response to Amy's telegram that Willie lies perilously ill, Reardon has no time to change into his better clothes and appears somewhat shabbily dressed. Gissing heightens the irony by juxtaposing Amy's expressions of affection and a desire for reconciliation, prompted in part by a sufficient income for their lives, with Reardon's mortal illness. Willie dies and Reardon dies. Beyond a certain point in the struggle, money cannot save either one.

When in *New Grub Street* Alfred Yule speaks to his daughter Marian about her supposed legacy of £5,000, he tremulously, almost fearfully, expresses his hopes that she will invest in a journal with him as editor (312–20). Seemingly craven in his approach to his daughter, who reluctantly hears him, Yule in reality reveals his deepest desires that his life will be saved, transformed, and redeemed from its bitter disappointments by this manna from heaven. Nothing less than a religious-like fervor lies at the heart of his words to Marian. Her rejection of his plan for her money and the substitution of her desire to marry Jasper Milvain and give him the legacy are destructive of Yule's last chance to achieve power in the literary world. Blindness and death follow soon after. Contrasted with the reality of what he would do as the editor of a new journal, to whose certain failure Jasper attests (332), Yule's language to Marian is pure hyperbole. It would not be too fanciful a comparison to contend that Yule creates a mirage, not some capricious illusion, but the surest description of what to him seems the most palpable reality: he the editor, Marian a valued contributor, Hinks and Quarmby his loyal lieutenants. If Yule did not consult a doctor and learn he suffered from cataracts, one would assume a psychosomatic blindness resulting from Marian's answer (409).

Gissing, to a certain degree, is a novelist of limits. Apart from his own personal liabilities, these limits reside in the physical and emotional conditions of his characters' lives, the extent of their intellectual capabilities, their knowledge and tastes, their degree of understanding life's complexities, and their abilities to imagine, to envision what they can accomplish and for what they can hope. Satire, irony, and paradox naturally fit with the idea of limits. George Orwell touches on Gissing's ironic sense of life's restrictions: "Understanding better than almost anyone the horror of a money-ruled society, he has little wish to change it, because he does not believe that the change would make any real difference" ("Not Enough Money" 3). The above figures shape, pull, control, and even distort, along with the allied figures of hyperbole and understatement, the literary contexts in which they appear. In these restrictive but suggestive figures, Gissing observes and explores limitations that charge his fiction and, paradoxically, open it up, linking it to other

ideas through the power of imaginative discourse. In *The Odd Women*, Alice
and Virginia Madden, in a scene of understated pathos, follow the latter's
suggestion: "'Let us review our position'" (15). What follows is a careful analysis of their money and expenses for six months against the possibility that neither spinster will obtain employment during that time. Alice suggests that
they could live on four pence a day for food, to which Virginia replies (noted
also by Selig, *George Gissing* 65), "'Is such a life worthy of the name?'" (16).
Lady Ogram and her secretary Constance Bride in *Our Friend the Charlatan*
present a linked pair exemplifying an exquisite balance of situational ironies
with money at its center. Lady Ogram, old and in poor health, comes from
a working-class background and, despite her infirmities, still desires to influence society, politically and intellectually. Though living retired in the country, her Liberal contacts extend far beyond it and include backing Dyce
Lashmar for a parliamentary candidacy for Hollingford. In addition to physical and class limitations that she transcends with varying degrees of success,
Lady Ogram's autocratic manner — assuredly based on money, her title, and
a lifetime's experience — conflicts with her secretary's sense of pride and self-
respect, warning Lady Ogram that she must not transgress the limits of assertion too far or too often (142–43).

Constance exists in a state paralleling Lady Ogram's. Educated but born
into straitened circumstances, she nonetheless feels herself endowed with great
gifts. This paradoxical condition is a constant theme in Gissing's fiction, developed with varied degrees of acceptance by his protagonists. From the agony
of a Godwin Peak in *Born in Exile* to the sad acknowledgement of Gilbert
Grail in *Thyrza* and Sidney Kirkwood in *The Nether World*, uneasy lies the
weight of poverty on those who feel it an unjust mark of fate or chance. In
The Paradox of Gissing (1986), David Grylls notes, "In [Gissing's] view, most
virtues depended on money: poverty demoralized" (105). With the sudden
discovery of her niece, May Tomalin, Lady Ogram plans to reduce the amount
of money for the trust that Constance, continuing her patron's charitable
work, will administer (*Our Friend the Charlatan* 183, 186–87). While not dis-
heartened by this unforeseen irony, Constance must adapt both her discourse
and her plans. Confronted with Lashmar's enquiries about the effects of May's
appearance and the intended diversion of money for the latter's future position in society, Constance continues to be sanguine, projecting a firm belief
that though reduced, Lady Ogram's charitable interests have not abated (188).
(See Chapter 8.)

Another monetary irony is that Lady Ogram presses Lashmar to ask Constance to marry him (*Our Friend the Charlatan* 182). All who see Lady Ogram
after even a brief absence notice her advancing illness, and her insistence on
arranging the lives of those beholden to her is in inverse proportion to the

time she feels remaining. When Lashmar speaks to Constance, he does so with feelings of trepidation. Not that he initially feels that she will accept him but that she will not agree to a subterfuge that, while they pretend an engagement, will outlast the autocrat's life. Much to his delight, Constance concurs with his plan and provides rationalizations for it (189–90). Thus, Gissing presents one person of presumed principle, Constance, and one of assumed principle, Lashmar, seemingly bending under the necessity and the hope of future largesse. However, the satire is not so broad as it would appear since Constance has apparently recovered her love for Lashmar; the disappointment she suffered six years before at his hands has not survived a new hope even when mixed with a surer knowledge of his unsavory character. Thus, both have mixed reasons for their collusion in frustrating Lady Ogram's hopes, e.g., Constance, ambition and love, and Lashmar, ambition and wealth, for if he can hold on long enough, May Tomalin might still be unmarried, an heiress, and available.

Obfuscation, deception, and concealment are Lashmar's methods of dealing with questions about his intentions. Once he receives May Tomalin's anonymous note, "'HAVE MORE COURAGE. AIM HIGHER. IT IS NOT TOO LATE'" (*Our Friend the Charlatan* 241), he correctly guesses her authorship and then attempts to pull May into his marriage deception, placing her on his side *vis-à-vis* both Lady Ogram and Constance (284–87). In the midst of the above complexities, Lashmar visits his parents, and against the background of his father's worries over money, they have an exchange, frank on the father's side and part openness, part obfuscation on Dyce's. Gissing's rhetorical strategies in this instance extend from the religious to social Darwinist discourse. Mr. Philip Lashmar, vicar of Alverholme, in reply to Dyce's statement, "'I'm afraid you're a good deal worried, father.'" says, "'I'm putting my affairs in order, Dyce'.... 'I've been foolish enough to let them get very tangled'" (233). When Mr. Lashmar shifts the conversation to Dyce's affairs, Gissing states that "Dyce drifted into verbosity," losing "from sight the impossibility of telling the whole truth about his present position and the prospects on which he counted" (235). Calling Dyce a "'post–Darwinian'" unable to believe in the Sermon on the Mount (236), the basis for his own beliefs, Mr. Lashmar says, "'To me your method of solution seems a deliberate insistence on the worldly in human nature, sure to have the practical result of making men more and more savagely materialist'" (237). Rather than the precepts from the Sermon on the Mount, Mr. Lashmar observes, "'You have to teach "Blessed are the civic-minded, for they shall profit by their civism." It has to be profit, Dyce, profit, profit'" (239). The father-son colloquy, a set-piece of revelation and concealment on the son's part, projects several things. One is that Dyce has not completely cut himself off from dialogue with a better vision that precludes treachery and dissembling. The other, as subsequent events show, is that Dyce cannot, in the larger world, translate his father's sincere Christian rhetoric into practical form.

Change is an essential part of the language of money in Gissing's work and evinces itself in many areas, e.g., social, personal, and intellectual. It is obvious that the Rev. Lashmar does not see change in a positive light while admitting that the New Testament speaks of "rewards" (*Our Friend the Charlatan* 239). His criticisms of the world his son hopes to inhabit center on the tendency of economic exchange to rob the world of spirit. Acknowledging the post–Darwinian environment and even admitting to an earlier belief in organic evolution as compatible with a broad Anglicanism, he nonetheless deletes this from his sermons because it is a view his parishioners could not understand (1). Paradoxically, he does not remove from his preaching Christ's historically profound teachings in the Sermon on the Mount. The Rev. Lashmar apparently believes that having heard these ideas all their lives, the parishioners will proceed to ignore them. Gissing exemplifies the Rev. Lashmar's views on the differential but inimical effects of society's materialist direction in two earlier novels, *The Town Traveller* and *The Paying Guest*. These two modern allegories, written in a comic, satiric style, demonstrate a basis for the Rev. Lashmar's belief that the modern world of profit and practicality has ineluctably arrived. Gissing focuses his portraits in these novels in two ways. First, he employs young women as the protagonists, one from the working class and one from the lower-middle class, respectively. Second, both women speak the language of money as almost an inherited character trait. Secluded from the London urban world of *The Town Traveller* and the suburban London environment of *The Paying Guest*, the Rev. Lashmar and later Ryecroft in *The Private Papers of Henry Ryecroft* incontestably perceive and speak of this new age as both arriving and sweeping away the values of the old.

In *The Town Traveller*, Polly Sparkes, a good-hearted vulgarian, sells "programmes at a fashionable theatre" (6). Grylls speaks in general of the characters' "rasping illiteracies" (*Paradox* 113). Understandably, as a young, self-supporting woman living alone who prizes her respectability, Polly must have her material welfare as a dominant concern. If she were to fail, the streets, a notorious receiver of impoverished women, might engulf her. Admittedly, Gissing has in *The Unclassed* sentimentalized to a degree the profession of prostitute, but this is an aberration in his fiction. Carrie Mitchell's portrait in *Workers in the Dawn*, undoubtedly based on his first wife Nell, remains the touchstone for understanding his views on the subject. Polly's manner of expressing her economic and other concerns rests on the volume used to state them. An increase in the auditory level of the utterance substitutes sound for thought, but Polly also uses sound to still anxiety. Functioning somewhat as a caricature of working-class life, she nonetheless represents a method of communal dialogue in which support is expressed and received. Gissing describes Polly early in the novel as "[m]eaning to pass an hour or two in quarrelling with Mrs. Bubb ... whom ... she had known since her childhood" (5). Though early reviewers note Gissing's awkwardness in dealing with middle-class life (Coustillas and Partridge 52, 56, 60–61, 83), he was at least knowledgeable of intellectual culture, if not all the distinctions of fashionable norms. But, he correctly reproduces the din associated with the crowded world of the London poor. Gissing's well-known description in *Workers in the Dawn* of Whitecross Street on a Saturday night; his portrait of the Mutimer household in *Demos*, especially the daughter Alice; the bank holiday mob in *The Nether World*; the celebrations in *In the Year of Jubilee* (1894); and the boat trip to Gravesend in "Lou and Liz" (1893) are just a few examples of the noise of the poor as they establish their levels of communication. In her rooming house in *The Town Traveller*, Polly moves from loud hilarity to equally loud hostility and frequently in regard to money. Paying rent is one of Polly's chief monetary concerns. And, when she decides to leave Mrs. Bubb's, she responds to her landlady's warnings with vituperation and haughtiness in an effort to preserve her precarious sense of self-respect. Overshadowing her assertiveness, based on a youthful, barely contained energy, a prospective bleakness looms, masked by her insistent rhetoric. Financial need traps and directs Polly as surely as in the lives of other characters.

Two males in these novels complement, respectively, the female portraits of Polly Sparkes in *The Town Traveller* and Louise Derrick, to be discussed below, in *The Paying Guest*. Gammon and Tom Cobb, respectively, reflect a decisive gender difference in relation to the rhetoric of money. Certainly, Gissing acknowledges the realities of economic life when granting men a greater expectation of and success in the struggle to earn a living. Gammon in *The Town Traveller* is an effective salesman, typed by Grylls as one of the "short-sighted smilers" (*Paradox* 4), who never seems to doubt his ability to acquire money. Consequently, his statements regarding money vary greatly from Polly's, to whom he is temporarily engaged. He expends energy and reaps his admittedly modest reward. Will the world always need and remunerate the traveling salesman, especially one who does not see his work as a burden? Evidently so, and confident of his abilities, he initially seeks to marry the seventeen-year old Minnie Clover. However, the mother has different social expectations for her daughter and refuses for her. Gammon eventually marries Mrs. Clover, whom he has continued to admire.

Tom Cobb, in *The Paying Guest*, expresses an equal certainty in his ability to survive and prosper economically. An electrical engineer (39), Cobb epitomizes the calm assertiveness of the technological expert and thus discloses his sense of a share in the world he inhabits. Lacking the gender-related uncertainties of the female dependent upon herself for sustenance, or even a salesman on his commission, Cobb harbors little misgiving about his economic future. He says to Louise Derrick, the woman he intends to marry, "'You seem to think I want to drag you down, but you're very much mistaken. I'm doing pretty well, and likely, as far as I can see, to do better'" (110). Luckworth Crewe, in *In the Year of Jubilee*, makes a similar statement to Nancy Lord in response to her observation about the high cost of portraits while they stand on top of the Monument: "'I know. But that's what I'm working for. There are not many men down yonder,' he pointed over the City, 'have a better head for money-making than I have'" (88). Both Cobb's and Crewe's rhetoric reveals the imagery of male sexual potency, the male's dominance through language when fully aroused. Gissing replicates this figure, though on a higher class level and with varying degrees of success, in *Our Friend the Charlatan* and *Sleeping Fires* (1895). In the latter work, Edmund Langley asserts his right to Lady Agnes Revill's love and her hand in marriage (96–97), while in the former novel Dyce Lashmar confidently, but mistakenly, assumes he can bend the independent Constance Bride to his will (336–48). The inescapable image in both novels is of a male bird flaunting its plumage in a mating ritual. Gissing grants occasional success to the man in this exaggerated dance.

   The Paying Guest's Louise Derrick is not in a higher class than Cobb but initially aims higher. Louise's stepfather, Mr. Higgins, has gained a small fortune in business, and she lives in relative affluence. Halperin states that Louise is a "girl from a family rich but vulgar and unrefined" (*Gissing* 223). Desiring to acquire social polish and refinement, Louise goes to live with Clarence and Emmeline Mumford, a middle-class London suburban couple with one child. The possession of money prompts Louise's desire for change and creates the possibility of her conceiving that change is possible. Much like Constance Bride's admission to the hapless Dyce Lashmar, after Lady Ogram's will has left her £70,000 and a paper mill, that the sudden possession of wealth has affected her (*Our Friend the Charlatan* 329, 344, 347), Louise demonstrates the power of money to generate thoughts and ambitions that would previously have been impossible to imagine or implement. In his introduction to *The Paying Guest*, Ian Fletcher notes generally "that attitudes to [money] are complex and often unconscious" (xiv). However, Louise's wish to remake herself does not equal the attainment of her goal. Cobb's insistent passion speaks to her apparently real desires, and she lapses back into her world, to the great relief of the Mumfords.

   Gissing's incorporation of the idea of money into the figurative patterns of his novels reveals money's omnipresence. Both overtly and covertly, money as the means of existence and exchange, the object of longing and the path to transformation, integrates itself into the characters' practical lives and emotional relations. Speaking of *New Grub Street*, Selig states, "Reardon feels obsessed by money's beneficent power, and even the tougher Biffen can write cadenced prose only about people short of money and simple creature comforts" (*George Gissing* 52). Rarely concerned with money as a physical object, Gissing instead writes of the social and psychological tensions and concerns that money engenders, creating a complex mixture throughout the range of his fiction.

10

Discovery and Disintegration: Figures of Disquiet

Halfway through his writing career, George Gissing published three novels that feature important male and female characters in sinister roles. *Denzil Quarrier*, *Born in Exile*, and *The Odd Women* portray figures who coerce and manipulate others either openly or secretively. Often these actions begin secretively and then become open, frequently without any apparent self-awareness as to motive. In *Manliness and the Male Novelist in Victorian Literature* (2001), Andrew Dowling discusses this process in relation to *New Grub Street*:

> In a novel dealing with success and failure, the idealists who believe in truth or beauty are left deserted or dead. Romantic love is as fatal as romantic notions of art and those who scorn both ideals are left happy and content [100].

A few pages later Dowling observes, "Amy's effect on Biffen is simply more rapid than her similarly destructive effect on Reardon" (105). Eustace Glazzard's expressed reasons for betraying Denzil and Lilian Quarrier, an act that leads to her suicide, are flimsy at best. Gissing does not explore them at any depth. Nominally, Buckland Warricombe in *Born in Exile* acts from class and family outrage at Godwin Peak's deception. However, Gissing does not sufficiently examine his character, leaving Warricombe's thoughts only sketched in during his pivotal moments in the novel. Edmund Widdowson's ominous manner and actions in *The Odd Women* toward his wife Monica parallel Everard Barfoot's ultimately manipulative conduct toward the passionate and serious Rhoda Nunn, which throws a more suspicious light on his explanation to his cousin Mary Barfoot of the earlier brief affair with Amy Drake. Finally, Lionel Tarrant and Samuel Barmby in *In the Year of Jubilee* portray somewhat milder, if nonetheless serious, examples of the sinister. These several male characters, with a few female ones, demonstrate the power of the sinister that lies both in the social structure and the individual lives acting within and by it.

Gissing's idea of the sinister briefly needs examining. As will be argued here, characters embodying it are usually male. This reflects the fact that males are still dominant in a society undergoing changes that will lessen that dominance. In addition to opening up the universities, clerical work, and professions to women, though still not the vote, the 1890s also witness a change in attitude on the part of women. For example, in 1890 and 1891, Gissing published two novels, *The Emancipated* and *New Grub Street*, respectively, that employ women who either find a new sense of life (Miriam Baske in the former novel) or who reveal their hidden capacities under trying circumstances (Amy Yule Reardon) in the latter one. Along with gender, the idea of the sinister emanates a certain sense of moral oppressiveness. No one particular moral lack appears in the male sinister but rather an air of unease threatening dire effects. This sounds melodramatic, but Gissing manages to avoid this by the use of psychological and social realism in both the characters and their motives. The occasional sinister female character contributes to the air of realism. Ultimately, the sinister figure subverts the traditional social order, and what one expects from a friend, a husband, or a potential lover is overthrown in the fulfillment of that always- feared threat that some harm might strike one. Akin to the Greek idea of fate, the sinister demonstrates the inability to suppress its revelations. Thus, its greatest power is the almost inevitable coming to light of these dark forces.

First, *Denzil Quarrier* is a novel replete with concealment, revelation, and betrayal, elements that mesh well with the sinister. Lilian Allen married Arthur James Northway years before meeting Quarrier. The marriage was not consummated since the police arrested Northway for embezzlement on his wedding day, and he afterward went to prison for several years. Lilian and her husband lose track of one another, and thus when she and Quarrier pretend to marry in Paris, Northway represents no immediate danger. Both she and Quarrier agree to this act, and her fear of exposure lessens over time. It is noteworthy that while Lilian lives with some degree of fear, it is Quarrier who first reveals their secret to another. When he does this, Quarrier does not feel that he takes any risk. His confidant is Eustace Glazzard, an old friend who still lives in Polterham where Quarrier grew up and where he has gone to stand for Parliament. This latter act upsets Glazzard since he has political ambitions himself and believes that Quarrier has usurped his rightful role. However, he conceals his feelings from Quarrier and also assures him that his and Lilian's secret is safe. On the contrary, Glazzard hires Tulks & Crowe, a private investigation agency, to find Lilian's husband. When they succeed, Glazzard meets with Northway and persuades him to come to Polterham to confront his wife. The outcome is that Quarrier's political career collapses, but more seriously, the revelation culminates in deadly consequences for Lilian. The source of these consequences emanates from Mrs. Wade, paradoxically a more sinister figure in the Quarriers' lives than Glazzard. In making the link between them, Emanuela Ettorre states, "As for Eustace Glazzard, he is a male version of Mrs. Wade" (79).

As with Glazzard, Mrs. Wade at first appears a most unlikely source of danger to the Quarriers. She is an independent, strong-natured woman who works for female rights. She reads widely, writes on gender issues, and speaks publicly on her views. Quarrier, a writer himself, converses as an equal to her, that is, as if speaking to a man. He finds her unfeminine, and thus she mildly repels him, even given her virtues. Quarrier, in another mistaken confidence, tells Mrs. Wade of his and Lilian's secret and asks her to interview Northway and mediate any meeting between him and Lilian. The upshot of Mrs. Wade's intervention is that she makes Lilian believe that she has ruined her husband's political career even though Quarrier has told her that it does not matter and that he only wants to live happily with her. Mrs. Wade urges Lilian to remove herself as a way to make up for her supposed wrongs to Quarrier and even watches, doing nothing to intervene, as Lilian drowns herself. Gissing inadequately presents the sinister nature of this manlike, at least to Quarrier, woman. Disappointed with her sterile life, she presumably fixates on Quarrier as a way to end her loneliness even though he evinces not the slightest attraction to her. But, the gap between these feelings as presented, however real, and her actions toward Lilian is too great for her emotions to serve as a convincing motive. It is the unexplainable forces behind these rather conventional answers that need analysis. Arlene Young in *Culture, Class and Gender in the Victorian Novel* (1999) states:

> Fictional characters are ... cultural constructions, shaped as much by the values and assumptions of the society for which they are created as by the author who creates them [45].

Although transferring the source of Mrs. Wade's actions from Gissing's explanation that her motives lie in her thwarted emotions and desires to the social structure does not illuminate them, it does suggest that the sinister threats represented by Glazzard and Mrs. Wade are dangerous and uncontrollable.

Glazzard and Mrs. Wade have come to know the Quarriers, and both have had a chance to observe how emotionally fragile Lilian is. Lilian functions best at home, in her and Denzil's private world. To reify her as they do is to cancel her as a person. Glazzard acts first against Lilian and Denzil and seems to bear the greater sense of responsibility for what happens. Glazzard also admits privately a sense of guilt for what he does but does nothing to avert the consequences. Admittedly, he has some will to act but fails to do so. This seems to imply that Glazzard cannot stop himself. It is not just a character flaw that allows him to destroy Quarrier's political career and endanger Lilian but forces outside himself as well. This latter conjures up a mystical source for the sinister qualities he demonstrates. However, saying it is neither mystical and other-worldly nor a semi-scientific social Darwinist force gets one no closer to discovering Gissing's thoughts on why Glazzard acts as he does. One is left to state that either the environment controls him or that he has a dark, unlovely aspect to his personality or a serious character flaw that allows forces to work from deep within his personality and emerge to dominate it. This suggests either madness or archetypal images that connect to the larger human social structure. A final idea, and one not to be easily dismissed is that this is Glazzard's, and the others,' fate revealed by their actions even if unaccompanied by a Delphic prophecy.

Mrs. Wade's situation parallels Glazzard's, and out of the welter of explanations mentioned above some may be more helpful than others in determining why she does what she does. Other reasons suggest themselves as well, partly to do with gender. To begin with, Mrs. Wade acts as she does because it is her fate to do so. Or, her biological or sexual needs determine what she does with regard to Lilian in her mistaken belief that she will win Quarrier for herself. However, two distinct determinisms do not necessarily lead to a convincing answer. Even though the biological or sexual determinism is more modern, both it or fate supplant her will, her individual character and personality that make her who she is and not someone else. If not exactly Descartes' mind-body dualism, opposing possibilities do seem to struggle for domination.

Much like Glazzard with Quarrier, Mrs. Wade is a seeming friend to Lilian. She suggests a path to her, insinuating that it would solve her painful moral dilemma and thus, Satan-like, tempting her to commit suicide. Gissing does not appear to suggest that Lilian thus loses her immortal soul to evil, but Mrs. Wade embodies the figure of the tempter to perfection. But can one be seen as totally evil? A true Satan figure? Gissing's realistic narrative prevents this without denying the possibility that the sinister actions by Mrs. Wade do derive from a profound evil moving and possessing her from within. The idea of possession parallels some of the speculation regarding Glazzard's motives and leaves a rich source if no definite answers.

At first glance, *Born in Exile*'s Godwin Peak seems an unlikely candidate for the sinister. After all, he just wants to marry up, and Sidwell Warricombe appears to be a pleasing vehicle for his social transformation from the lower-middle class to a county family. However, as Simon J. James observes, "Peak's nature is noble; his actions are not" (*Unsettled Accounts* 107). His aims focus inwardly with an almost aesthetic quality. The Warricombe family represents peace, culture, and harmony, all functioning in a beautiful setting outside Exeter. The distance from this goal and the vulgarity of his family relations and his radical London life are measured in more than miles. The sinister intrudes when Peak decides how he will achieve his aim. To begin with, he "discovers" a calling to be an Anglican priest. Next, knowing earlier Sidwell's deep religious faith, he plans to gain her emotional and mental acceptance through this bogus calling, an act, according to Davis Grylls, of "moral hypocrisy" (*Paradox* 136). Of course, Buckland, with Marcella Moxey's unconscious aid, exposes his lies, and he fails. However, the sinister nature of Peak's actions lies in their implications, which Sidwell herself, even after he confesses his falsity to her, comes close to enabling. What if marriage and children had come before exposure? Gissing does not show the intellectual Peak contemplating any specific future but rather enjoying the fruits of the environment. Peak is so consumed with what he lacks that Sidwell never factors into his calculations as a human being who could suffer from his actions. Sidwell explains to her friend Sylvia Moorhouse:

> "I know ... that he cannot in that first hour have come to regard me with a feeling strong enough to determine what he then undertook. It was not I as an individual, but all of us here, and the world we represented. Afterwards, he persuaded himself that he had felt love for me from the beginning. And I, I tried to believe it — because I wished it true; for his sake, and for my own" [489].

As it turns out, she asks him to come to see her before he runs away from his humiliation and offers the chance to try to make it work. Buckland has exposed his radical past and his active disbelief. Peak rejects her offer and flees. His disgrace and anger overwhelm him. After he receives Marcella Moxey's legacy, Peak renews his suit to Sidwell, but after much painful deliberation, she breaks off contact with him (489, 495). Would he have reacted any differently if she were his wife and mother to their children? The question does not involve the supposed sanctity of the institution or the trueness of the person betrayed. The question involves his apparently complete lack of awareness that what he does might seriously harm another person. Peak represents Gissing's talented but alienated young man who has the brains but no means to rise in the world. However, the weakness of that as a justification for his actions toward Sidwell becomes apparent in the telling.

While the sinister nature of Peak's proceedings lies largely in their potential harm, Buckland Warricombe's relentless efforts to expose Peak suggest a darker source, one finding its sinister power in a deep class hatred, what Grylls terms "intense and atavistic class prejudices" (*Paradox* 140). The mindlessness of it is most apparent.

John Keats' "The Eve of St. Agnes" (1820) furnishes a good analogy. Family hatred rather than class spurs the furious passions of Madeline's kinsmen against Porphyro. Keats lays out his danger in Stanza X as he arrives at the castle:

> He ventures in: let not buzzed whisper tell: All eyes be muffled, or a hundred swords Will storm his heart, Love's fev'rous citadel: For him, those chambers held barbarian hordes, Hyena foemen, and hot-blooded lords, Whose very dogs would execrations howl Against his lineage: not one breast affords Him any mercy, in that mansion foul, Save one old beldame, weak in body and in soul [St. X. lines 82–90].

Angela, the beldame, names two of them in Stanza XII, "Hildebrand" (line 100) and "old Lord Maurice" (line 103). In Stanza XL, Keats describes the whole group as "sleeping dragons" (line 353), possessed of a visceral, unreasoning hatred for Porphyro. There lies the connection to Gissing's novel and Warricombe's reaction to Peak. Warricombe does not consider his sister Sidwell and any feelings she may have for Peak nor does he consider any ideas she may have about him; she is, Gissing seems to imply, to be disposed of as a family possession much like Madeline, though neither faces any immediate pressure to marry. Warricombe wishes to erase Peak from Sidwell's life. However, much like Madeline's escape with Porphyro, "For o'er the southern moors I have a home for thee" (XXXIX. line 351), Sidwell acts by asking Peak to come to her, but he turns out to be a weaker reed than she and cannot respond to her when she acts independently of her brother. Simon J. James states:

> In one of Gissing's characteristic reversals of expectation, even after Sidwell becomes intellectually independent through losing her faith, and Godwin financially independent following Marcella's death, a happy ending still does not take place. Although Sidwell loves Peak, the barriers of class are too strong for the success of their union, and the possibility of forgiveness by the Warricombes can be no more than "an idea out of old-fashioned romances" [*Unsettled Accounts* 117].

Earlier at Whitelaw College, Warricombe and Peak compete in a friendly rivalry for academic prizes. Warricombe seems to recognize Peak's intellectual gifts and treats him as an equal, inviting him to Exeter during one vacation. Yet, Warricombe has the offer of equality to give, and Peak knows this. He never forgets his lower-middle-class origins, and recognizing his status, it would make no sense to say Peak treats Warricombe as an equal. The balance of power in this class struggle tilts in Warricombe's favor until Peak makes the bold move to come to Exeter and recreate himself. An antagonist other than Buckland Warricombe might not have stopped Peak. After Whitelaw College, Warricombe's only occupation, besides his unsuccessful pursuit of Sylvia Moorhouse, is his function as his father's oldest son. This suggests that Warricombe acts against Peak in order to repel an interloper, a social climber, someone rising from a lower social level to infect their world. Yet, Gissing fails to emphasize this wider possibility, instead representing his actions only as efforts to protect the family. Warricombe does appeal to his father and Sidwell, but neither accepts his authority to interfere. Warricombe's exposure of Peak's falsity regarding his religious vocation and his discovery of a pamphlet Peak wrote supporting atheism function merely as weapons to use against Peak, not as heartfelt assertions about Peak to Sidwell in order to protect her from him. Sidwell goes to Peak with full knowledge of what he has done and professes her love for him, but Peak, as empty as her brother, leaves Exeter, rejecting her offer. Peak and Warricombe are emotionally and ethically dangerous people, not to be trusted or relied on by others.

The middle class lies as a colossal sphere across a straight line between the upper and lower classes, obscuring their views of one another and it. This somewhat fanciful geometric analogy confers a feeling of its immobility and potential power and it also suggests a marginalization of whatever lies outside the middle class, extending the dramas within its own area to the rest of society and drawing from other, less important areas whatever suits its needs. To three attributes of a deity, i.e., omniscience, omnipresence, and omnipotence, can be added omnivorousness, the latter a power in the social sphere that the middle class utilizes. The closer to the lower class, and thus the further from the center of power and wealth and the nearer to the edge of social uncertainty, the more one lies vulnerable to the conscious and even unconscious operations of those at the center. Reference is made above to Everard Barfoot's involvement with Amy Drake in *The Odd Women*. Barfoot, educated and well-off and from a good family, suffers from rumors that he took advantage of the unattended Miss Drake on a train trip to London. He leaves the city because of these rumors but later returns and visits his cousin Mary Barfoot. There, he defends himself from the accusation that he is the father of Amy Drake's child.

According to Everard Barfoot, Amy boarded the train by entering his compartment. Evidently, each compartment stretched across the width of the cars with no outside corridor running length-wise that allowed entry into other compartments once the train started. Naturally, this was, at the end of the nineteenth century, highly compromising for an unmarried woman traveling alone. Barfoot alleges that she was very forward, and that once in London, they repaired to a hotel for the night. The next day they parted. Amy became pregnant, but Barfoot, admitting the relationship, denies her claim that he is the father. He asserts to his cousin that she is known to be free with her favors and that she attempted to trap him as the better financial prospect. He does pay her a sum of money but says it is only to help her out and shows no admission of guilt.

The connection between Everard and Amy's dilemma and the beginning idea in the first part of the previous paragraph is that Amy's place in society is precarious at best, coming as she does near the lower edge of the middle class. Is Barfoot's story true, and is Amy the female predator he pictures to Mary? Mary earlier dismissed Amy from her business school for middle-class women, the odd women of the title who have little hope of marrying, and appears predisposed to believe Barfoot since she feels Amy's previous conduct would threaten her school's reputation. Added to this, Mary is attracted to him, an attraction that leads to her and Rhoda Nunn's temporary estrangement when Mary learns they have been seeing one another. Judging Barfoot is difficult since he is so suave and self-assured. Not far below the surface lies a desire to rule, a desire that cannot fully hide his feelings of superiority toward women. This attitude leads him to confront and pressure Rhoda as well as ultimately marry the placid Agnes Brissenden. John Halperin remarks, "When he discovers that [Rhoda's] will is equal to his own and that he cannot rule her, he backs off too and the affair is ended" (*Gissing* 185). Barfoot seems to have carefully planned his approach to Mary and his later confrontation of the unsuspecting Rhoda, although at the time he protests that his strong feelings for her have caused him to invade her solitary vacation.

Gissing specializes in the conflict between a man and a woman, involved or potentially involved in a romantic relationship. From the first novel to the last, revelations, disappointments, rejections, and triumphs swirl about most couples and affect their feelings about one another. The romantic emotional life means nothing but trouble for most Gissing characters, which is why, to critics from Morley Roberts and Frank Swinnerton onward, the retired life of Henry Ryecroft in Gissing's *The Private Papers of Henry Ryecroft* represents Gissing's real aspiration. However, Barfoot does not seem caught up in the romantic swirl. He and Rhoda Nunn have spoken about forming a free association with none of the restrictions of marriage. They both seem to want this, and yet, when Barfoot goes to Rhoda, he asks her to marry him. This appears a calculated attempt to disturb her feelings and certainties and thus display an exploitable weakness. He also reveals his desire to break off

any understanding they previously reached. When Rhoda at first indig-
nantly rejects his offer, he claims he was only testing her. Their chance at a
union disintegrates when he again changes his mind and says he will live with
her without benefit of clergy and she responds that she will agree to marriage
only.

Neither one comes off well, but to Rhoda, Barfoot seems relieved that
the ordeal is over. One suspects that, with his greater experience in romantic matters, Barfoot played on her inexperience and womanly pride. Rhoda
is the only one of the two deeply moved by their brief connection.

In *Workers in the Dawn*, the protagonist Arthur Golding attempts to
mold his wife Carrie Mitchell, whom he has rescued from the streets, into a
companion who meets more than just his sexual needs. Since she is barely literate, Golding begins to teach her to read and also corrects the way she speaks.
Eventually, Carrie cannot stand his attempts to improve and control her, and
she turns at intervals to old friends and habits. (See Chapter 3 for an earlier
discussion of their dilemmas.) Their relationship resembles that between
Edmund Widdowson and Monica Madden Widdowson in *The Odd Women*
and Lionel Tarrant and Nancy Lord in *In the Year of Jubilee*. Broadly, the
theme of redemption occupies an important place in Gissing's fiction and
appears in different guises. In *The Unclassed, Demos: A Story of English Socialism, Thyrza, The Nether World*, and *The Emancipated*, one character attempts
to change another in ways that please one and could benefit both. Not all
cases before *The Odd Women* involve an elevation from a lower moral plane
to a higher one. This is certainly not the situation between Widdowson and
Monica. However, he needs a woman who will fill his sexual needs, furnish
companionship, and bend to his will. Monica at first seems willing to answer
those wishes but eventually fails in every area. She cannot stand for him to
embrace her, she cannot endure a life in which he is the only person with
whom she interacts, and she discovers a ravenous desire to be free from him.
Widdowson ultimately becomes a dark, sinister force in her life. He hires a
detective to follow her and learns of her visits to the building in which Everard Barfoot lives. In fact, Monica intends to run away to France with Mr.
Bevis who lives one floor above Barfoot. Monica "naturally" dies after giving
birth to a child that Widdowson believes is Barfoot's. Unlike Widdowson,
Tarrant's and Barmby's focuses on Nancy Lord in *In the Year of Jubilee* do not
have the same ominous air. Contiguity leads to complications, more serious
in Tarrant's case than in Barmby's. The one redeeming feature of Nancy and
Lionel's unconventional marriage is that Nancy does not have to deal with
Tarrant on a daily basis. Admittedly, she wants a more normal married life.
Samuel Barmby, the son of her father's friend and business partner, wants to
marry her but gives her little trouble over that or the violation of her father's

will. From a potentially threatening position, he subsides into complicity with her deception.

A common thread in the lives of these sinister figures is an intense self focus on their thoughts, feelings, angers and humiliations. As a consequence, little emotional room is left for the other. If not sufficient explanation for this malign force, this thread does accompany any attempt to fathom the havoc left by them.

11

Romantic Love, Sexuality, and Convention

Ideas on romantic love and sexuality permeate Gissing's fiction and enter into a sometimes desperate struggle with convention. The power that convention exercises in these two intimate areas of human contact creates the desperation that characters feel in attempting to find a way to live without undue suffering. Some reject the sensual life, e.g., Maud Enderby in *The Unclassed* and Jane Snowdon in *The Nether World*, and some are overcome by their overindulged senses such as Carrie Mitchell in *Workers in the Dawn*. As an example of a passionate but thwarted character in the same novel, Helen Norman suffers from an overwrought sense of sexual convention. Gissing may, subconsciously, want his readers to take Helen's case as a warning to the denied life. Yet, he intertwines portraits of men and women in his novels of the 1880s who conquer, to some extent, convention's strictures and find outlets for love and desire. Arthur Golding in *Workers in the Dawn*, Ida Starr in *The Unclassed*, Adela Waltham in *Demos*, and Ross Mallard and Miriam Baske in *The Emancipated* demonstrate that Gissing knows of a many-faceted response to human dilemmas growing out of one person's desire, though often failing, to find another with whom to share some sense of joy and fulfillment.

Difficulties abound when Gissing's characters attempt to establish a romantic relationship. Michael Collie states:

> Romantic love and social realism for Gissing turned out to be incompatible: only when he negated romance by showing his characters as alienated from each other was he able to locate a story about people in the actual world he wanted to describe [*Alien Art* 21].

However, the drive to connect romantically, even if the path is circuitous, is often more powerful than obstacles to its fulfillment. In *Thyrza*, Gilbert Grail has loved the beautiful Thyrza Trent for some time before Walter Egremont comes to their part of South London and opens a free library in which he gives lectures on literature to the local members of the working class. He even offers to put the studious Grail in charge of the library. However, Thyrza falls in love with Egremont, someone above her class, and thus finally rejects Grail's proposal and in turn suffers rejection from Egremont. Luke Ackroyd, also a part of the working class, marries Lydia, Thyrza's older sister, though earlier he too loved Thyrza. Ackroyd also is involved with Totty Nancorrow before choosing Lydia. Little is romantically satisfying to any character in this novel. Egremont proposes to Annabel Newthorpe, a woman of his class, who somewhat coolly accepts him. Their union resembles that between Everard Barfoot and Agnes Brissenden in *The Odd Women* after Rhoda Nunn says no to Barfoot and decides to continue working for women's improvement rather than ever marry. So many diversions present an underlying theme on the difficulty in finding love no matter how great the desire to do so. Rhoda responds strongly to Barfoot's embrace and is willing to flout convention and live with him, but neither can hold to their initial decisions. The sexual by-play and power struggle suggests that in this realm, just as in that of politics and business, conflict and either triumph or defeat, but little in between, are the norm.

Gissing intuits the difficulty in making the transition from isolation to a romantic relationship. Marian Yule and Harold Biffen in *New Grub Street*, each in their own way, illustrate this. Many commentators have noted Gissing's theme of the educated but alienated young man who feels cut off from his rightful place in society. Godwin Peak in *Born in Exile* lives out this condition in all its painful detail. The wall of money and class, however transparent, is nearly impenetrable. Yet, Peak is not emotionally isolated in his own world; he has a circle of radical friends and admirers (see Chapter 4) that he turns away from in order to make his fruitless attempt to force his way into a higher social class. Stephen Ogden observes, "Peak's doomed efforts to win Sidwell amount to the first Darwinian tragedy in literature" ("Darwinian Scepticism" 177). Ogden expands on this: "Godwin Peak, in his reach for Sidwell, commits the Unpardonable Darwinian Sin: he attempts a Lamarckian evolutionary adaptation through exercise of will" (177). Marian and Harold suffer in quite a different fashion. They are all but alone in the world and want to end this state of affairs. Marian lives with her parents and works as a research assistant for her embittered father Alfred Yule, minor critic and failed editor. The British Museum Library is her place of suffering while her home, with her estranged parents, is an extension of this condition. Marian has not one female friend her own age until she meets Dora and Maud Milvain, Jasper Milvain's sisters. Marian accidentally encounters them in Finden, a village near Wattleborough. She and her father come to see his sick brother John. From this adventitious meeting, Marian gains two friends and a potential lover in Jasper. From her Uncle John Yule's death she receives a possible £5,000, but the figure reduces to £1,500, and she loses not only money but Jasper, who apparently loves her but cannot contain his ambition enough to marry her on so little money. In consequence, Marian drops back into isolation when she leaves London for a library position late in the novel. It must have been a bitter irony that she moves from one library to another in order to find a way to make a living. Her mother and now-blind father accompany her, and she loses all contact with Dora and Maud. Marian wants to love and be loved, but moving from a state of emotional isolation to one of fulfillment is nearly impossible in Gissing's world-view.

Although Biffen's situation seems much bleaker than Marian's, he does have one friend at the beginning of the novel, a friend who has seemingly crossed that boundary between loneliness and a loving companionship. Edwin Reardon is a writer, formerly a successful one, but now struggling to compose his novels. In addition, Reardon is in the "foolish" position of wanting to be loved for who he is and not for what he does. His wife Amy operates on an opposite system, loving and excited by him when he showed promise of even more success but coldly withdrawing as he weakly asks for her love, support, and encouragement. After Reardon dies, Biffen puts on his new wardrobe and visits Amy in London. She initially accepts his condolences in a friendly manner but on his second visit subtly lets him know that she will not respond to his interest in her. Unlike the ever-hopeful Whelpdale who has frequently lost out in the battle for love, Biffen has not hoped to find it since he was a young man. When he recognizes the folly of his actions toward Amy, his eventual suicide in Putney Heath Park seems inevitable. Better to have plodded on than to have begun to hope. Maud Milvain's calculated marriage to Dolomore for wealth and social position and Whelpdale's overwhelming joy at being accepted by Dora Milvain are more realistic outcomes but hardly rival Gissing's matching Jasper Milvain with the equally ambitious Amy Reardon. Except for Marian Yule and possibly Dora and Whelpdale, no other characters appear to have the faintest experience of loving someone.

In one area, as shown above, Gissing's portraits of romantic love and sexuality are supreme, i.e. unfulfilled desire. This would not include someone like Emma Vine in *Demos* who evinces little desire. She is an admirable character in her patient care for her family, her initial trust in Richard Mutimer, and her uncomplaining acceptance of his rejection of her in favor of Adela Waltham. Ultimately, she negates herself even as she presents the image of

Mutimer's ideal mate. And, with the inheritance from his grandfather, he has no financial need, as contrasted to a social one, to cast off Emma. One might infer that Emma wants to marry or would have married Mutimer, but this does not equal a passionate wish to have him as a lover and a husband. Sometimes Gissing is too circumspect to acknowledge that the lover is as important as the husband or wife. Men and women frequently want to match up with one another in his fiction, but sexual desire is not always apparent. When one can separate those circumstantial situations from the ones in which desire is present, Gissing's thinking on this theme comes into clearer focus. Iris Woolstan in *Our Friend the Charlatan* seems besotted with the untrustworthy Dyce Lashmar for no discernible reason except that he is young, attractive, ambitious, unmarried, and tutor to her son Leonard; Lashmar, in other words, is presentable and available. Gissing indicates little more on Iris's part than emotional neediness. However, this state is not passion. After Dyce disgraces himself, he reluctantly marries Iris when she gratefully accepts him. Lashmar's above attributes are not unimportant as conditions on which to base an involvement, but Iris does not appear as a sexual being anymore than the calculating Lashmar does.

Gissing deals with female sexual desire in an elusive manner. While it is tempting to resort to his life, letters, diary, and journals for answers, a focus on his creative work will give one a deeper insight into the life of this theme in late-Victorian England. Perhaps almost unconsciously, Gissing develops situations in which women unmistakably exhibit physical passion. If the assertion of this idea seems too tentative, it is because the society did not encourage, especially for middle-and upper-middle class women, the open acknowledgement of sexuality. This, of course, could be countered by references to expectations generated by courtship rituals. *Workers in the Dawn* provides an important example of this complex situation in the relationship between Carrie Mitchell and Arthur Golding. Carrie is attractive, has borne a child out of wedlock, and is about to be thrown out of her Aunt Pettindund's house, a house in which Arthur also resides. They marry and, generally, live unhappily ever after. Young and pretty are probably enough to attract the equally young and attractive Golding, but what role does Carrie's previously illicit sexual activity play in this attraction? Golding does not think her immoral for having a child outside marriage, but he does seem to think of her as a sexual being who could answer his sexual needs. He has no family and can please himself as to whom he marries. Admittedly, Gissing does not pronounce his own ideas on sex and then match Carrie's and Arthur's to them. Rather, he presents their youthful dilemma as they experience it.

The concept of unfulfilled desire in Gissing's fiction obviously does not mean that men and women neither have nor express desire. Rather, it focuses on the ability of one character to connect sexually with the object of his or her desire. Even when, as in the case of Arthur and Carrie, Arthur connects with the woman he desires and initially finds a sexual response in her, other problems occur to thwart their relationship. In the category of the plain but passionate woman, one finds a different kind of impediment to fulfillment. *Isabel Clarendon*'s Ada Warren projects a stubborn, almost sullen resistance to Isabel Clarendon's attempts to exercise her role as Ada's guardian. Without revealing to Ada that she will inherit most of Clarendon's money, Isabel feels obligated to act as a parent even though Ada opposes her. Independent of Isabel's control and risking Vincent Lacour's rejection, Ada still shows her desire for a relationship with him. He plans, instead, to go to India. Both are young, but Ada is young, plain, and dependent with no apparent expectations to inherit anything. After all, Isabel is the widow, and it comes as a surprise to all when Ada learns of her good fortune. Both Ada and Vincent talk about literature, and she at least feels drawn to him. If he had known what was in store for her financially, would he have left so abruptly? Ultimately, Ada rejects both Isabel and the money and plans a future as a professional writer. In fact, she gives Isabel the money. Bernard Kingcote, the protagonist, has also broken off with Isabel. She offers to resume their engagement, but he cannot accept her social world and refuses. Stripped of any physical beauty and seemingly lacking much personal charm, Ada is no ideal heroine. However, she feels passionately about people and what they do to her. If this is not sexual passion, although her physical feelings for Lacour cannot be ruled out, it is nonetheless a basis for it.

Marcella Moxey in *Born in Exile* and Constance Bride in *Our Friend the Charlatan* are two other examples of the plain but passionate woman. However, they come to far different ends. Marcella and Constance have one important element in common. Both are rejected as desirable by an attractive man, Godwin Peak and Dyce Lashmar, respectively. Marcella is part of a group of radical friends, among whom are her brother Christian, John Edward Earwaker, and Peak. Until Peak leaves London for Exeter and his pursuit of Sidwell Warricombe, the group has a certain cohesion and camaraderie. However, Godwin never responds to Marcella's obvious interest in him. Part of this has to do with his dislike of intellectual women. Gissing has foreshadowed this in his portrait of Marian Yule in *New Grub Street*. Marian has reluctantly become a good researcher and literary critic in helping her father Alfred. However, she only wants to love and be loved, and almost as if she senses that she will never attract someone if the British Museum Library circumscribes her life, she rejects what she does. In contrast to Marcella and Constance, Marian is very attractive, especially to Jasper Milvain, but her manner of living and working erodes her beauty. Milvain comments to his sisters Dora and

Maud on her fresh beauty and attractiveness when he first meets her in the country and its lessening on her return to the city and literary labor. While Constance lives outside a small town and works as the personal assistant to Lady Ogram, she has little beauty either to lose or regain. Not unattractive, Constance affects Dyce with a sense of her too manlike nature. If she looks in part masculine, in the manner of his description of Amy Reardon, Gissing does not mean to characterize this negatively, but if there is a sense of assertive competence, as in Constance's case, his male characters remain cold toward them. Marcella contrasts too strongly with the ideal represented by Sidwell, and Peak's coldness apparently stems from the intellectual aspect as much as the physical. In *Women and Marriage in Victorian Fiction* (1976), Jenni Calder characterizes Peak's attitude to both types:

> In Gissing's *Born in Exile* (1892) the hero asserts that he hates emancipated women. His picture of the ideal wife is cosily traditional, and he feels that a woman without good looks is incomplete. In his view women are selfish, materialistic and severely limited, and in spite of the fact that the woman he loves is of superior and sensitive intellect he can only think in terms of dominating his future wife [169].

Denzil Quarrier's reactions to Lilian Quarrier, his wife, and Mrs. Wade, a proponent of female equality, demonstrate this idea in *Denzil Quarrier*. Quarrier has saved Lilian; she needs him and leans on him. Outwardly, Mrs. Wade does not appear to need his masculinity, and as much as she would like to attract him, nothing she does can reverse this contextual given.

Gissing's ideal relationship in which romantic love, convention, and sexuality converge occurs in *The Crown of Life*. This sometimes painful novel, painful in the characters' mistakes and their suffering penance for them, a penance not always leading to a successful conclusion, has a distinct parallel to his life. The letters Gissing wrote to Gabrielle Fleury in the late 1890s demonstrate an astonishing idealization of women that no human being could support. Piers Otway literally throws his life into Irene Derwent's lap and abases himself before her in a way that leaves one searching for the combination of elements that could provoke such fervor. Gissing establishes Otway's fixation on Irene early in the novel when he first meets her and turns from grinding for the civil service exam to a consecration to the goal of winning Irene as his wife. Whatever Otway does after this event focuses on her and her hoped-for approval. John Halperin remarks:

> From beginning to end *The Crown of Life*, one of Gissing's most interesting books, is imbued with the novelist's feeling that perhaps he was destined to love and be loved after all. Love is everywhere, on every page [*Gissing* 295].

The moments in the narrative that shift one's attention from Otway's actions to Irene's responses or lack of them reveal a stark emotional contrast. From seeing Irene as the center of his life to seeing himself as one of her many acquaintances shows the gap that Piers must close. As peerless as he sees her, Irene has moments of conventional response to Piers' failure to observe the proprieties. Piers is invited to an evening at her home, but prior to this he meets his two disreputable brothers, Alexander and Daniel. Piers and they drink too much, and they insist on accompanying him to Irene's door. Irene hears their loud good-byes in the street and observes Piers' flushed face when he enters. It does not take long for him to realize that he is not welcome, and he withdraws. There is no doubt that Irene's rejection of his behavior sobers him and directs his future actions. He decides to take a business position in the Crimea and leaves England. However, Otway does not give up his life's aim to win Irene, though he judges his chances of success are now much slimmer.

Gissing presents Irene as a beautiful, emotionally restrained young woman controlled, if not obsessively, by social convention. She unconsciously lives within its rules as most other women do on her class level. It is important to note that Gissing does not portray her as merely prim and proper. She has feeling and shows it. However, early on she is not romantically or sexually awakened by any man. This may seem a too passive way to present her, but in general, Gissing's middle-class women do not often exhibit strong feelings until they are in a committed relationship. When the opposite occurs, the feeling arises from a significant conflict in their lives as happens in *The Odd Women* to Monica Widdowson with Bevis and to Rhoda Nunn with Everard Barfoot and *In the Year of Jubilee* to Nancy Lord with Lionel Tarrant. The dilemma that Irene raises for Gissing is in moving her from this settled and socially supported stance to one that exhibits a greater degree of passion. Gissing resolves this problem in characterization through Irene's relationship to two women, Olga, Hannaford and Helen Borisoff, and two men, Trafford Romaine and Arnold Jacks. Through their involvement in her life, Irene encounters people and situations that she cannot easily control through social convention and to which she must respond at a deeper level. Once she undergoes these experiences, she is ready to recognize her love for Piers Otway and marry him.

Irene's transition to a fuller life is not as mechanical as this evenly balanced arrangement might appear. And, her relationships with the above women extend from early in the novel to near the end. Olga Hannaford is Irene's first cousin, the daughter of her father's unhappily married sister. Lee Hannaford, Olga's father, is a wealthy inventor. He and his wife have become estranged with unhappy effects on Olga as well as Mrs. Hannaford. Olga is a nervous, somewhat unstable young woman approximately Piers' age. He lived with Mrs. Hannaford and Olga for several years in Geneva, Switzerland, while attending school. Piers is never attracted to Olga though when Irene becomes engaged to Arnold Jacks, the son of his father's friend John Jacks, Piers thinks he might want to marry Olga. However, he soon changes his mind, a change that Olga encourages. She later marries Florio, an Italian shopkeeper living in London. Irene and her father, Dr. Lowndes Derwent, try to help Olga and Mrs. Hannaford but to little avail. However, Irene sees and sympathizes with their difficulties. This is especially true with Mrs. Hannaford who has fallen in love with Daniel Otway. He attempts to obtain money from her for the return of her letters to him. Irene's intimate knowledge of these problems and Piers' efforts to help Mrs. Hannaford lead her to greater awareness of the complexities of the emotional life. Her friend Helen Borisoff whom she meets on a ship returning from the colonies also adds to her emotional education. Helen sometimes lives apart from her husband and apparently has discreet affairs. At least, this is the inference to be drawn from remarks Helen makes to the long-inexperienced Irene. Yet, it is more in Helen's exposure of Irene to the idea of female independence that changes her from her father's daughter and her brother's sister to an identity all her own.

Trafford Romaine and Arnold Jacks contribute to this transition from a grown child to a mature woman. Irene has become accustomed to male adulation, but both men introduce the serious idea of marriage. Romaine is the champion of British imperialism and is widely admired for his views, especially by Arnold Jacks. When Irene declines his offer of marriage, he goes without a murmur. It is others who regard her rejection of the much older man as a surprise, implying the honor is in her being asked by such an esteemed man. However, Irene's actions reflect real growth in her character. She can examine her own conscience and find an answer for her actions. Arnold, Romaine's disciple, gives more trouble, but she ultimately says no to him as well. At first, Irene seriously considers his proposal and accepts him. She does not seem greatly attracted to him, but they have much in common, especially in terms of their class level and acquaintances. Jacks is also emotionally untouched by Irene. His lack of much response to her seems more constitutional than personal. Irene is an ornament to him and once gained becomes of less importance than other aspects of his life. During their brief engagement, he rarely sees or writes her and appears satisfied at the arrangement. It seems that Jacks, if society had sanctioned it, would have consented to marriage by post. Irene, meanwhile, has resumed thinking about Piers Otway and contrasts him to Jacks, finding the latter wanting. Partly, she rejects his imperialist politics for a wider view of peoples and cultures resembling Otway's. (See Chapter 16.) More importantly, Irene realizes she cares nothing for Jacks as a possible husband and breaks their engagement. His reaction confirms her own ideas about him, since he is almost wholly concerned about the social repercussions of Irene's actions and, after some resistance, gives in to her firm stance that nothing will compel her to marry him. Almost as a revelation, Irene discovers that she has slowly grown to love Otway (343, 359). Piers, of course, is ecstatic at this sudden, unexpected reversal in his romantic expectations. Neither his illegitimacy nor her rejection of two imperialist luminaries affect what appears to be a mutual love for and desire to be with one another.

The crown of Otway's life is always to win the love of a beautiful, cultured woman. As the novel demonstrates, achieving that end involves a dynamic process of advance and retreat, acceptance and assertion of one's claims, and a patient, fervent hope that it will occur. For Irene Derwent, Piers Otway is the last man standing, but the right one, in this battle for romantic and sexual fulfillment. Piers and Irene do not render social convention insignificant, but they do make it pliable and adaptable to their own lives. As the experiences of other characters often show, full happiness is neither imagined nor achieved, but *The Crown of Life* functions as a Rosetta Stone for what is possible in romantic affairs.

12

The Dubious Sex: Women in George Gissing's Fiction

Women figure prominently in George Gissing's fiction. In positive and negative roles, they interact with men and other women to develop the novels' plots. Female protagonists' names form the titles of four novels. In probably his most important portrayal of the sex, *The Odd Women*, Gissing uses a certain category of women for the title, i.e., women who, for whatever reason, do not fit into the general social pattern of marriage and family. In addition, the plots in other works principally revolve around women. The dubiousness of the sex is felt mostly by men but also by some women. Certainly Mary Barfoot and Rhoda Nunn in the above mentioned novel take a judgmental stance toward any woman who would threaten their attempt to teach women skills they need to earn their living. One such skill is how to operate a typewriter, a comparatively recent invention. For the most part, Gissing narrates his third-person novels from the viewpoint of one or more males. Robert L. Selig states, "In *The Odd Women*, in short, Gissing's considerable sympathy with the movement for women's emancipation remains essentially ambivalent because of the opposing aims of his masculine egoism" (*George Gissing* 65). Consequently, the dubious nature of women originates more often than not from men, and even when women castigate their own sex, one is always aware of the male author behind the scenes. The sense of dubiousness about women, more covert than overt, reveals a genuine change occurring in the 1880s and 1890s in the relations between the sexes, and far from being programmatic, Gissing shows his sensitive awareness of the change and his own struggles about how to dramatize it.

One aspect of this change appears as new longings. Many and varied vistas seem to open for women. The lower class female owner of a boarding house is not unknown in nineteenth-century fiction, but Gissing uses three strong examples and thus raises their profile: Mrs. Pettindund in *Workers in the Dawn*, Mrs. Peckover in *The Nether World*, and Mrs. Bubb in *The Town Traveller*. Each woman functions as a center of power in her respective sphere. It is true that their type was personally a source of great bother to Gissing, but he is objective in these characters' portraits. Mrs. Pettindund is absolute in her rejection of Carrie Mitchell when she discovers that her unmarried niece is pregnant. No amount of Carrie's pleading touches her aunt. It is winter and Christmas is near but out Carrie goes. Her child dies of exposure, and Carrie nearly does until Arthur Golding, the protagonist, rescues her. An anonymous reviewer in the *Spectator* for September 25, 1880, comments:

> With an exceedingly low standard of morality, for themselves, if one outside
> their immediate circle should, through greater poverty or temptation fall
> below it, people of the Pettindund [sic] class will always be found ready to
> cast a stone, and there is nothing that has been said against the working-
> class, but can find a counterpart in words and actions ascribed to some of
> them by Mr. Gissing [Coustillas and Partridge 63].

Contrasted with this harsh treatment is Gissing's rich description of Mrs. Pettindund's Christmas feast for friends and relatives. A bacchanal, the cast of characters eats for nearly a whole day. Mrs. Peckover tyrannizes over her maid, the very young Jane Snowdon. Her cruelty toward Jane and the encouragement in her daughter of the same behavior proves to be the mark of her character when one adds her severe manner toward the Hewetts. Finally, Mrs. Bubb, lacking Mrs. Peckover's harshness, still controls and overworks Moggie, her general. Men, unless as favored customers (Bubb) or reflections of their hosts' generosity (Pettindund), play minor roles. Sarah, Mrs. Pettindund's daughter, and Clem, Mrs. Peckover's, exactly reflect their mother's exercise of power in their houses. Their callous indifference to suffering suggests their awareness of the inefficiency of other sentiments.

Dickens, and before him Shakespeare, are important predecessors for these lower-class female holders of power. Mrs. Gamp in *Martin Chuzzlewitt* and Mrs. Bumble in *Oliver Twist* prefigure later nineteenth-century examples, always accompanied by ominous overtones. Falstaff's contests with Mistress Quickly in Shakespeare's *Henry IV Part I* and Mistress Ford and Mistress Page in *The Merry Wives of Windsor* demonstrate that women, in a certain sphere, can hold their own with men. Gissing may be one of the last nineteenth century authors who portray the sheer maliciousness of some women's

actions. The aforementioned women in Gissing's novels are not prim uphold-
ers of middle-class morality and respectability. Not even Mrs. Pettindund fits
that description. The certainty of their possession of property supports their
stance toward everyone within their world. Mrs. Peckover abuses Jane with
the knowledge that no one can nor will interfere to help her. Sidney Kirkwood attempts to mitigate Mrs. Peckover's and Clem's physical and emotional abuse, but they know he can do nothing. Jane becomes their property
to dispose of as they will. As long as they do not kill or severely harm her,
Kirkwood cannot succeed in changing Jane's condition. It is fruitless to appeal
to the better sentiments of the Peckover women who fairly erupt into their
position of control as if destined for this role. Except for Moggie and the
presence of the landlady's young children, *The Town Traveller*'s Mrs. Bubb
primarily deals with adults who work and who thus could live somewhere
else. Polly Sparkes, her youngest lodger, becomes a target of her desire to control, but Polly has a temper of her own, and neither her father, Mrs. Bubb,
nor Mr. Gammon can prevent her having her way and eventually leaving Mrs.
Bubb's. Polly has desires to exercise power and control over a husband, and
when she realizes that Mr. Gammon is stronger than she, shifts her attentions
to the ever-attentive Christopher Parrish whom she proceeds to mold to her
wishes. This sentiment is also not without precedent, but Polly has a job on
which to rely as she negotiates Christopher's surrender, and this gives her an
unassailable position with her young lover. Essentially, Polly has nothing but
her own efforts on which to rely. Her waiter-father cannot help. Polly makes
the men with whom she engages recognize her will and accept it. Gammon
wishes her well even as he states that she is too headstrong for him.

Another example of the change between the sexes during the late
nineteenth-century is the emergence of an increased desire for independence
on the part of lower middle-class and middle-class women. Literary examples
of this type occur as well, but in Gissing they are not always limited to the
desire to be independent of parents. Nor, as is the case in Jane Austen's *Emma*
(1816), do they relapse into marriage after experiencing independence. One
could not legitimately claim that Eve Madeley relapses into marriage with
Robert Narramore in *Eve's Ransom* (1895). Comparing the benefits from Maurice Hilliard's gift of money, supposedly offered with no strings, to Narramore's
greater wealth, she chooses Narramore. In fact, Hilliard seems destined to
return to his drudgery as a technical engineering draftsman. Gissing does not
narrate the results from Eve's choice but gives the impression of a woman with
a hard core and one not easily dominated. In *The Unclassed*, Gissing takes a
different attitude toward female independence. When Osmond Waymark meets
Ida Starr, she is a paradoxical figure for Victorian sensibilities, i.e., a cheerful
prostitute. Gillian Tindall writes in *The Born Exile*, "In *The Unclassed* the per-

sonality of the prostitute heroine, Ida Starr, is so romanticized that it is hard
for a modern reader to see why the book was widely considered shocking"
(85). However, she has had a hard past. Her mother was rejected by her own
father, the wealthy Abraham Woodstock. Lotty Starr turned to prostitution
to support herself and Ida. Lotty enrolls Ida in Miss Rutherford's school until
Harriet Smales, a classmate, informs the school head of Ida's mother's profession. Patricia Ingham remarks on Harriet's other and later depredations regarding Julian Casti "whom she tricks into marriage" (145), Osmond, and Ida:

> The full measure of her degeneracy appears in her determination to destroy
> Casti's friendship with Waymark; her instinctive reversion to alcohol, "low"
> companions and prostitution; and most of all her malicious and successful
> plot to have Ida wrongly imprisoned for theft, so returning her to a world of
> criminals and prostitutes [*The Language of Gender* 146].

After Ida and Osmond meet, Ida begins her expected penance, and Osmond
ultimately redeems her through his love. Before Woodstock's death, he and
Ida reconcile, and she and Osmond, who now works for Woodstock, plan to
marry. Rather than achieving independence, Ida forfeits it for a different, and
possibly better, condition. Sally Fisher, a prostitute friend of Ida's, marries
Philip O'Gree, a former teacher with Waymark at Dr. Tootle's school.
Although Sally and O'Gree open a chandler's shop and settle down, she never
goes through the purgatory to which Waymark, maybe inadvertently, con-
signs Ida. O'Gree is happy to have her, even knowing her past. The different class positions between the two couples might account for Sally's aura of
independence even after marriage. Ida has to pay a price for her past life, even
for refusing to go with Woodstock after her mother's death, whereas Sally
incorporates her past into her present. Before Waymark, literally, can make
an honest woman of Ida, one sees her at Woodstock's giving a garden party
for poor girls. Ida's mother dies in a hospital, presumably from the effects of
her profession, and Ida earns her newfound respectability with a vengeance.
(See Chapter 3 for a discussion of Ida's recovery of moral authority.) Gissing
was ill at ease with many middle-class sentiments, social and religious, but
he could not legitimately show Ida moving back into the middle class, where
she belongs by birth, unless she thoroughly purges herself of her and her
mother's profession and rebellion against their class. Pierre Coustillas's description of Ida suggests her transformation to type:

> Like Nell [Gissing's first wife] in real life and Carrie Mitchell in fiction, Ida
> Starr is a street walker, but unlike them, she succeeds, through sincere love,
> in resuming the position of an honourable woman and devotes herself to
> philanthropy ["Gissing's Feminine Portraiture" 93].

Some women from the lower and middle classes are independent by nature
but do not fit clear patterns. For instance, the cynical Maud Gresham Waghorn

in *Workers in the Dawn* knowingly marries a man of her class for whom she
has little respect. When he begins striking her, she leaves him. She tells Helen
Norman that she has resources of her own and will not stand for his mistreat-
ment. Her father is Helen's guardian, and they have known one another since
the Rev. Norman's death. Helen is financially independent but uses her money
quite differently than Maud. Gilbert Gresham, Maud's father, is a self-indul-
gent society painter and so makes little trouble over Helen's desire to study
in Germany. Later, Helen rejects his marriage proposal and also breaks off
relations with Arthur Golding when she learns of his marriage to Carrie
Mitchell. Gillian Tindall observes:

> In the book, Helen is the female antithesis to Carrie, a pure, not to say smug
> and cold heroine, admired by Arthur — and presumably by Gissing himself —
> but distinctly unattractive to most twentieth-century readers [*Born Exile*
> 83–84].

Whatever the reasons for or the effects of her decisions, including working
for the poor in East London, Helen makes them and carries them out. Though
coming from totally different circumstances, Helen's pursuit of her own ends
regardless of the consequences resembles Carrie Mitchell's. Carrie is an alcoholic prostitute who probably dies from venereal disease, and Helen has some
wasting disease similar to emphysema, quite respectable, but both lose whatever happiness Arthur could provide and suffer lonely deaths. Although Gissing does not set up a cause-and-effect relationship, he shows that no matter
the results, both women will have their way. Even Carrie seems stronger than
her husband Arthur when they are together, and he winds up throwing himself over Niagara Falls after Helen Norman's death. Ada Warren in *Isabel
Clarendon* starts from a different social position than either Maud, Helen, or
Carrie. Initially, everything works against Ada's developing as an independent woman. Left as the ward of a woman with whom she shares no sympathy and apparently penniless, Ada is sullen toward everyone she meets until
her surprise inheritance and her rejection of it propel her into adulthood.
(See Chapter 11.) She falls in love with Vincent Lacour, but he rejects her affections and goes off to India. When she learns that she and not Clarendon's
widow Isabel is to inherit nearly everything from the man who is supposedly
her real father, and thus dispossess Isabel, she chooses to earn her living as a
professional writer. While not very sensible, this is in keeping with her character.

Women disrupt, dislodge, and discomfit some men with whom they
come into contact by merely existing. Since these women's modes of living
may be different from these men's previous experiences, men may have no
way of understanding how they should relate to them. Gissing is careful in
The Whirlpool not to give Harvey Rolfe much understanding of women before

he marries Alma Frothingham. The nearly middle-aged Harvey has retired
from the world with a competence. He has his few men friends and some
female acquaintances he encounters in social settings. Harvey is settled and
seems to want little more from others. However, he meets Alma and her
mother, learns of the father's embezzlement from the insurance company he
runs and his subsequent suicide, and ends up marrying the pretty, musically
talented daughter. Over the next few years, Alma will upend his comfortable
life so that he feels compelled to take his young son Hughie, leave London,
and settle in Gunnersbury, near the small town from which he originally came.
Before they make the final shift from London to Gunnersby, her musical career
dries up, and she must admit she lacks the talent to make it as a professional
violinist. Lloyd Fernando describes their marital dilemmas:

> His child awakens him to a sense of parental responsibility and to the gen-
> eral problem of educating children for a society which had lost much of its
> sense of tradition. It also brings him to a realisation of limits that must be
> drawn to a woman's independence, since Alma, nervously wrapped in the
> pursuit of her musical career and in the social life accompanying it, leaves
> her domestic relationships to founder as they may, or uses them to further
> her own ambition ["Gissing's Studies" 115].

In addition, Hugh Carnaby, Harvey's old friend, kills Cyrus Redgrave in a
jealous rage over Redgrave's affair with his wife Sybil and goes to prison. Alma
is present the night of the killing; she also feels some degree of jealousy that
Redgrave is sleeping with Sybil though she refuses to sleep with him herself.
Alma's death on her final return to Harvey and her son after the failure of all
her aspirations soon follows from an accidental narcotic overdose. It is clear
that Harvey has no idea what to make of Alma, a seemingly quiet girl when
he first met her. From what in her life does all the turbulence come? She has
no explanation herself and may not even see it as turbulent. One could say
that she leads a life of unquiet desperation. And, Harvey could no more have
planned for it than he can divert her from living it out to its fullness. As Fernando astutely observes, "Rolfe slides into marriage with Alma Frothingham"
("Gissing's Studies" 115).

The disruption of male hopes for marital bliss develops into an important theme in Gissing's fiction. The details vary from novel to novel but usually display the strength of character needed by women to change their
circumstances. Monica Madden in *The Odd Women* provides a dramatic example of this. The pretty younger sister of Alice and Virginia Madden, older
spinsters who seem to have nearly run out of choices in life, Monica is their
hope that through marriage she can save them from an increasingly impoverished existence. They all formerly lived as a middle-class family in the west
of England. By a freak accident, Dr. Madden dies days before he can insure

his life, and the Madden daughters are left with a tiny income. Alice, a lady's companion, and Virginia, a governess, gradually lose the ability to obtain work, and one sees their extremely frugal lifestyle in a one-room London boarding house as the last step before the grave. Only Monica, working in a draper's establishment in London, offers any hope to them. Her position has no future either, given its low pay and the long hours that sap her strength. (See Chapter 7 and below for further discussion of the Maddens.) From that low point, Monica, in effect, takes charge of her life. First, she speaks to a strange man on her free Sunday. In the late nineteenth century, unchaper-oned middle-class women did not do this. Edmund Widdowson pursues Monica and persuades her to marry him. This second step liberates her from the draper's establishment but sends her into Widdowson's increasingly stul-tifying idea of marriage, two people cut off from the world. Monica rebels and goes out for visits on her own. Widdowson cannot fathom why she acts this way. Unknown to him, she meets and falls in love with Mr. Bevis and is ready to go with him to France where his wine merchant employers have decided to send him. A private investigator misinforms Widdowson that Mon-ica goes to the rooms of Everard Barfoot, who lives in the same building as Bevis. Monica earlier met Barfoot at his cousin's on one of her excursions into central London. When she becomes pregnant, Widdowson charges her with committing adultery with Barfoot, never learning about Bevis. Monica swears to Widdowson that it is his child, but he refuses to believe her, and after Monica's death gives Alice and Virginia money to raise the child and start a school for children. Not unlike Harvey Rolfe with Alma, Widdowson has no way of coping with, controlling, or understanding Monica. The morose Wid-dowson demonstrates no ability either to assess his actions or begin to deal with the wreck of his hopes. Every step Monica takes to free herself casts him increasingly into the shadows. Sandra R. Woods sums up their dilemma, "After they marry, Widdowson attempts not only to prescribe Monica's read-ing but also to regulate her contacts. Monica resists; Widdowson persists; the marriage degenerates" ("Dangerous Minds" 112).

A final category of female dubiousness shows women emerging from obscurity and claiming a role in society that, however indirectly, overturns male expectations. For example, Alice and Virginia Madden, who hope that their sister Monica will save them, counter the passive image discussed above and gradually gather strength to control their own lives. (See also Chapter 7.) First, the two sisters arrange their circumstances in London so that even with-out Monica's help they can survive. True, they barely continue to exist, liv-ing on the edge of destitution. Second, they confront Virginia's alcoholism, and together begin to control it. Selig comments on an episode when Alice and Monica find her drunk:

> In their different ways, each sister recognizes that alcoholism is a calamity for a self-respecting woman: Virginia's pathetic denial that she is hopelessly drunk, Monica's anger, and Alice's tears. One underlying element makes the scene extraordinarily touching: the humiliated Virginia, the angry Monica, and the tearful Alice all care deeply about one another and about each other's good opinion [*George Gissing* 66].

At the end of the novel, Virginia plans to go to an institution and get help for her drinking. This is a domestic drama but one of heroic proportions. Gissing makes no doubt that unless they turn to themselves they will not last. He leaves it to the reader to imagine from where they obtain the courage to do it. When Alice first comes to London and acquires a room, necessity forces her to bargain with the landlady and have her rent reduced by preparing her own meals. She and Virginia live on the small legacy they received after their father died. Virginia joins her when she loses her job as a lady's companion. She was only receiving room and board in return for the onerous task of teaching several young children. Obviously, Gissing has reduced them as low as they can go and still maintain their independence. Neither is strong enough to work anymore. Next would be the street and/or the river. Against all odds, they summon the will to stabilize their lives and then improve them.

A number of women emerge from social or religious backgrounds to discover a stronger sense of themselves. Sidwell Warricombe in *Born in Exile* responds to Godwin Peak's ideas about religion, and, as she tells him before their final separation, she no longer accepts religion in the same way. She has begun to think about what she should or should not believe. She even has enough self-confidence to reject him when he presses his suit a final time after inheriting money. Sidwell has decided to stay in her own world, but no one now guides her thinking, especially her brother Buckland who exposed Peak's religious pretensions. Rather than the formerly dutiful daughter and sister giving way to male authority, she has become an independent presence in her world. (See Chapter 10.) In a similar fashion, Miriam Baske in *The Emancipated*, discussed earlier in Chapter 8, wintering in Italy for her health, abandons her rigid evangelical roots and, with Ross Mallard's help, discovers art and culture. Finally, Irene Derwent in *The Crown of Life*, an upper-middle-class woman, must extract herself from a deadening social world and an unfortunate engagement to the imperial automaton Arnold Jacks. Prior to the crisis when she breaks off her engagement to Jacks and takes the first step toward her emancipation and eventual marriage to Piers Otway, Irene's involvement in the emotional lives of her cousin Olga Hannaford, the latter's mother Mrs. Hannaford, and her friend Helen Borisoff helps break the congealing social grip in which she lives. (See Chapter 11.) Irene couples her recognition of

Piers' worth with a clearer recognition and acknowledgment of what she wants as a woman. Marriage to Piers is a taking up of life against the strictures of a world she no longer fully accepts.

In his many novels, Gissing employs a complex array of male and female characters. His sympathetic interest and understanding might lean more toward the difficulties of the talented and alienated young man without financial and social resources, but the portraits of women shifting themselves and society out from under the seemingly impermeable layers of social custom also strongly draw attention. In a society still tilted in favor of men, women begin the work of equalizing the expectations and outcomes in many areas. They have the world before them, and Gissing shows them taking their proper places in it.

13

Conflicted Identities: The Individual and Society

The concept of the individual in society or out of it, for it or against it pulls together ideas from the entire range of George Gissing's fiction. Individuality is a theme whose difficulties undergird many of the problems Gissing's characters face. Each novel attempts to deal with a theme or themes that taken together portray his complex, multilayered perspectives. His fiction never rejects the view that most people can function and survive in society, but seldom does he ignore the hardships that survival entails. *Will Warburton* demonstrates this eternal dilemma. As he dons the apron and goes behind the counter, Warburton transcends his partner's earlier financial miscalculations. Robert L. Selig observes, "The now-bankrupt hero becomes a grocer, so that he can continue to pay the interest that his family expects and needs. But to save them from worry, he conceals his business troubles and his fall into grocerdom" (*George Gissing* 91). But is transcendence a dominant element in Gissing's fiction? His novels do not ultimately tend that way. Yet, pessimism is only part of what his characters exhibit as they react to the travails they undergo, for they frequently demonstrate a hard kernel that rebuffs defeat as a preconceived end to their lives. The few suicides in his novels, e.g., Arthur Golding (*Workers in the Dawn*), James Hood (*A Life's Morning*), Harold Biffen (*New Grub Street*), and Lilian Northway Quarrier in *Denzil Quarrier*), only take that step after many disappointments. Lurking behind their decisions, as John Halperin argues, is also the "terrible power" of social

132

convention (*Gissing* 170). Usually, difficulties are struggled against, endured, or ignored. The vexing question is whether society in all its manifestations is largely benevolent or harmful. Sidestepping this either/or position, one can say that Gissing's characters for the most part do struggle, do endure and preserve a sense of identity while often experiencing the despair of their existences. The title of Gissing's posthumously published essay, "The Hope of Pessimism," captures this paradoxical stance that lies at the center of his fiction.

Pragmatic considerations are important when analyzing the role of the individual in society. Just as in religion the one may be asked by the many how he or she can doubt when so many believe, so in more secular terms the weight of the world generates self doubt as to what one should think or do. If so many think or act in a particular way, how can one stand against their position or even think of doing so? Gissing's heroes frequently reveal so much about these conflicts because they are on the edge of nonconformity and, through their painful struggles, show the cost. John Yule, Amy Reardon's brother in *New Grub Street*, visits Reardon after their separation and upbraids him regarding his conduct toward his sister. Reardon is isolated and alone while Yule has society on his side. Reardon can only feel his way toward the right direction for himself in this situation, knowing and accepting that not only Yule and Mrs. Yule, Amy's mother, but also Amy herself reject his course of action that will, in their eyes, drag Amy down in class. And, Reardon senses that the right personal solution will only bring opprobrium to him. Far from the image of the Byronic hero admired for his rebellious stance, Reardon suffers alone with only the even more long-suffering Biffen for support. Amy, surprisingly, gives little attention to their strong differences of opinion after she returns to her mother's home except when Reardon comes to see her. Comforted by the relief from Reardon's gloomy pessimism and their previous struggle over money, she is too happy to be out of the deteriorating situation to expend much energy on remonstrating with him. Not surprisingly, society approves of her actions and condemns his. Even the sympathetic Biffen feels that Reardon's only recourse is to reconcile with Amy, in effect surrendering his will to hers.

In *The Private Papers of Henry Ryecroft,* Ryecroft reels from life's difficulties but has sufficient strength when he receives a legacy from an admirer of his writing to shelter himself in rural Devon for the last few years of his life. Ryecroft wrote for a living. So much independence as that confers was his. He was able to live, but the struggle to survive was deadening. He chose the career so could not legitimately complain of the difficulties, but once committed, it held him in its grasp. This personification of writing as a compelling force is Ryecroft's weight of the world. Like Reardon, Ryecroft maintains a sense of self before his retirement but finds difficulty in doing so. Both men die relatively early, but Ryecroft has the joyful shock of the legacy and the several years of peace. Reardon, while seemingly near a complete reconciliation with Amy, dies before it can be effected. For both men, the idea of living as free individuals, while technically possible, would function as a supreme irony. It is hard to imagine that it would previously have mattered to either man as they struggled to hold on to their lives. At such impasses, death seems the only rational way to solve their problems. Even the retired Ryecroft dies from the effects of his early struggles. Before this event, he lives quietly and sees almost no one except his housekeeper. A writing friend from his early days visits infrequently. Ryecroft attunes himself to nature's cycles and beauty. However, Gissing is adamant in his portrait of the former author that nothing could regenerate an ability to live, although Ryecroft's desire to do so is not gone. John Goode portrays Ryecroft's Janus-like position: "The celebrated possession of privilege, the tame utopia of the detached intellectual is lit with the flickerings of oppression and struggle that constitute his past and the world outside" (*Ideology* 48). Ryecroft's is the paradox of a life lived freely even though it is not his fully to control.

Dyce Lashmar in *Our Friend the Charlatan* reveals a different outcome in somewhat analogous circumstances. As in Ryecroft's case, Lashmar chooses his life and keeps to it, but events manipulate him as well. Lashmar suffers his own weight of the world but in a tone very different from Ryecroft's. *Our Friend the Charlatan* is one of Gissing's few satiric comedies, *The Paying Guest* and *The Town Traveller* being two others. Lashmar has two distinct needs that depend on the good will of others, i.e., the need for money and the need to succeed. By themselves, these two needs do not necessarily provide subject for satire, but in a personality such as Dyce's, they do. Smoothly attempting to deceive Constance Bride and Lady Ogram, his need overbalances him, revealing the hustler and con artist. Only the foolish Iris Woolstan, who previously hired him as her son Leonard's tutor, remains true if blinded to his real nature. Lashmar must go into the world, and all individuals who do are subject to its very practical corrections if their needs clash with those they wish to manipulate. For all his miscalculations, Lashmar is an admirable figure in that he cannot be kept down. (See Chapter 7.)

The idea of a free individual living in a community, sustaining it and sustained by it, is possible but problematic in Gissing's fiction. Of course, this may be a natural response to complex, layered artistic portraits. Not ideologically driven, Gissing pursues the twists and turns of character, action, and motivation. Sharp, clear-cut stances give way to deeper, more variegated insights into personality. In *Demos*, Richard Mutimer, unlike Westlake, Hubert Eldon, or even Adela Waltham, moves from clear stances on family, love, and trade unions to more and more complicated intellectual and emotional situations. His sudden inheritance separates him from past clarity of purpose and substitutes, initially, new clarities. However, circumstances either open up even newer, more tempting possibilities or overcome past desires. Mutimer cancels his engagement to the faithful Emma Vine; plans striking uses for the money, uses designed to help the workers but that unsettle them instead; and quarrels with his family — mother, sister Alice, and younger brother Harry. At every juncture, Mutimer has to make a choice; stasis is seemingly not an option. From sure control over his life, Mutimer goes from certainties to unforeseen difficulties. John Sloan remarks:

> It is one of the novel's paradoxes that what is clearly meant to support its thesis that working people given instant wealth will be corrupted, should so nearly become a criticism of the alienated life-style of the owner of capital, and a recognition of the real human contact and community enjoyed by the urban poor [*Cultural* 64].

Adela grows to despise Mutimer for his commonness; a new will disinherits him; his family, even his mother, desert him; and a working-class mob stones him to death. The problematic nature of Mutimer's ability to live as a free individual in a community comes not from any one circumstance but rather a confluence of choices made and actions taken. No one can foresee the outcome of possible directions in which to shape one's life. Thus, the chorus's warning at the end of Sophocles' *Oedipus Rex* that only after death can one decide whether a particular life was happy or sad appears justified in Mutimer's case.

Rhoda Nunn in *The Odd Women* moves from an independent youth to an adult with an even stronger sense of self. Bolstered by her connection to her friend Mary Barfoot and the young women who come to their agency for training, Rhoda represents the fulfillment of the independent ideal. An important part of this independence is freedom from reliance on men. As a youth, Rhoda knew the Madden family, consisting of Dr. Elkanah Madden and three daughters, Alice, Virginia, and Monica. Three other daughters died earlier. As a fifteen-year-old girl, Rhoda holds her own in conversation with Dr. Madden, when he will deign to talk seriously with her. Shortly afterwards, Rhoda receives a legacy and decides to use it to train for a career in office work. Her energetic portrait contrasts sharply with the Madden sisters after their father's death. Alice and Virginia, a lady's companion and governess, respectively, are beaten down by the sudden death of their uninsured father. They have a small legacy that they invest and that gives a meager addition to their income. Their one hope lies in their pretty younger sister, Monica.

Neither Monica nor her sisters, who now live in London on their limited income, and under the most exacting frugality, actively work to control their lives but rather react to circumstances. Rhoda, who meets the Madden sisters again in London, has joined with Mary Barfoot to train young women for office work, especially on the newly invented typewriter. Both Mary and Rhoda are strong, independent women, and the latter's love affair with Everard Barfoot, Mary's cousin, is seen by her as a test to her independence. (See Chapter 7.) Her ability to say no to a man she loves, a man who she understands wishes to control and dominate her, confirms her own strength and the rightness of her work with Mary. As Rhoda exults in her power, Monica declines, more from an inability to defeat Widdowson in their domestic battles than from any clear medical reason. At her death, her sisters raise her child. It is clear that Rhoda's independence is contingent on her relationship with Mary and the mission to save the "odd" women in late-Victorian society, those who like the Madden sisters can find no clear place from which to discover their lives. Monica's death, therefore, affects Rhoda's success since it represents a loss to part of her community. At the very end of the novel, Rhoda sits alone with Monica's child: "And as the baby sank into sleep, Rhoda's vision grew dim; a sigh made her lips quiver, and once more she murmured, 'Poor little child!'" (*The Odd Women* 386).

The Whirlpool presents a society that the very title of the book calls in question. The circling descent and powerlessness suggested by a whirlpool argue that the characters lack the ability to live freely. Alma Frothingham Rolfe conveys this meaning more than anyone else in the novel. Free individuals have some ability to make choices and resist the pull of circumstance and others' demands. From a protected environment, Alma becomes socially vulnerable following her father's death. Harvey Rolfe, however, falls in love with her and is unconventional enough to marry her. (See Chapter 12.) Harvey's passivity indirectly exposes Alma to her weaknesses. She is nearly good enough to make a name for herself and continues working at her music, leaving Harvey to take care of their son Hughie, even though she knows that she will never be one of the best. Her vanity and near-talent, coupled with Harvey's acceptance of her decision to continue or not in her profession, seduce her into moving out into experiences in which she cannot find her own self. Nominally acting from her own choices and pursuing an artistic career because she must, Alma in fact does not discern her true nature in the welter of voices and events surrounding her. She cannot stop events long enough to assess what she wants and can accomplish.

It may seem impossible to write, other than ironically, of free individuals existing in a community when considering *Thyrza* and *The Nether World*. The oppressive social conditions, especially in the latter novel, tend to rob the idea of individual freedom of any power. Sidney Kirkwood, Clara Hewett, and Jane Snowdon represent three separate, but overlapping, areas of oppression.

Each character struggles to achieve a sense of individuality in a community that constantly acts to deny it. Unlike Sidney Kirkwood, Clara and Jane are strongly affected by their families. Initially, Clara is the only one facing an ongoing family controversy. Her father, the over-protective and emotionally unstable John Hewett, attempts to keep her close to the other family members, all beaten down by poverty and John's inability to hold a job and to deal with this fact. Clara eventually runs away and becomes an actress. Grace, another actress and jealous of Clara's success, throws acid in her face, and John brings Clara back home. In the early part of the novel, Jane undergoes more suffering than Clara. In effect orphaned, but with a living father who knows of her condition, Jane works as a maid in the house of Mrs. Peckover, who is also the Hewett's landlady, and is abused daily by Mrs. Peckover's daughter Clem. Jane is patient and long-suffering, but her manner only further encourages Clem to harm her. The Hewetts help Jane before her grandfather returns wealthy from Australia and rescues her. Jane's father, Joseph Snowdon, appears when he learns of his father's good fortune and hopes to profit by it. Unluckily, he marries Clem and suffers the consequences of her violent temper. Sidney Kirkwood, who befriends the young Jane and who eventually falls in love with her, betroths himself to Clara and marries her, thus denying his love for Jane. She in turn, controlled by her grandfather's will, turns to charity work.

The intertwined lives of Sidney, Clara, and Jane, pulled and pushed by their community and their living conditions, make a mockery of the idea that one can only become a free individual in a community. Sidney first seeks friendship with John Hewett, who becomes so filled with rage at his and his family's hardships that he drives off Sidney, rebuffing his overtures of aid. Hoping for love, Jane still turns away from Sidney, and he marries the disfigured Clara out of a sense of obligation. Clara seeks liberation through acting but has her beauty and her chances taken away by the acid attack. She little values Sidney's sacrifice in marrying her. Jane wants a human response from those around her, but except for Sidney and her grandfather's initial manner toward her, she suffers only rejection and denial. They are still separate beings, but their community disvalues and rejects their most admirable qualities. *The Nether World* becomes a low point in Gissing's portrayal of the individual life seeking to liberate, to let flow its deepest and best self.

In *The Form of Victorian Fiction*, J. Hillis Miller states:

> In most Victorian novels there is relatively little detached self-consciousness, the self-consciousness of a single person becoming aware of himself in separation from other people. In Victorian novels, for the most part, the characters are aware of themselves in terms of their relations to others [4–5].

In its absoluteness, Miller's position raises objections, yet there is an element of this relation to others that is borne out by Gissing's fiction. In *Thyrza*, Luke

Ackroyd and Totty Nancarrow achieve a sense of themselves as individuals but connect with another through marriage, Ackroyd to Lydia Trent, Thyrza's sister, and Totty to the anti-religious Mr. Bunce. Characters realize who they are as individuals through a struggle to liberate themselves from past conditions or entanglements or to escape from situations, sometimes alluring, that do not correspond to their sense of identity. Not every liberation or escape has positive overtones or is achieved by an admirable person. Lionel Tarrant in *In the Year of Jubilee* is an example of someone who achieves at least a partial liberation from an onerous condition but who does not stand as any model of good conduct. After impregnating Nancy Lord, a young woman with whom he little more than dallies, Tarrant feels constrained to marry her. However, he wants neither her nor the child as a continued presence in his life. At first, he travels, ostensibly on some business venture, and when he returns to London, he persuades Nancy to make permanent their separation while remaining married. She reluctantly acquiesces, and Tarrant, now living largely on his writing, feels pleased that she accepts the idea that they will thus not grow tired of one another. His manipulations reveal a man thoroughly self-concerned, one willing and able to create around him a world that adjusts to his needs. The self that he has liberated, while no positive social model, appears to be his true nature. Tarrant, at one level, is little different from Horace Lord, Nancy's younger brother. Stephen Lord, their ailing father, attempts to restrain Nancy and Horace, but Horace struggles to break away from this restrictive environment. He pursues and later marries the intemperate Fanny French. The similarity between Tarrant and Horace lies not in the type of woman with whom they involve themselves, for Nancy has greater strength of character than Fanny, but in their escape into a revelation of shallowness. Like Fanny, both men are willful, pushing aside anything to assert that will but having no substantive goals beyond the assertion. In contrast, Nancy takes a strong stand in bearing a child unknown to her father, in concealing her marriage from him, and, after his death, in violating the terms of his restrictive will.

Godwin Peak in *Born in Exile* hopes for liberation or escape from his present existence but does not accomplish it. In addition to his presently unsatisfactory life and the relationship he hopes to create with Sidwell Warricombe (see Chapters 8 and 10), the novel eventually presents the ironically wealthy Peak who has inherited an income of £800 per annum from Marcella Moxey, a woman he found unappealing and thus rejected. (See Chapter 4.) Godwin Peak, as several critics have noticed, is one of Gissing's best pictures of the educated but alienated young man with no means to make himself known. Peak believes that if he can change this state he will achieve happiness and fulfillment. Escaping his past life represents the path to liberation and a full selfhood. He will not be a complete individual without this. Sidwell's nearly complete acceptance of and satisfaction with her family and her life emphasize the difference between one who lives her true life and one who hopes to find that state. However, Peak's lack of authentic selfhood becomes clear when Sidwell, contrary to the wishes of her family, goes to see Peak and, essentially, offers to continue their relationship. The falseness of Peak's position surfaces in his rejection of her offer. Sidwell has achieved her individuality, but Peak has nothing left when his lies are exposed. With Marcella's money, he wanders in Europe and dies of a mysterious illness in Vienna. Not a heavy moralist, Gissing nonetheless seems to argue that a desire to liberate oneself, to escape from restrictive circumstances that stunt one's growth to a fuller life as a free individual, cannot be achieved through a false image. Liberation of self only comes through an honest facing of one's beliefs and conduct and an honest statement of them.

Some characters in Gissing's fiction achieve their individuality through antagonism towards those nearest them or in opposition to circumstances that threaten them. Both situations release a flood of emotions and energy that seemingly propels them away from threats to self but can also lead to greater personal danger. Carrie Mitchell in *Workers in the Dawn* is Gissing's first extended character of this type. Although Ada Warren's social behavior in *Isabel Clarendon* is far more respectable than Carrie's, Ada has an even greater antipathy to her situation and to those around her. The primary focus of her resentment is Isabel Clarendon, a wealthy widow and Ada's guardian. Unknown to Ada as the novel opens, she is to inherit the bulk of the former Mr. Clarendon's wealth. Before she learns of this, Ada sees herself as forced to live in an unacceptable state of dependency. She chafes at Isabel's attempts to guide her life. Robert L. Selig succinctly states Gissing's resolution of their dilemmas:

> But Ada, who now supports herself as a professional writer, nobly and unexpectedly renounces her inheritance for Isabel's sake, and the now-secure widow offers Kingcote another chance. Employed at last as a humble bookseller, he rejects her pitying offer to marry him after all. As a result, she marries her friendly rich cousin [Robert Asquith], and the closing pages hint that the hero may eventually marry Ada [*George Gissing* 37].

Ada has found a sense of herself once money has been given and returned. She has liberated herself from a past that included Isabel as a guardian and the money by means of which she performed that chore.

The idea that antagonisms form some part of one's self identity may help explain Edwin Reardon's refusal in *New Grub Street* to follow Jasper Milvain's and his wife Amy's advice, first touched on in Chapter 2, regarding the direction of his literary career. Gissing pictures Reardon sunk in gloom as he slowly fails as a novelist, having no possible way to recover the energy or desire to write. When offered suggestions that reflect definite, sure ways to overcome his lack of success, Reardon feels that it is impossible. He cannot follow his wife's and friend's advice because to do so would either violate his artistic integrity or be emotionally beyond him. To take the latter instance first, Milvain believes that Reardon needs to promote himself and success will follow. He must go to literary evenings and meet editors and opinion makers. Essentially, Milvain urges him to sell himself just as he does, and he offers to start the process by pushing Reardon's latest novel, *Margaret Home*, a work that the author thinks of with little more than contempt. In fact, Reardon states to Amy that he is washed up, finished, left with no ability to create. Amy advises him to work at fiction as one would work at a job. For his next novel, he should do so many pages a day and send it off to the publisher when finished. It is irrelevant that it will not be a great work of art. Amy's advice resembles Jasper's, and she uses the latter as an example to follow. Urging their financial necessity, she reminds him of their lack of money and offers to stay with her mother while he goes away for three months and writes a work that will sell. Reardon's antagonism reveals itself as he stubbornly refuses to let Milvain help him and accuses Amy of knowingly asking him to violate his artistic conscience.

At the beginning of the novel, Milvain states to his family that Reardon could write well if he had no financial worries but that with a wife and child he is doomed to failure and possibly to suicide (*New Grub Street* 6). However, Reardon stops writing, takes a clerk's job at a hospital through his and Amy's mutual acquaintance, and moves to cheaper but socially less advantageous lodgings. He and Amy never live together again, something he predicted when they first separated. Reardon might seem the picture of obstinance, but making the above changes, even in his unhappiness at living estranged and apart from Amy, seems to allow him a chance to regain an inner balance and certainty about what he wants and what he must do to achieve it. He says to Amy that he cannot write, but he once achieved a lifestyle that allowed him to become a moderately successful writer, financially and artistically. It is not that Reardon must be alone to become a free individual, but this appears to be his route to a clear self-identity; a stubborn antagonism to others' attempts to direct his life is the mark of his individuality. Before they separate, Amy tells him not to worry about where the money to live will come from; she will manage all those cares in the future. Reardon cannot live with that arrangement, and their break-up is inevitable. He must tell her who he is and what he can do and not the reverse. Amy's strong assertiveness is no match for Reardon's antagonism to her attempts at control and direction.

It could be argued that Reardon rejects the advice of Amy and Jasper for artistic reasons. His disgust with his last novel, as well as his careful attention to his earlier work, suggests that possibility. However, as Milvain clearly shows, following a clear path to success will give him all the time and money he needs to write as he wishes. He only has to sacrifice his personal standards for a short time. This is the difficulty; Reardon cannot accept this suggestion even if it would allow him to continue to write and keep his wife and child with him. His artistic principles are important to him, but going his own way is even more important. To allow Amy to assume financial responsibility for their daily lives or to let Milvain show him the direction to literary success is too much personal sacrifice. Reardon's deep response to both Amy and Milvain is to hold on to his sense of himself, lashing out at both of them. He completely rejects Milvain, as friend and adviser, and accuses him of alienating Amy's affections. He only sees Amy in circumstances that suggest a reconciliation when she telegraphs him that their son Willie lies gravely ill in Brighton. Amy now has the £10,000 legacy from her uncle and no longer fears living in poverty, but both Willie and Reardon die within a day of each other. Reardon's conduct seems maddeningly willful, but he knows his emotional life and fights off claims to mold him.

Gissing is concerned with the individual man or woman. He knows something of the struggles of Beatrice Redwing in *A Life's Morning*, Beatrice French in *In the Year of Jubilee*, Alfred Yule and Mr. Duke in *New Grub Street*, Rhoda Nunn and Mary Barfoot in *The Odd Women*, as well as Monica Madden and Mr. Bevis in the same novel, and Mr. Wyvern in *Demos*. The panorama of characters in his fiction, along with the many false starts he makes to find a subject on which to write, reflect his imaginative engagement with a world pressing on his everyday life. The characters struggle from his subconscious, almost as if they compete for a chance to live. In *The Form of Victorian Fiction*, Miller is partially right when he claims in writing on Dickens' *Our Mutual Friend* that fictional characters exist only in words, but only partially: "Veneering, his guests, his table, and his mirror exist only in words and can be encountered nowhere else" (39). This reductionist approach misstates the lived feel of the imaginative experience that continues to generate responses and speak to other minds from other times. The various individuals do not walk in the world and cannot be questioned, but their fictive lives can be examined.

PART THREE

The Cultural Imagination

14

Against the Modern: Rural Idylls and Urban Realities

In George Gissing's *Workers in the Dawn*, the child Arthur Golding flees from the Rev. Edward Norman's home in Bloomford, where he was taken after his father's death, to London and the building and the very room in which he lost his father. It is a grim scene, an urban hell in its bleak squalor, and Arthur's life can, by comparison, only improve even if he remains for a while alone and friendless in the city. Henry Ryecroft, the title character in *The Private Papers of Henry Ryecroft*, reflecting, as John Halperin observes, "Gissing's deep love of the English countryside" (*Gissing* 309), retires with an unsuspected legacy to rural Devon from a hard life as a writer and to the rhythms of nature experienced in a quietness hardly broken by Mrs. M, his housekeeper. Golding, too young to appreciate the rustic retreat to which the Rev. Norman takes him and where he meets Helen Norman, and Ryecroft, long too ill to enjoy a peace that he never expected to know, both suffer in the city and from the city. In *Demos: A Novel of English Socialism*, a work that Jacob Korg calls "an extensive examination of lower-class character" (*George Gissing* 87), Gissing sharply dramatizes the incompatible worlds of country and urban-industrial England in the conflict between Hubert Eldon and Richard Mutimer and their competing visions over the future of the valley near Wanley in the west of England. Gissing shifts the novel from a pastoral setting to an industrialized outreach of urban forces represented by New Wanley to the valley's complete restoration to its original state at the beginning of the story, paralleling the ascendancy of either Mutimer or Eldon. In these and other novels, Gissing draws positive cultural and physical portraits of rural environments, but in most instances the modern city ultimately dominates, determining the destinies of people and societies.

First, Arthur Golding's return to London, his blind desire to be where his father was, is a significant comment on the dominance of the city in Gissing's fiction. In *Victorian Cities* (1963,1968), Asa Briggs states, "Nearly all his characters are London characters, and when he talked about social problems, as he often did, he saw them in a London context. London provided him with his facts, his experiences, and his ideas" (350). When Golding finally leaves, it is ultimately to meet his death in Niagara Falls, a place of wildness and even greater blindness in the water's roar. Nearly forty years before in *American Notes* (1842), Charles Dickens had written of the splendor of the American and Canadian falls (228–30). (See Chapter 18.) It was one of the last places he saw in his westward swing as he returned to New York City. Golding has no similar aesthetic response. For him, one place of sound and struggle replaces another, both having obliterated all hope of life. His loss of love and the loved one when Helen dies is only a concomitant to the unavailing struggle that the city represents. David Grylls summarizes their plight:

> And yet in spite of all their striving, their passionate concern for art and philanthropy, both come to miserable ends. Radical unhappiness infects their rapture, as they lurch between surges of co-operative zeal and pacing their rooms in isolation and despair [*Paradox* 12].

Gissing draws the portrait of Arthur undergoing his trials as a child in London, but these trials do not have decisive effects on his ultimate decisions. Before he meets and comes under the protection of Samuel Tollady, Golding's picaresque experiences in the city represent potential dangers only. One gets a sense that these are preliminary exercises before his real life begins. Helen has lived abroad in Germany and has studied religion and philosophy and learned German. With activity reminiscent of George Eliot's early years, Helen, nevertheless, moves in a different direction when she returns to London to work with the poor. Arthur's life before he receives the Rev. Norman's legacy consists almost entirely of urban experiences. Mr. Tollady raises and educates him, encouraging his early artistic talent. However, Arthur never leaves London until the end of the novel, and what he knows of life comes from within its boundaries.

Carrie Mitchell contributes profoundly to Arthur's education as a young man in London. Her importance lies in the fact that she is London made, and made from the lower-middle class. Chapter 3 discusses her pregnancy and eviction from her Aunt Pettindund's home. Arthur is an innocent bystander until he marries Carrie. However, his kindness and sense of humanity, derived in part from Mr. Tollady's influence, are no match for Carrie's fundamentally intemperate character. Not only her vulgar relatives but the city as well have reinforced her natural desire to indulge herself. When Arthur tries to teach her better ways, a fatal error, Carrie endures his instruction only so long and then rebels against what she sees as a too-constrictive lifestyle:

> "Why don't you let me speak as I'm used to?" cried Carrie, starting up with flashing eyes, one night when Arthur had interrupted her in every sentence for a quarter of an hour. "What's the good of tormenting me in that way. If you wanted to marry a grammar-machine you should have looked somewhere else, and not have taken up with me!" [*Workers in the Dawn* II.148].

Her dilemma is a moral one with which she cannot cope nor begin to understand. Trapped in the city and his marriage to Carrie, Arthur subsequently loses Helen, with whom he has fallen in love, after he reveals his relationship to Carrie. All three characters die young. Melodramatic as it sounds, the novel shows Gissing's unrelenting attention to his story as it unfolds. For these characters, the city offers no respite.

As Gissing finishes *Workers in the Dawn* with the waters of Niagara Falls overpowering Arthur Golding's senses and ending his life, his fiction offers no stronger instance of nature's force, and this hyperbolic image seems a fitting closure to a novel of extremes situated in a London literally and metaphorically destroying the lives of many of its inhabitants. John Sloan states, "Directing the novel is an overriding pessimism and sense of urban degeneration that lies beyond explicit correctives to middle-class philanthropy" (*Cultural* 19). The question arises as to whether Gissing literally sees the city as a moral problem. The above reference to Carrie's moral dilemma and Sloan's concept of "urban degeneration" present two opposed sources of moral difficulties, i.e., the individual and the environment. Gissing complicates matters by suggesting that Carrie's problems derive both from her own moral failings and from the environment. Few of Gissing's novels present such a bleak picture. In fact, Osmond Waymark helps redeem Ida Starr from a life of prostitution in *The Unclassed* (1884), but no escape is available for Carrie or Arthur. Gissing generally rules out redemption as a thematic means to rescue his characters. Other Gissing novels than *Workers in the Dawn* use the idea of the roar, the fray into which various characters plunge in different ways but not always in London. *Denzil Quarrier* is set in Polterham, Where Quarrier runs for election as a Liberal candidate. One indirect effect of his action is his "wife" Lilian's suicide. Mrs. Wade, who wants Quarrier for herself, convinces Lilian that the revelation of her marriage to Northway will ruin her husband's political career. *New Grub Street* opens with Jasper Milvain's visit to his mother and sisters in Finden near Wattleborough. He goes to the quiet village to recuperate as much as to see his family. London is his scene of struggle, and the train, in the incident with Marian Yule on the bridge, is an outreach of the city. Marian, as her father's literary helper, views herself, unfortunately, as a part of that city. Rachel Bowlby observes, "Marian sees her work as a writer as an anachronism, something which ought to be done not by 'such poor creatures as herself,' but by 'some automaton' perfectly programmed to meet the requirements of present-day industry" (*Just Looking* 98–99). In *Our Friend the Charlatan*, Dyce Lashmar's every visit to his parents in Alverholme or to the London home of Iris Woolstan, the lady he eventually marries, is a lull in his efforts to make himself known. In contrast, every moment at Lady Ogram's home near Hollingford is a combat. Lashmar stands to win or lose through the sharp-eyed autocrat's favor, and since he generally deceives her as to his intentions at every level, he never relaxes his tense watchfulness. With his skeptical friend Constance Bride serving as Lady Ogram's private secretary, Lashmar has little chance to succeed. Although *New Grub Street* is primarily set in London, it and the other two novels above offer examples of the projection of the central city's conflicts into the rural world of small towns and villages. Intentionally or not, characters bring London and its problems and concerns with them.

Second, the natural world not only acts as a force opposed to the urban environment, but it also occasionally produces a position from which to efface it by remembering it and by that act partially contain it. One initial effect of this effacement through memory is to balance both rural and urban portraits, surrounding them with language. If the rural is the viewpoint from which the urban is observed, the latter diminishes in power. *The Paying Guest* suggests a need for such containment but shows that urban invasions cannot easily be resisted. Clarence and Emmeline Mumford live in the suburbs of London. Though the situation presses them financially, they determine that their lives are better away from than in the city. However, the city arrives in the form of Louise Derrick who comes to be improved by the Mumfords and the society of their friends. (See Chapter 9.) Perhaps this could be successfully accomplished, but Miss Derrick appears with her lower-middle-class accent and attitudes strongly in place. The Mumfords manage to survive her presence but not before part of the house catches fire; Louise's vulgar parents visit unexpectedly; Emmeline becomes jealous of Clarence's attentions toward Louise, however innocent; and Tom Cobb, a no-nonsense electrical engineer, arrives to claim Louise. For the Mumfords, the money is not worth the contention. After Louise departs, they gratefully return to their peaceful lives, far from the world that produced her. The city has the ability to injure the Mumfords in their personal and social relationships, but whether the injury be emotional, physical, psychological, or moral, distance and desire lessen the city's impact on their lives. Bringing Louise into their home opens them to the city's entanglements and thus requires strong action to restore their suburban calm. Proximity to London is one of the dangers to that calm, and in *The Private Papers of Henry Ryecroft*, Ryecroft moves to Devon, nearly two hundred miles from his scene of suffering.

Physically, the city no longer looms over Ryecroft, but mentally and emotionally it still reverberates in his life. Kevin Swafford observes, "Ultimately, Ryecroft's sense of loss is directly related to his perception of art. For Ryecroft, the capacity to know and enjoy art recedes through the experiences of modernity" (1). Thus, Ryecroft must actively efface memories of the city by writing about it and its attendant miseries, mixed with the visual, olfactory, and aural presence of the rural world. Divided into the seasons, the autobiographical novel usually begins each chapter with an appropriate description and comment on the physical world's rich profusion before being drawn back into the past and the city. The effect of this literary structure is to attenuate the city's menace, its ability to do harm even when the person remembering is so far away. The more Ryecroft weaves his descriptions and images of the natural world with the past urban struggle, the more that struggle lessens in intensity. Gillian Tindall remarks on "its theme of a self-centered and quiescent identification with the British landscape" (*Born Exile* 126). But, Ryecroft must fully unburden himself. He is his own best therapist, knowing that he cannot withhold any part of his former fight for survival as a writer. The quiet and silence of his retreat are essential to him, but he knows that silence as to his past will not further his quiet. Adrian Poole argues, "the Utopian calm so affectionately pictured here can only be considered as a deplorable but logical capitulation." He refers to it as an "indulged withdrawal" (*Gissing in Context* 204). However, the coexistence of past and present is not possible. Ryecroft's tools are words, and with them, he can change the balance to his present favor. Obviously, he is now safe, but the very extremes of his two worlds require preemptive action. Just as he has moved to Devon and limited his human contacts to his housekeeper Mrs. M, occasional visits from N, an old friend, and infrequent trips to nearby towns, Ryecroft must now put the past between the covers of a book. In one way, his memoir allows him to enfold his Grub Street existence into nature's rhythms just as he has enfolded himself, burying both in the peace not so much of the grave as the quiet life. Yet, this is a too passive construction. And, Ryecroft's "sharply marked out circle" (Poole 206) that separates him from the world is a far more active image that leads one to perceive what he accomplishes in his book. *The Crown of Life*'s Jerome Otway and his study of Dante in his Wensleydale retreat enlighten one as to Gissing's appreciation of the engaged withdrawal.

Six years earlier, Gissing employs two characters that illuminate Ryecroft's duality. *The Whirlpool* dramatizes the temporary estrangement of Harvey and Alma Rolfe when it becomes evident to the former that his wife cannot give up her desire for a successful music career even when it appears obvious that she does not have the talent to reach the first rank of performers. Alma is a daughter of the city, and her life is replete with its sufferings. Michael Collie remarks, "Harvey Rolfe is himself on the edge of the whirlpool, is not independent of its motion." Collie continues:

> It is the whirlpool of materialism, in which the individual, however frugal, however adventurous with money, struggles for financial independence in a world whose capitalist mechanisms make independence from the system virtually impossible [*Alien Art* 157].

Her father Bennet Frothingham was exposed as a fraud and embezzler in the conduct of his insurance business and subsequently committed suicide. Not quite twenty-one years old, Alma studies at the Royal Academy of Music and tries to make her way as a musician, but success comes slowly. She and Harvey marry, and they have a son. Eventually, Harvey realizes that her unrequited obsession will not allow her to enjoy life. They are reasonably well off, but Alma only reluctantly gives up her hopes for a career when she falls ill. Her suburban sojourn with Harvey and their son Hugh at Gunnersbury near Richmond and Kew lasts briefly, and she dies from an accidental drug overdose (448). Ryecroft also dies soon after he moves to the country. Both Alma and Ryecroft come to these venues marked by their urban experiences. In an 1893 letter to Eduard Bertz written from Exeter, Gissing states, "Before long, I shall go back to London for good. I want the streets again" (Mattheisen, Young, and Coustillas 5: 105). While Ryecroft would shudder at such a thought, Alma lives in the suburbs by default. Ironically, both Ryecroft and Alma reject the idea of community as a saving grace. The structure of Ryecroft's life precludes it, and Harvey and Hughie cannot replace what Alma has lost.

The rural world's effacement of the looming, menacing city may often be no more than shutting one's eyes to it. Given enough distance, the illusion of control will be successful. In *The Odd Women*, after Monica leaves her husband Edmund Widdowson, gives birth, and dies, her sisters, Alice and Virginia Madden, the latter presently institutionalized for alcoholism, plan to set up a school for young children and with the financial help of Widdowson raise his and Monica's daughter. They live far from London and the pain endured there. The city with all its strife and struggle still exists, but their small world of three, along with Rhoda Nunn's moral support, faces in a different direction. Of course, Rhoda and Mary Barfoot, mutually supporting one another, and the "odd women" they train to be self sufficient, create an urban community that denies the city's heretofore omnipresent control of women's lives. Rhoda falls in love with Everard Barfoot, Mary's cousin, and he becomes a threat, but one finally avoided. Annette Federico states:

> Gissing seems finally to suggest, though, that however brave and attractive the New Woman may be (and clearly he feels she is potentially ideal), she cannot fulfill men's desires completely if she does not consent to subdue her will to his [*Masculine Identity* 94].

Rhoda and Mary, as it were, look away from the world that grinds on around them. If the city still ultimately controls these two female communities, it is a loose control, one that allows some to escape if not triumph over it. A more problematic urban dominance occurs in *Born in Exile* with the Warricombe family and their circle of friends and acquaintances. Buckland Warricombe exposes Godwin Peak's attempt to deceive Sidwell Warricombe and his parents by claiming to be sincere in his desire to become a Church of England priest. In reality, Peak is an atheist and a representative of the new, urban culture threatening the rural peace and harmony of the Warricombes' Exeter life. However, the Warricombes' strength lies more in the traditions of life to which they adhere than to any overt turning away from the city. Even Sidwell's reaching out to Peak after his exposure suggests more the solidity of her character built on family and religious belief than a defeat of the urban world's influence. However, Peak is an intrusion into her society and a dangerous one. In *The Haunted Study*, Peter Keating contrasts him to *New Grub Street*'s Jasper Milvain:

> Godwin Peak in *Born in Exile* is also set on getting to the top through marriage. He is more devious, more fastidious, and less successful than Milvain. Peak could never be satisfied with an Amy Reardon: the quality he seeks in a wife is "refinement" [203].

The Warricombes' community maintains its cohesion by rejecting him, but just barely.

Finally, if Henry Ryecroft, exhausted in his rural retreat from the worst the city could do, represents a modest effacement of the city's power, Hubert Eldon's triumph in *Demos* over the forces of urban industrialization raises more questions than it answers. As discussed in Chapter 5, Wanley undergoes dramatic changes as New Wanley, an outpost of the modern industrial world, before once more presenting a pristine natural image, one that competes against that of the modern city in *Workers in the Dawn* and *The Nether World*. Should not *Demos* take primacy over these earlier and later figures of urban desolation? An examination of this latter novel and two others, *The Town Traveller* and *Will Warburton*, reveal's the city's ability to open the dialogue to other ideas. After Eldon starts to restore Wanley, a mob kills Mutimer in London. Mutimer's death and Eldon's action operate as darkness and light, respectively. The city appears in its most repellent aspect while the rural world gleams with its own rebirth. In addition, Eldon hopes to wed Adela Waltham Mutimer, the dead man's widow. After Eldon proposes to Adela, the novel ends with the two "natural" partners finally planning to marry. (See Chapter 3.) Mutimer's dynamic personality succumbs to the static one of Eldon who now has exactly what he originally desired, i.e., Wanley and Adela redux. Removal and replanting on the one hand and marriage on the other supposedly return innocence to place and person. Nevertheless, the urban world, standing for a larger reality, however flawed, still exists in Wanley even if as no more than past echoes.

The Town Traveller and Will Warburton have no such difficulty with competing rural images that unsettle choices and enjoyments offered by their urban settings. With two such ultimately positive stories, one wonders, given Gissing's consistently ambivalent relation to city and country, what their effect is on the rural image of peace and harmony in his fiction. The Town Traveller is generally a novel of struggle, choice, and settlement within an urban, lower-middle-class environment that gives fulfillment to many of its characters. There is, literally, no hankering after lost pastures. Everything is contained within the city, even the missing Mr. Mark Clover, Louisa Clover's errant "husband" who turns out to be Lord Polperro and a bigamist. Mr. Gammon, the traveler of the title, is the core of the novel. His life satisfies him greatly — his work, his home life, and his recreational pursuits. Gammon lives in Mrs. Bubb's boarding house and takes great enjoyment in the swirl of activity there, especially in the morning as the house awakens and sends Moggie, the general, careering with hot water from one room to another (1–4). The gloom of working-class life in Workers in the Dawn, The Unclassed, Demos, Thyrza, and The Nether World is gone. Gammon temporarily engages himself to Polly Sparkes, another inhabitant of Mrs. Bubb's establishment. However, they part since Polly intends to rule in any relationship she forms, and so does Gammon. She eventually accepts Christopher Parish whom she plans to reform, and Gammon marries Louisa Clover, who owns a china shop, after being rejected by her for her daughter Minnie's hand in marriage. An improbable plot, it even contains at least four upper-class characters who exude great vitality and discover no disgust with London. Except for Lord Polperro-Mark Clover's preference for "a humbler station" (Town Traveller 269), there is no alternative world to which the other characters wish to escape. (See Chapter 19.) In reality, The Town Traveller erases the country more thoroughly than the reverse examples in Born in Exile, The Odd Women, The Paying Guest, The Whirlpool, and The Private Papers of Henry Ryecroft. Not only do the characters not wish to flee the city, they do not travel — except for Lord Polperro who demonstrates a character flaw in abandoning his "wife" and daughter.

Gammon also reveals no anxiety regarding his work. He is good at what he does, enjoys it thoroughly, and if one employer does not suit him, another will.

Will Warburton, a novel of middle-class life, also focuses its story on London with hardly a notice of the outside world. (See Chapter 4 for a more extensive discussion of the novel.) Warburton goes behind the counter in a grocery store after his partner Godfrey Sherwood defrauds him of his and his family's money. But, Warburton shows his hardihood by making a success of his venture. Known as Jollyman, Warburton hires his former housekeeper's brother-in-law, Mr. Allchin, and together they not only prosper but also demonstrate values of friendship and loyalty that Norbert Franks and Rosamund Elvan, Warburton's former friend and fiancée, singularly lack. Bertha Cross, a book illustrator, admires Warburton's courage and sense of responsibility towards his family after he loses his money (91–92). Jane, Warburton's sister, earns her living at horticultural work. The five working-class novels from the 1880s show a city destroying the people's lives, but the novels from the 1890s to the early 1900s, while often revealing the country as a haven, also show the city as a place of energy and life. This mixed perspective on modern and traditional life, usually represented by the city and country, respectively, demonstrates an evolution in Gissing's thinking. The competing visions of these years allow Gissing to trace out his characters' lives in a slightly more objective manner.

New Grub Street furnishes strong examples of this balancing of forces. Jasper, Dora, and Maud Milvain go to the city and succeed; Edwin Reardon and Harold Biffen either die from the city or in it. Biffen collapses the city-country image into one by poisoning himself on Putney Heath (492–93). Along with Marian Yule and Dora Milvain, Reardon and Biffen are two of the best people in the book, and even the occasionally obtuse Jasper recognizes Biffen's fine nature and the hopelessness of his chances in the modern city. John Goode states:

> Biffen, who has a more serious interest in the aesthetic potential of fiction, is determined to write about life without rearrangement, and echoes one of the other great topics of the 1880s, the influence of French naturalism. Like Flaubert, he sets out to make art out of the banal; like Zola, he confers epic seriousness on the everyday. Naturally it is going to be a commercial failure [Introduction *New Grub Street* xvii].

After receiving a letter from Amy Reardon regarding Biffen's death, Milvain remarks to his sister Dora:

> "Really, one can't grieve. There seemed no possibility of his ever earning enough to live decently upon. But why the deuce did he go all the way out there? Consideration for the people in whose house he lived, I dare say; Biffen had a good deal of native delicacy" [495].

As he lies in his little copse immediately before taking the poison, Biffen only has the light of the moon, a sense of "ineffable peace," "thoughts of beautiful things," "the memory of his friend Reardon," "but of Amy he thought only as of that star which had just come into his vision above the edge of dark foliage — beautiful, but infinitely remote" [493].

In the Year of Jubilee presents several examples in which neither rural nor urban life appear to good effect. Nancy Lord of Camberwell, while on vacation in Teignmouth, becomes pregnant by Lionel Tarrant. After they marry and Nancy discovers her condition, she goes to Falmouth, far from London and prying friends, and has their child. Unhappily for her, circumstances relating to the provisions of her father's will and Tarrant's absence from the country prevent them from openly cohabiting, and Tarrant, on his final return to England, convinces Nancy to make that arrangement permanent. Beatrice French and Luckworth Crewe, in apparent contrast, make a success of their businesses in the city, with Crewe's helping Beatrice, but he reveals a hard side to his personality when he ultimately dominates Beatrice and shows no interest in her as a woman. Gissing appears to make Crewe's career in advertising a symbol of the falseness of the modern world. Crewe wishes to paper over his environment, substituting image for substance and establishing the former, paradoxically, as the essence of the modern world. Goode remarks:

> The particular line of business is important here. For Crewe is not like those self-made men of the mid–Victorian novel: he does not produce goods, does not even work in their sense. Rather he sells, and what he sells are images — advertising — the modern science which makes suburbia what it is — clean, healthy, endlessly aspiring to greater consumer power [*Ideology* 174].

This essence-less, paper-thin, but nonetheless powerful vision reminds one of Hubert and Adela in *Demos* as they view New Wanley's new-old picture. Have there been too many changes ever to see again the original valley? In Samuel Johnson's *Rasselas* (1759), the protagonist returns to his happy valley, chastened by experience and ready to accept what he formerly rejected. Of *Demos*, Robert L. Selig states, "The novel allows aestheticism a final triumph: Eldon demolishes the mines once run by the socialist and remakes the valley into a natural work of art, a place for the happy few who appreciate good things" (*George Gissing* 30). At this final point, Gissing makes too little of Hubert's and Adela's earlier experiences to know whether they can truly dislodge the modern and escape its possibly harsh echoes.

What is the modern? What can one do to deal with it successfully? Gissing clearly shows the modern most intensely in an urban environment and dramatizes one solution after another for its stringencies only to leave his readers with *The Private Papers of Henry Ryecroft*, the last novel published in his lifetime, not so much a *Notes from the Underground* as a "Ms. Found in a

Bottle," a final communication from a brief survivor of the modern world, an ominous place gaining energy as he writes. In *The English Novel: A Short Critical History* (1954), Walter Allen notes, "His general view of his times was very close to Flaubert's; he too might have used the word *muflisme* to characterize the age, which he found vulgar, shallow, naively self-satisfied, and which, like Flaubert, he judged by standards drawn from his notions of classical antiquity" (343). If he could not be in another time, Gissing could think himself there, and *Veranilda: A Romance* (1904) is the vehicle even if, ironically, set in the decline of the Western classical world.

15

Gissing and Morley Roberts: The Life of Writing in Late-Victorian England

George Gissing's picture of the writing life in *New Grub Street* and his retrospective on that same world twelve years later in *The Private Papers of Henry Ryecroft*, each novel incorporating significant aspects of his life, contain some of his sharpest observations and most profound sentiments about the lived experience of writing for a living. Michael Collie argues for the need to see Gissing as a literary artist:

> Gissing, the writer, quite obviously thought a great deal about how to write a modern novel. He experimented a lot. He revised his early work. He adopted new techniques at various stages of his career. He wrote a range of books that few others could emulate. It is on this level, as a writer, that it seems best to try to meet him [*Alien Art* 171].

Robert L. Selig states of *New Grub Street* that it "stands as Gissing's masterpiece and also one of the finest novels of the late-Victorian era. Part of its strength comes from his finally having restricted all his major characters in a novel to an occupation that he knew firsthand — that of a writer" (*George Gissing* 46). Most of his other works that include authors do so in a way that looks glancingly at their struggles as writers. In *Born in Exile*, Godwin Peak, ironically, tries to escape the notoriety of having written an attack on Christianity. It is true that Julian Casti in *The Unclassed* works seriously at his poetry, but Gissing allows his disastrous marriage to Harriet Smales to swallow his life's aim to write and eventually this destroys him. Morley Roberts'

The Private Life of Henry Maitland (1912) is a novel based on Gissing's life. Roberts, Gissing's fellow schoolmate at Owens College in Manchester and lifelong friend, traces Grissing's struggles as a person and a writer. These struggles included two failed marriages and a fear that he would be reduced to poverty. Gissing apparently worried about the latter even though toward the end of his life he was reasonably successful. Both Gissing and Roberts, from slightly different perspectives, depict a bleak picture for anyone who pursues literature with aesthetic ideals as the dominant focus.

Whatever Gissing's motivations were to write after he returned from the United States in 1877, and Barbara Rawlinson makes a good case in *A Man of Many Parts: Gissing's Short Stories, Essays and Other Works* (2006) for the publication of the twenty stories written in 1877 as a primary source for this, he soon produced a three-volume novel that he paid to have published. *Workers in the Dawn* depicts the lives of the struggling poor, the first of five such works. Tired of tutoring and producing a monthly political letter about England for *Vyestnik Evropy*, the periodical edited by Turgenev's friend Mikhail Stasulevich, Gissing writes on what he observed among London's poor. However, except for Carrie Mitchell and Samuel Tollady, the major characters are from the middle class. Two, Gilbert Gresham and Arthur Golding, are artists. Both Osmond Waymark and Casti in *The Unclassed* are interested in literature and writing. Casti represents the failed artist, a theme that Gissing explores extensively in *New Grub Street*. More ominously, Casti is the failed artist pulled down by a dissatisfied wife, a theme that Gissing also includes as a central element in his portrait of Edwin Reardon in *New Grub Street*. This latter novel exhibits the widest variety of writers in any of Gissing's works, e.g., Reardon, Jasper Milvain, Harold Biffen, Alfred Yule, Marian Yule, Whelpdale, Quarmby, Hinks, Sykes, Dora Milvain, Maud Milvain, and various other writers who do not appear in the novel but are used as types, often successful ones. Collie remarks:

> He depicts a small group of hacks, literary idealists, unsuccessful writers of fiction, litterateurs, and critics, who live partly in the British Museum reading room, partly on the fringes of literary London, whether for mercenary or idealistic reasons eking out a living as best they can [*Alien Art* 111].

While the above list suggests that the novel is more a survey of literary types than a work of literature, that is far from the truth. Gissing focuses mainly on writers but includes wives, lovers, family members, and friends as they add to, develop, or detract from writing as a profession.

Just as Roberts remarks in *The Private Life of Henry Maitland* that Maitland is not naturally a writer of fiction or other literary work destined for a wide audience, in *New Grub Street* Gissing describes the pedantic critic Alfred

Yule in a similar vein, his labored style not saved by his wide learning nor helped by his often caustic tone. His daughter Marian, who wishes anything but the reputation of a literary critic, writes for him when he is too pressed for time. Selig observes that Marian "does literary slave work for her embittered old father, the hack writer Alfred Yule" (*George Gissing* 47). In *Gissing in Context*, Adrian Poole states, "With his 'peculiar croaking' laugh and 'seamed visage,' he inhabits an angular, desiccated world of his own, in which a complimentary footnote from a friend is worth more than his daughter's love" (143). Yule's frustration lies mainly in his inability successfully to edit a literary magazine. Thus, failed ambition is a major theme in *New Grub Street*, but one explored in a wide variety of ways. Yule exhibits a natural limit to his talent. He begins his career as an assistant "at a London bookseller's" (18), and through struggles to educate himself thoroughly, succeeds more than one might expect. However, he does not feel successful. Not only does he not prosper when he once becomes a journal editor, but his own writings fail to receive the respect he feels they deserve, especially from Clement Fadge, a rival critic and editor.

When Marian eventually receives some of the money due her from her uncle's will (469), she has already refused to let her father have it to start a literary journal and has said she plans to offer it to Jasper Milvain, her intended husband, a man who Yule believes has deserted him for the detested Fadge (399–402). Yule's subsequent blindness seems an apt judgment on his life. He tells Marian, "'If you marry, I wish you a happy life. The end of mine, of many long years of unremitting toil, is failure and destitution'" (424). Quarmby and Hinks, long-time British Library veterans who look to Yule for success, especially as they discuss the hoped-for new journal that Marian's money will launch, struggle along as minor critics who publish slim volumes and endure Yule's benign condescension. Gissing studied in the British Library and was acquainted with the backwaters of literature by means of which one could survive, if barely.

Jasper Milvain, Whelpdale, and Sykes represent another group of writers who focus on markets other than those of Alfred Yule and his friends. While the latter largely restrict themselves to writing about literature, Milvain, Whelpdale, and Sykes have a broader subject, that of culture in general. Dora and Maud Milvain might be included with these three. After their mother's death and the cessation of her income with her life, Dora and Maud face a bleak picture as teachers in nearby Wattleborough. The ever-innovative Jasper has assured them that he will not abandon them when that unlooked-for event occurs. Jasper is at times almost heroic figure. When he makes this statement to his sisters, he cannot fully support himself in the manner necessary to break through as a writer and editor of a prestigious journal. He has explained that he is learning his profession and slowly making his way. One thing becomes clear in the novel; he knows what he is talking about, and he knows what steps he must take. If no one else, Jasper has told himself to be bold. Consequently, he first suggests that Dora and Maud think about writing religious stories for children and then, the riskier step, agree to move to London to meet people who will help them in this new career. Both young women have been well educated and are fitted to supply this market, one that Jasper assures them is there to be exploited.

Jasper is the new man in the modern world of writing, perfectly adapted to meet the needs of a wide variety of magazines and newspapers. Beginning with Gissing's view that Dickens identified closely with his period, Poole compares Milvain to Dickens: "Dickens had indeed been the 'man of his time,' and good luck to him. But the 'man of the time' now was, in Gissing's version, Jasper Milvain, the shameless entrepreneur" (*Gissing in Context* 110). He admits to his family that he cannot write novels (*New Grub Street* 9), but he adds that for the educated readers he can supply enough matter to give them a sense of being in the know (14). He is studious as far as he needs to be and clever, the sine qua non for his ambitions. In addition, he works hard at his profession, and this means working hard across the whole spectrum of what it takes to succeed. Jasper cultivates editors and hostesses at whose entertainments he makes contacts. When Jasper meets Marian Yule and her father in Finden, the latter, as one learns later, is cautious towards him (99–100), as if he knows that Jasper's desire to succeed transcends everything else. Later in the novel, Jasper tells Marian this when he visits her home in London (120). Near the end of the novel, she assures him that he has "more energy and more intellect" than to act, as Jasper supposes she thinks, like a "brute" (499). Earlier, Alfred becomes suspicious that Jasper has written a disparaging article about him (184). While this is not true, Jasper abandons Marian when she inherits only £1,500 instead of the expected £5,000 and says that she cannot neglect her mother and her now-blind father (471–74, 501–04). Disgusted as Dora and Maud are at his falsity to Marian, nothing shifts Jasper from his intended path. Whelpdale, whom Dora eventually marries, presents a more positive image of someone pursuing a career path similar to Jasper's. He both attempts to write fiction and then, with no success, to advise others on how to do so. After each failure, he tries something else. Journalism is the career in which he succeeds. Writing for *Chat*, he suggests it be renamed *Chit-Chat* and helps launch a success. Eventually named its editor, Whelpdale, with the sure instinct for appealing to the "quarter-educated" (460), is able to marry (478–79). Whelpdale merely wishes to satisfy a remunerative market and leaves any higher ambitions to his friend Jasper.

Sykes is the true denizen of Grub Street as he desperately writes any-thing that will bring in money; he resembles Samuel Johnson's portrait of Richard Savage and other inhabitants of the original Grub Street (*New Grub Street* 377–80). Written some years before the *The Lives of the English Poets* (1779–81) but incorporated into that work, Johnson's essay on Savage (1744) shows the sometimes frantic writer barely surviving in London and eliciting the reader's sympathy through his many woes. Sykes does the same, especially when Reardon and Biffen visit him and he begs them to give him a "quarter of an hour" (378) to dash off something. While Milvain might be above Sykes' necessary struggles, Gissing notes the former's efforts when he tells Marian at one point that he must go home rather than stay longer with her since he has several hours of hard writing "before seven o'clock" (473). How-ever, Sykes remains the unromantic warning for all who dream of writing for a living without some other monetary support. Henry Ryecroft miraculously comes forth from a life such as Sykes endures, but neither Reardon nor Bif-fen survive even when some chance beckons to both men. Whelpdale, given some of Gissing's own experiences in America, talks lightly of his serious difficulties (390–95), but neither Reardon nor Biffen offer an opportunity for any distancing from their tragic ends.

Edwin Reardon and Harold Biffen, especially, are the only two writers in *New Grub Street* who write novels with aesthetic criteria primarily govern-ing the process. John Goode notes, "whereas Reardon only writes fiction because he feels that it is the only way for the modern writer who can't jour-nalise to make a living, Biffen embraces his own modernity with a modern aesthetic commitment" (*Ideology* 139). They are not averse to success, and Reardon actually achieves some with his fiction that is the occasion for his risking marriage to Amy Yule. But, as Milvain tells his mother and two sis-ters at the beginning of the novel, Reardon now has no leisure to publish a novel every other year. The more pressure he feels to write, the less able he is to respond. (See Chapter 13.) Milvain's opinion is more convincing than critic Michael Collie's: "Reardon does not fail because literature had become a trade or because something outside himself prevented his writing a master-piece. He fails because of himself. He is just one part of the larger scene that Gissing is describing" (*Alien Art* 112). Fittingly, Reardon appears in his decline, a decline so thorough that he cannot even write a pot-boiler on demand; he cannot enter the world of trade as Milvain describes literature in the present day (8). John Sloan states, "In portraying the actual toil and frustrations of the professional writer, Gissing's aim is clearly to question the conditions which have reduced literature to a commodity" (*Cultural* 86).

Reardon's wife is one of the last to advise him to write something, any-thing, so long as it sells. In this, she repeats Milvain's advice on previous occasions. To the literary tradesman, it seems so simple: produce the work for the market and prosper. To the artist, it is truly death. John Halperin writes, "Nowhere else in Gissing's work is the malignity of matter so emphasized or the life of the artist characterized so despairingly" (*Gissing* 148). Milvain knows Reardon's creative abilities and also knows that he will fail if it takes two years to write each novel. The economics of the situation work against him. In *The Paradox of Gissing*, David Grylls states the general problem:

> *New Grub Street* deals with Gissing's most pressing dilemma. Convinced that art, by its very nature, should transcend material desires and cares, he could also perceive that in a market economy it was impossible for this to happen. The artist was compelled to make concessions [81].

Milvain acknowledges that genius will force its way to the public's attention and acceptance, but to him, neither Reardon nor Biffen are geniuses though he accords due recognition to their artistic aims. Unlike Reardon, Biffen never expects to live by his pen. He has striven for years to write his novel, *Mr. Bailey, Grocer*. His work is a realistic portrayal of the life of the ignobly decent. Aesthetic criteria are the sole governing principles in the production of the book, and he, deservedly, makes little or nothing from it in the burgeoning age of advertisement. Who did you think would buy it? one might ask of Biffen. However, he expects it to fail. The act of writing it governs him throughout. Earlier, running into his burning building to save the manuscript symbolizes the value he puts on literary creation (*New Grub Street* 430).

The Private Papers of Henry Ryecroft is an autobiographical novel that functions as an aberration. Not only is there a distance between Gissing and the hero of the volume he "discovers" among the writer's papers and edits, but the general tone of the work at times masks Ryecroft's harsh struggles before receiving his legacy at fifty years of age. The well-loved home he leases near Exeter, the books, the quiet, the leisure to become a participant in the workings of nature — all of these belie the jarring experiences of his earlier life and, along with his resignation, deprive one of the sharp sense of anger and outrage that would be expected. Thus, one senses a tension at the core of the novel. Gissing was briefly a widower after his first wife Nell died but seems to have rushed to marry again. The silence that Ryecroft relishes in his home is not always what Gissing yearned for, especially if it meant that he was generally alone in that silence. Another difference between him and Ryecroft is that eventually Gissing was, regardless of his worries, a successful and admired writer. Ryecroft is a mix of Milvain and Sykes in that he little valued what he wrote but had some critical and economic success. Gissing, also, neither had nor expected any legacy to rescue him later in life. Both love Italy; both love the sun, Ryecroft initially in an earlier holiday in Devon; and both love the English countryside. Despite these and other similarities, Ryecroft is no complete match with Gissing, and this distance might underlie the strength of the book. In an April 5, 1903, letter to Eduard Bertz, Gissing writes, "Remember that, after all, 'Ryecroft' is a fictitious personality.— Though, bye the bye, a lot of English readers are stupidly believing that the man really existed, & I receive letters inquiring about 'his works'" (Mattheisen, Young, and Coustillas 9:75).

Ryecroft employs an elegiac tone and this, potentially, indicates the conflict between the feel of more energy in re–experiencing past difficulties and what the reader would expect Ryecroft to generate. He, thus, has not closed off his earlier life, in the midst of his present comforts, to what amounts to an investigation of its hardships. Protected by his legacy and buoyed by the relief at being where he is, Ryecroft goes back to that time and feels what he felt then. With all the pain of his memories, he does not lament or regret their existence. The very act of writing the book suggests that everything is still alive to him. Gissing, as the putative editor, remarks that Ryecroft wrote the book because he used to be a writer and could not refrain from writing. He even notes that Ryecroft possibly intended to publish it, suggesting that his retirement was not total. Ryecroft does not so much exorcise the pain, a pain that at times seems in inverse proportion to the small number of his complaints, but brings it out to air. He speaks of his once strong will to work and in his declining years, paradoxically, resurrects it. He now has no deadline to meet nor editor to please but surrenders to the creative impulse when it matters. Consequently, Ryecroft seems to address the future or a clear present instead of a past that is finished, closed off, there to be handled but not relived. Tennyson's *In Memoriam* (1850), as an evolving elegy, comes to mind. Tennyson's loss of his friend Hallam was present and had to be dealt with, and so he writes the poem until he rounds off his feelings and gets beyond them enough to continue his life, a progression of anticipation at Hallam's return, despair over his death, resignation at what cannot be changed, and acceptance of all that these feelings entail.

At the risk of overstatement and after so many various judgments by others on the book, it seems clear that most critics miss the substance of *The Private Papers of Henry Ryecroft*. Not all, of course, and Jacob Korg's statement in his *George Gissing: A Critical Biography* (1963) should orient one toward a better understanding of the novel: "Though it is often difficult to tell where the character, Ryecroft, ends, and the real Gissing begins in these pages, the important fact remains that Ryecroft is a fiction distinct from his author" (244–45). In *The Born Exile*, Gillian Tindall perceptively discusses the connection between the facts of his life and the literary uses that either Gissing in *The Private Papers of Henry Ryecroft* or Roberts in *The Private Life of Henry Maitland* makes of them and asserts that "fiction often has a coherence, a probability and a truth of emphasis which the muddled 'true facts' lack" (24). Gissing states that the manuscript

> was not intended for the public, and yet in many a passage I seemed to perceive the literary purpose something more than the turn of phrase, and so on, which results from long habit of composition. Certain of his reminiscences, in particular, Ryecroft could hardly have troubled to write down had he not, however vaguely, entertained the thought of putting them to some use. I suspect that in his happy leisure there grew upon him a desire to write one more book, a book which should be written merely for his own satisfaction [*The Private Papers of Henry Ryecroft* xx].

Gissing also remarks that Ryecroft was a man whose sufferings had clearly marked him (xx). Beginning with this "editorial" observation, one can start to examine the character in ways that set aside many of the statements Poole makes. He writes, "*Ryecroft* will seem lacking in all but the thinnest emotions, of self–indulgent, self–caressing sentimentality" (*Gissing in Context* 204); he asserts the work is "the relief of a perfectly defined distance between Self and the World" (206) that "can go hang" (206); he observes the book's "tone of haughty, magisterial judgment on a world that can provide only objects for ironic, self–satisfied contemplation" (206–07); he remarks on "this shallow but seductive structure of desire" reflected "in its state of advanced debility" (207). Clearly, this moral condemnation intertwined with a class-based perspective distances itself from the text with every statement.

Ben Jonson's "To Penshurst" (1616), Alexander Pope's "Windsor Forest" (1713), and John Dyer's "Grongar Hill" (1726) are country-house or topographical poems in which the authors describe the ideal life of reading, writing, or infrequently visiting friends. The urban noise and squalor are conveniently left behind. *The Private Papers of Henry Ryecroft* resembles these works but only superficially. The poems' principal characters have the means to retire and contemplate nature when and if they so choose; Ryecroft is the survivor of a shipwreck, but far from being the "self–indulgent" retreat alluded to above, his removal from London creates another life. He connects intimately with nature in all its seasons and aspects; he reads deeply and with real pleasure; he discovers himself as a fuller human being in his many moods and ideas; and he remembers, in the process creating a work of social, literary, and cultural criticism that reveals a coherent philosophy. Events and ideas blend in a powerful statement of who he is and what he believes. Godwin Peak's pursuit of Sidwell Warricombe in *Born in Exile* demonstrates the same yearning that Ryecroft realizes, that of escaping into a better, a fuller life. Ryecroft, using his own statements regarding his past, is living a more complete life, even granting his love of peace and silence (*Ryecroft* 61). He writes, "I remember the London days when sleep was broken by clash and clang, by roar and shriek, and when my first sense on returning to consciousness was hatred of the life about me." He adds, "but worse still is the clamorous human voice" (61). In assessing Ryecroft as a character, one must absorb the concrete details of his life; this will still the superficial ideological reaction.

In his Introduction to the 1958 edition of *The Private Life of Henry Maitland*, Morchard Bishop speaks of Roberts' fictional presentation of Gissing's life in somewhat negative terms while extolling its general quality. Bishop says that "the book in its execution is strikingly original" (3) but adds that "its true excellencies were then [1912] gravely obscured by the fictional draperies that encumbered it: draperies, moreover, that merely irritated the instructed, since in fact they impeded without concealing" (3). Whether Roberts, as Bishop earlier states, "by allowing his book to bear the outward semblance of a work of fiction, deprived it of any pretension to authority" (1), is a matter for readers and critics long after 1958 to decide. However, Bishop's different assessments reveal the difficulty in approaching the work as an imaginary construct. Roberts changes names but uses information on Gissing's life, as far as he knew it, in the guise of writing a novel. In *The Born Exile*, Tindall observes that Roberts' work "gives, in my view, a better and truer overall impression of Gissing the man than many subsequent and more scholarly writers have done." She adds, "In fiction, the view is longer, the perspective better" (25). Biographical or autobiographical novels are not unknown and many admired works such as Dickens' *David Copperfield* and Mrs. Humphry Ward's *Robert Ellsmere* (1888), autobiographical and biographical, respectively, explore and reflect real lives. In an attempt to understand the significance of actions and ideas in one's own or another life, fiction can be a creative way to accomplish this. A too strict adherence to the chronological order of the events in a person's life without a concomitant probing may make the work seem mechanical. Roberts and Gissing had known one another since they were youths and kept in fairly regular contact, and this helps him as he struggles to balance the portrait of the man and the writer.

It is not absolutely clear whether Roberts wants to write a biography or a biographical novel, though the evidence appears to tilt in the direction of the latter. In the Preface to the first edition of 1912, Roberts states, "There is no book quite like it in the English tongue, and the critic may take what advantage he will of that opening for his wit" (245). He goes on to say, "Here is life, not a story or a constructed diary, and the art with which it is done is a secondary matter" (246). However, in Chapter I, Roberts, writing as J. H., whom he says "dictated" the book "mostly in my presence" (245), reports: "Once I proposed to him to use his character and career as the Chief figure in a long story" (20). Roberts reveals something of his approach to the complex portrait of Maitland at the beginning of Chapter VI: "Out of the many times in many years that I saw Maitland comes the intricate pattern of him. I would rather write a little book like "Manon Lescaut" than many biographical quartos lying as heavy on the dead as Vanbrugh's mansions" (103). Early in Chapter I he states, "I am far more concerned to write about Henry Maitland for those who loved him than for those who loved him not, and I shall be much better pleased if what I do about him takes the shape of an impression rather than of anything like an ordinary biography" (21). Thus, Roberts the literary artist figures in the book with Roberts the memoirist. He generally narrates the events of Maitland's life in chronological order. Speaking of the real individuals rather than the fictive narrator and subject, it seems clear that writing this work helps Roberts understand his friend Gissing and interpret him to others. Roberts, as J. H., sees Maitland's life as an exemplary one: "If Henry Maitland bleeds and howls, so did Philoctetes, and the outcry of Henry Maitland is most pertinent to our lives" (246). Roberts portrays Maitland's pain and suffering as inevitable. He observes, "His whole life, as I saw it and shall relate it, is but a development of the nature which made his disaster possible" (34). However, he does not judge Maitland's life from a moral perspective but rather through his own eyes assesses his actions and qualities as an experienced man of the world. Roberts was a professional writer of fiction and nonfiction, and through the use of chronology, letters, selected memories of events and conversations, explorations of motives for particular actions, and the manipulation of time, he creates something akin to a historical novel with Gissing as its subject. As Roberts states in the first Preface, "At any rate we have a portrait emerging which is real" (245).

Roberts' strongest statement about Maitland as a writer is that fiction did not come natural to him: "Fiction, even as he understood it, was not for a man of his nature and faculties. He would have been in his true element as a don of a college, and much of his love of the classics was a mystery to me, as it would have been to most active men of the world, however well-educated" (*The Private Life* 104–05). This much-contested claim does not seem believable of a man, as Bishop states, "who wrote as many novels as Gissing, and who took such obvious pains with them" (6). In this Bishop follows Frank Swinnerton's judgment in *George Gissing: A Critical Study* (1912): "The fact that he continued to produce literary work is a proof that it was his chosen occupation, and in the end he was justified by the fame that was his in the last years of his life" (194). Against his own opinion, Roberts offers other aspects about Maitland as a writer. On Maitland, who he observes is "perhaps a great man of letters" (42), Roberts remarks that "He rejoiced in every form of Art, in books and in music, and in all the finer inheritance of the past" (42). Roberts later writes on the care Maitland takes with his fiction: "He always wrote with the greatest pain and labour" (79); in order "to perfect his control of the English tongue" (82), Roberts says, "he often destroyed the first third of a book. I know he did so with one three times over" (82). Roberts states further on, "There are, indeed, very few of his books of which a great part was not destroyed, re–written, and sometimes again destroyed and again re–written" (135). Maitland's typical writing day started at 9:00 A.M. and, with short breaks, ended at 10:00 P.M., and in that period he wrote for nine hours (159). Roberts also speaks about Maitland's "sincerity" (79) in his work and states, "In many ways writing to him was a kind of sacred mission" (83). Yet, against his many observations of Maitland the writer of fiction, Roberts appears to hold that "he was a scholar and a dreamer" (82) and felt that his inhuman work schedule "shows, in a way that nothing else can, that he had no earthly business to be writing novels and spinning things largely out of his subjective mind, when he ought to have been dealing with the objective world, or with books" (159). Roberts affirms that Maitland "gave me the most definite permission" (20) "to write his life and tell the whole and absolute truth about him" (20). This possibly explains Roberts' ambivalence about Maitland and his fiction, seeing him as both a careful artist and a misplaced one.

These three writers, i.e., Edwin Reardon, Henry Ryecroft, and Henry Maitland, all based substantially on George Gissing, furnish the concrete experience, the self–conscious awareness of writing for a living in the latter part of the nineteenth century. Along with *Isabel Clarendon*'s Thomas Meres, *Born in Exile*'s Godwin Peak, *In the Year of Jubilee*'s Lionel Tarrant, and *The Crown of Life*'s Piers Otway, figures such as *New Grub Street*'s Jasper Milvain, Whelpdale, Harold Biffen, and Alfred Yule fill in the portrait of late-Victorian authorship. Commenting on Gissing's difficulty in *In the Year of Jubilee* on writing about his age, William Greenslade states, "This novel, in memorable set-piece descriptions, renders a world Gissing would rather shut out, but which his commitment to realism cannot do without" ("Writing Against Himself" 271). Experience transformed into language permeated the culture to an extent that transcends its recorded feel in many other ages. However, it is a culture in which the mass of what is written is disposable and deserves to be. Grylls remarks that Gissing "did ... subscribe to the view that newspapers spread infection" (*Paradox* 77). Though a few writers who aspire to create art do not outweigh the numberless others who crowd them out, to the modern reader Gissing succeeds as a writer while his own authors often fail if they attempt to achieve more than the mediocre.

16

Nationalism, Imperialism, and the Idea of England

The Crown of Life is Gissing's strongest attack on militarism, war, and imperialism. Jacob Korg states, "Gissing, who blamed Imperialism on 'the syndicates,' hated and feared it as a mingling of greed and violence" (*George Gissing* 231). Although not isolated instances in Gissing's fiction, Piers Otway's statements bring into sharp focus the conflict between nationalism and internationalism. When Otway replies to the bluff, outspoken chauvinist in the Liverpool hotel, he introduces several important issues (*Crown of Life* 279–81). One is that the life of a people is not contained in one's clichés about them. This position asks for a large view of others, a recognition of their separate existence, history, and culture. It posits that those unknown to one have an equally serious engagement with life that may be largely beyond one's comprehension and asks for an awareness of this separateness. This fundamental operation must occur for one to have a true understanding of their lives. Second, Otway implies that one must possess accurate knowledge about another country before one can make any judgment about it. Starting with *Workers in the Dawn*, Gissing infuses his novels with ideas on England's position relative to other countries, but it is especially in his novels from the 1890s and early twentieth century that he dramatizes the conflicts inherent in nationalist and internationalist themes and includes the evils of imperialism and jingoism as negative factors that move his fiction toward an almost hopeless portrait of his country's future.

Paradox illustrates Gissing's use of any of the three parts of this chapter's title. Many of his characters feel strongly attached to England and yet spend time learning about other countries or traveling to them. The time spent in these activities is not incidental to their lives. In *New Grub Street*, Edwin Reardon and Harold Biffen long to travel to Greece and Rome, for Reardon a return journey and for Biffen a first trip. However, neither feels that he will be able to go. In *Workers in the Dawn*, Helen Norman goes to Germany to study philosophy and theology. She returns convinced that Christianity does not answer her needs. And yet, she spends the remainder of her life serving the poor in London's East End as a supporter there of the Rev. Edward Heatherley's ministry. Aside from her changed beliefs, Germany and what she gained from it hardly figure in her future plans. Characters such as Harvey Rolfe in *The Whirlpool* and Henry Ryecroft in *The Private Papers of Henry Ryecroft* speak, respectively, either for or against imperial adventures, but neither does anything about them. Michael Collie observes:

> Preoccupied throughout his lifetime by the problems of individual liberty, Gissing saw that the arrangements of modern society inevitably denied it. Thus the calamities of modern life were not primarily the fault of the individuals concerned. It was not a moral matter. Rather the individual, unless he was extraordinarily lucky, was sucked into the processes of society where he was at the mercy of economic and social forces for the most part beyond his comprehension [*Alien Art* 157].

Others dislike living in England because of the weather or the conditions under which they are forced to exist. The city of London is the entire country to most of the former and many of the latter as well. In *New Grub Street*, Reardon and Biffen feel that the city is killing them, yet neither takes serious steps to leave. Miriam Baske in *The Emancipated* temporarily resides in Italy, the setting for most of the novel, because in England her life in a provincial city and in the world of Protestant Dissent has made her ill. (See Chapter 8.)

Except for Denzil Quarrier in the 1892 novel by that name and the dubious Dyce Lashmar in *Our Friend the Charlatan*, none of the other major characters in Gissing's fiction has or desires a political career. Politics is not the only way to fulfill one's obligations as a citizen, but other than minor figures in *Denzil Quarrier, Our Friend the Charlatan*, and *The Crown of Life*, few have any wish for public service. Not by voting, by working for national and local governments, by serving as policemen, judges, and city clerks, or by joining the military do many characters perform a public duty. Yet, some experience a real joy in being in England and participating in the culture and responding to the beauty of the English countryside. Even if they express a disgust at the society, they often appear to long for what life in England offers. John

Sloan remarks, "His most popular work of these last years, *The Private Papers of Henry Ryecroft*, is dominated by a note of chronic melancholy and nostalgic longing for English food and English virtues" (*Cultural* 146).

The sense of superiority and contempt felt and expressed by some characters toward other peoples and cultures demonstrate another paradoxical element connected to the themes of nationalism, imperialism, and the idea of England. Arnold Jacks, an official in the foreign office in *The Crown of Life*, is a stereotypically upper-middle-class figure who assumes British superiority as a first step in dealing with foreigners. John Halperin states, "His nature is meant to represent those forces of the English character Gissing struggled to portray in *The Crown of Life* as responsible for Imperialist ventures" (*Gissing* 294). The illegitimate Piers Otway, with his disreputable brothers Alexander and Daniel, and the almost unconsciously supercilious Jacks contrast sharply in their attitudes to other countries and to Irene Derwent, a woman to whom Jacks is temporarily engaged. Of course, not every English character who lives abroad demonstrates a sense of superiority to the citizens of the country he or she inhabits. Ross Mallard, a working artist in *The Emancipated*, has none of this feeling. However, Arnold Jacks' official position makes him able to create difficulty between England and other countries. Contrasting his attitude to that of Otway's, one notices an entirely different orientation to foreign cultures. Educated partly in Geneva, Otway joins a business in Russia when he realizes that Irene does not return his love. There, Otway learns Russian and absorbs the customs. He admires their writers and begins to understand their worldview. Eventually, he returns to England, and after Irene breaks her engagement to Jacks, they marry. One thing that forces her to take special notice of Piers is the manner in which he enlightens Jacks about Russia, demonstrating greater knowledge and understanding of the country but not assuming an air of superiority toward Jacks during their discussion. The favored son of Jerome Otway, the old radical and friend of John Jacks, Arnold's father, comes into his own and shows himself a man in Irene's eyes.

It is probably an overstatement to say that most of Gissing's characters who experience dramatic changes in their lives do so in foreign countries. However, many do. For instance, in *Workers in the Dawn*, Arthur Golding goes to the United States to commit suicide by jumping over Niagara Falls while Helen Norman returns to Germany and dies of a weak heart. These are only Gissing's first examples, and others later, often less dramatically, demonstrate the pull of being elsewhere. The reasons that they go abroad vary widely, frequently with social or moral overtones. In *Demos*, while out of England, Hubert Eldon was wounded in a duel in a quarrel over a woman. He returns home surrounded with an air of mystery to be nursed back to health by his mother. Eldon's downfall and restoration in Adela's eyes parallel that of Wanley Valley's industrialization and liberation from any taint of those activities. John Goode argues that Eldon "finds no contradiction in restoring the cosy feudal facade of the rentier class to its pristine pastoral beauty" (*Ideology* 89). Whatever "intellectual 'rebellion'" (*Ideology* 89) Eldon felt has vanished in his new role as preserver of the natural world. While life certainly does not lack drama in England, other places often provide the sharp edge of experience to Gissing's characters. Whelpdale's recitation of his American exploits (mostly Gissing's own) near the end of *New Grub Street* give him an air of excitement, rather than failure as in his attempts to write fiction and then to advise others in doing so. America, thus, becomes a place of danger that he survives, further attracting Dora Milvain whom he wishes to marry. Whelpdale has odd adventures, e.g., living for a day or two on peanuts, but he triumphs over his adversities and looks less a fool than before. Even Jasper Milvain afterwards relents, admittedly under pressure from Dora, and accepts their marriage.

Foreign countries often provide Gissing the locus for change in the form of redemption, escape, or development. Everard Barfoot in *The Odd Women* is "seduced" by Amy Drake. On a train to London she gets, unaccompanied, into his compartment, presumably one with doors on either side of the train and with no communicating corridor. They come to an understanding and spend the night in a hotel with the result that she tarnishes his reputation, having herself little left to lose. Barfoot soon leaves England, but after some period of time and an "explanation" by him, he is able to return and recover his place in society. His cousin Mary Barfoot, while admiring the changes in him after his travels, seems the more reluctant to accept him but does so because of their family connection. Barfoot does not suffer while abroad, but his very absence is essential for his rehabilitation. The complexity of Barfoot's romantic relationship with Rhoda Nunn, Mary Barfoot's friend and business partner, leads to their breakup, but Everard, after inheriting money from his brother Tom, marries the beautiful and ornamental Agnes Brissenden. In *The Nether World*, Michael Snowdon also undergoes important changes because of his experiences abroad. He went to Australia and became wealthy. On returning to England, he looks for and finds his granddaughter Jane Snowdon. Jane, abandoned by her father, lives in an abusive situation in Mrs. Peckover's house where, at thirteen years of age, she is the maid of all work. Mrs. Peckover and her daughter Clem deprive her of any sense of belonging and harm her physically and emotionally. Michael takes her into his own home and thus saves her.

For Gissing, England seems to have no place that is sufficiently other to effect the necessary redemption. Both time and distance produce this quality. In *The Crown of Life*, Piers Otway's experiences in Russia over many years help him win the love of Irene Derwent, redeeming him in hers and others' eyes. (See Chapter 11.) It is ironic that he would appear to need redemption since his youth, his family circumstances, and his overwhelming love for Irene, unresponsive until the end of the novel, send him to Russia on two occasions. Otway's illegitimacy and his disreputable brothers, Daniel and Alexander, who cheat him out of a share of his father's will, damage his chances for a successful career. However, his father Jerome, despite his irregular family circumstances, wins the admiration of many prominent people, especially John Jacks. In business with Marchmont in Russia, Otway learns the language and begins to write about the country, gradually earning a reputation as an expert on its problems and possibilities. As mentioned above, he demonstrates this knowledge to Arnold Jacks, at that time Irene Derwent's fiancé. When Irene breaks her engagement to the astonished Jacks, she leads up to it by silently contrasting Jacks to Otway and finding the former wanting. It takes this foreign experience for Otway to be seen fully. He has not changed in his adoration of Irene and what she represents of the best of English womanhood, but others, starting with Irene, have developed an ability to appreciate him, matured and tempered in foreign lands.

The last two decades of the nineteenth century were the heyday of imperialism. Queen Victoria celebrated her Gold and Diamond Jubilees. In 1876, she was proclaimed empress of India. Rudyard Kipling and W. E. Henley were celebrated for their work extolling the empire, and Great Britain fought wars in Afghanistan, Sudan, and South Africa. After the Indian Mutiny in 1857, the Raj had no serious threats to its rule until the passive resistance campaign led by Mahatma Gandhi led to independence following World War II. Yet until the latter part of his career, Gissing makes no significant references to war or the empire. He has no important characters that perform military service. And unlike the silent veteran in Book Four of William Wordsworth's *The Prelude* or Margaret's husband in "The Ruined Cottage," Book One of *The Excursion* (1814), no returning or absent soldiers represent the personal effects of war. Gissing introduces the themes war and empire in the late 1890s with the publication of *The Whirlpool*. As noted above, he presents Harvey Rolfe, a somewhat weak man, as a supporter of empire and the use of force against native peoples who threaten British control. Gissing possibly employs him in this instance for the ironic image of a man urging violence and yet incapable of carrying it out. Sloan states, "Imperialism has emerged, as Rolfe recognises, not so much from a collective sense of moral superiority and national achievement, but from a consciousness of waning power in the face of colonial competition" (*Cultural* 143). In a letter to Eduard Bertz on December 11, 1899, Gissing complains that the German critic Dr. Friedrich Wilhelm Foerster does not recognize that Rolfe's words were spoken "in bitterest irony"

(Mattheisen, Young, and Coustillas 7.412). It is only in *The Crown of Life* that Gissing introduces a serious portrait of the conflict over empire. Robert L. Selig observes, "Imperial competition among the powers of Europe intensified their nationalism and military belligerence" (*George Gissing* 88). Piers Otway and Arnold Jacks, respectively representing anti–and pro-empire positions, dramatize Gissing's views on the dangers of war and imperial adversities.

Prior to these two novels and *The Private Papers of Henry Ryecroft*, Gissing's only warlike references are to the wars between books, authors, and publishers, the above novel especially including this area of conflict. As discussed in Chapter 11, Gissing sets his ideas about war and empire in *The Crown of Life* within the desire of three men to marry Irene Derwent, i.e., Trafford Romaine, Arnold Jacks, and Piers Otway. Ironically, Piers has become a respected writer, and if not triumphing over Jacks or Romaine in the literary world, he has demonstrated in his writing a more humane attitude toward Russia than theirs and has also countered their senseless praise of the imperial position that he thinks will lead to war. In *London in the 1890s: A Cultural History* (1992), Karl Beckson makes a fundamental observation regarding the idea of imperialism during that period:

> As an "ideology or political faith," British imperialism was in part a substitute for the decline of Christianity and an expression of confidence in Britain's economic and political future. In effect, the empire provided a stunning example of the social Darwinists' conviction that, among the various nations, Britain was the fittest to survive [345].

At his best, Gissing combines themes, bringing forward his political ideas in the resulting intensity. Setting the marriage struggle against the battle over empire and the looming war in South Africa, Gissing uses private passion and self–interest in conflict with public positions to heighten the drama.

Drama is largely missing from *The Private Papers of Henry Ryecroft* or at least any sense of it equaling the degree it motivates the action in *The Crown of Life*. In the Autumn chapter, Ryecroft remarks, "My life is over" (141). Consequently, the novelist is only left with memory and ideas with which to insert a degree of feeling into the work. Ryecroft's use of the natural world and his genuine love for all its seasons and manifold beauty set the stage for memory and ideas to awaken him to life. The sordidness of his struggles to live by writing, the few periods of success, and his visit to Italy are strong memories fused with the peace of his Exeter existence. Along with these factors, Ryecroft addresses current ideas on war and imperialism, locating them primarily in the natural human need to engage in conflict. He states:

> "It is so difficult for human beings to live together; nay, it is so difficult for them to associate, however transitorily and even under the most favourable conditions, without some shadow of mutual offence" [71].

He sets this observation in a paradoxical framework. He writes that "angry emotion is [not] the ruling force in human life" (71) and argues that "dire experience" has led to "a remarkable degree of self control" (71). However, Ryecroft compounds the paradoxical quality of his statements by extending the tendency of conflict to nations and says, "It passes the wit of man to explain how it is that nations are ever at peace!" (72) Yet, just as experience convinces individuals in a society that compromise is necessary, Ryecroft supposes, "A hundred years hence there will be some possibility of perceiving whether international relations are likely to obey the law which has acted with beneficence in the life of each civilized people" (73), thus also enabling nations to look for peaceful compromises.

Speaking of "one of those prognostic articles on international politics which every now and then appear in the reviews" (73), Ryecroft sketches the author in such a manner as to suggest the character of either Trafford Romaine or his follower Arnold Jacks in *The Crown of Life*. This self–referential quality in Gissing's work, either to episodes in his life or earlier fiction, is not uncommon. However, Ryecroft quickly draws back and states, "But I will read no more such writing. Why set my nerves quivering with rage, and spoil the calm of a whole day, when no good of any sort can come of it?" (74) Ryecroft's reaction to these outside provocations is not peaceful; they conjure inevitable images of mass slaughter that the article writer, foreseeing "the certainty of a great European war" (73), would surely share if he had an ounce of imagination. World War I, in which Gissing's older son Walter died, was only eleven years in the future. Ryecroft relinquishes the field to the forces of destruction, placing his hopes in "some silent few, who go their way amid the still meadows, who bend to the flower and watch the sunset; and these alone are worth a thought" (74). He does not commit an act of solipsism in his withdrawal to the peace of Exeter and away from the conflicts of the wider world. He is quite conscious that the conflicts continue and that his is an individual act, not one that determines the course of society. He seems to imply that others will have to make their own decisions on engagement or withdrawal. He has done with the outside world except in memory.

Although Gissing usually focuses on the individual life, he is not unaware of the world around him. His early fiction is in response to a desire to depict the real life of the London poor even though he increasingly felt that they could not be raised from their condition. Almost before he published his first novel in 1880, Gissing rejected the beliefs of Auguste Comte's Positivism that taught that the application of reason to social problems could improve all human life. One way that Gissing handles this social awareness is to focus on the individual in the midst of chaos and despair. An Ida Starr (*The Unclassed*), a Gilbert Grail (*Thyrza*), or a Sidney Kirkwood (*The Nether World*) stand out from their societies' backgrounds. Thus, ideas on nationalism, imperialism, or the idea of England do appear in a polemical structure but rather as aspects of the characters' holding or living them out to their consequences. The difficulty that Gissing had in achieving a sympathetic critical response to his work comes from this aesthetic stance in which the author removes himself as much as possible. Pierre Coustillas states, "Some national traditions in literary criticism may not be compatible with a full appreciation of some forms of originality. The handicap of most Victorians when it came to passing judgement on innovative forms of art which placed truth above puritan aesthetics amounted to a national infirmity" ("Gissing the European" 9–10).

17

Religion and Morality

George Gissing was a confirmed atheist throughout his adult life, notwithstanding the controversy that ensued as he lay dying in the Pyrenees. The Reverend Theodore Cooper, an English clergyman from a nearby town, claimed in a letter to the *Church Times* that Gissing accepted the Christian tenets before he died. Later, the clergyman backtracked and played down the suggestion, especially after Gissing's friend Morley Roberts wrote to the *Church Times* in January 1904 absolutely rejecting the idea (Korg, *George Gissing* 253–54; Halperin, *Gissing* 354). Atheist though he was, Gissing employs religion and religious believers in nearly half of his twenty-three novels. In *Workers in the Dawn*, three clergymen appear in secondary roles but ones that involve them directly with the main characters, Arthur Golding and Helen Norman. However, Samuel Tollady is the principal exemplar of a nonreligious moral life in his care for Arthur and others. John Halperin observes in *Gissing: A Life in Books*:

> Arthur spends most of his adolescent years as the informally adopted son of a stationer named Tollady, who seems to be Gissing's idea of what his father might have been like in old age had he lived. Tollady's library, significantly, is large on the literary side, sparse on the scientific side except for botany, and bereft of theology [32].

In other novels, religious professionals function as friends or confidants, e.g., *Demos: A Story of English Socialism* and *Isabel Clarendon*, or are related to the protagonist as in *Our Friend the Charlatan*. In several novels, protagonists come to reject some or all of their religious beliefs. This occurs with Miriam Baske in *The Emancipated* and Sidwell Warricombe in *Born in Exile*. However, Gissing does depict two characters, Maud Enderby in *The Unclassed* and Jane Snowdon in *The Nether World*, fervently embracing some religious or

175

moral calling and rejecting (Maud) or being deprived of (Jane) the possibilities of love and marriage. Moral conflicts tend to dominate many of the plots and often, with the exception of Godwin Peak in *Born in Exile*, with no reference to religion as a basis for morality. Jacob Korg goes so far as to state, "He despised Christianity as a retrograde superstition, but he was opposed to militant atheism, because he realized that religion did much to soften human nature and cultivate its possibilities" ("George Gissing: Humanist in Exile" 241). As a social realist, Gissing uses religion in many aspects, but for the most part, his characters seek answers in this world and through moral systems that are more humanistic than theistic in origin.

Religion or religious figures lie in the background of most of Gissing's novels. While the struggle of a religious figure is not central to any of his novels as it is in Mrs. Humphry Ward's *Robert Elsmere* or Anthony Trollope's *Framley Parsonage* (1861) and *The Last Chronicle of Barset* (1867), the movement away from or toward religious belief often plays an important role. In *Workers in the Dawn*, Helen Norman, the daughter of the Rev. Edward Norman, on her return from her studies in Germany, volunteers to help the Rev. Edgar Walton Heatherley in London's East End. (See Chapter 14.) Religion underlies his moral stance and, as a westerner, Helen also operates, in part, under Christianity's influence. The Rev. Heatherley is a model of one who serves his fellow man by following Christ's admonition to help the poor. Gissing presents no crowded Anglican or Dissenting churches, but he does insert into *Born in Exile* the institutional structure and philosophical impact of religion. Godwin Peak, a thorough atheist, wishes to join the upper-middle class and for his path into that life chooses a pretended religious calling. When he comes to Exeter and ingratiates himself into the Warricombe family, he follows a perilous course that his many vulnerabilities help overwhelm. (See Chapter 10.) Contrasted with his pretended religious belief is the Rev. Bruno Chilvers' position as an Anglican priest. Does Chilvers believe any more than Peak in the tenets of Christianity? Does Gissing show Chilvers undergoing any religious crisis that either strengthens or weakens his belief? The answer to the first question is unknown and to the latter a clear no. Chilvers is a professional Christian. He plans to rise in the church hierarchy and, apparently personally unaffected by any serious theological issue, has caught the proper look and tone of someone on his way up the clerical ladder. His position is in sharp contrast to that of Mr. Warricombe, an amateur scientist. He is troubled by ideas that challenge the Christian belief system but in the end lapses into, at least, the religious formalities that he has known. His daughter Sidwell, resisting both her brother Buckland and her mother, announces that she now doubts some of what she formerly believed. After finally rejecting Peak's second offer of marriage, she decides to continue with her traditional religious observances. Surprisingly, Gissing does not present Sidwell's actions as a defeat. Rather, she responds to the pull of her family and its class traditions. The church exerts no authority over her or anyone in the novel, but the Christian religious philosophy lived out over time by her family and members of her social class has a power to hold her.

Ineffectual clergymen form part of the religious background in Gissing's fiction. Two striking examples appear in *Workers in the Dawn*. The clergyman as a figure of fun is not a common figure in his work, but the Rev. Orlando Whiffle provides a promising model. Jacob Korg describes him as "the self-important and heartless curate" (*George Gissing* 37). He is the Rev. Norman's curate, and his unfocused energy contrasts strongly to the former's depressive manner. Whiffle is efficient in one area, and that is in his and his wife's production of children. One suspects that Gissing uses him to satirize the utter uselessness of the clergy. Whiffle also has scholarly pretensions and works on a number of religious topics in which he strongly believes. One unfortunate product of his marriage is his oldest child, Augustus Whiffle. While at King's College in London, Augustus squanders much of his father's spare money. He might be termed, to echo Dickens in *Hard Times*, a brainless whelp since his supposed friends dupe him out of most of it. He and Maud Gresham Waghorn, Helen Norman's former friend, begin a liaison near the end of the novel but eventually separate. The cynical Maud appears to find her proper level with the seemingly reformed Augustus. The Rev. Whiffle, Augustus, and Maud are minor characters but reflect a social focus seldom explored by Gissing. Certainly, the somber Rev. Norman and the earnest Rev. Heatherley counterbalance any comic tone the Whiffles suggest. Gissing's mother and sisters were very religious and deplored any irreligious tone in his works. That and his temperament may have affected his decision only occasionally to employ religious satire. The Rev. Philip Lashmar in *Our Friend the Charlatan* hints at a return to the image of clerical uselessness. His discussions with his son Dyce about money, while practical, suggest a life largely circumscribed by the mundane. (See Chapter 9.) Dyce, a political plagiarist and the charlatan of the title, is in sharp contrast to Augustus Whiffle in that he purposely, and almost successfully, sets out to con the public and his supporter Lady Ogram in a parliamentary election. Augustus and Dyce, two of the very few clerical offspring in Gissing's fiction, suggest the parsonage as an unpromising background from which to start one's life.

Since Gissing depicts so few children in his fiction, one rarely sees, with the striking exception of Maud Enderby in *The Unclassed*, any struggle over what to believe as a character passes from childhood to adulthood. Similarly, few adults recall religious difficulties that deepen their faith or that lead to humanist positions. Miriam Baske in *The Emancipated* and Sidwell Warricombe in *Born in Exile* come closest to this latter kind of experience, but Gissing does not explicitly state in either novel, though they struggle over their faith, that they have given up every vestige of theism. Halperin comments on Gissing's clear attitude toward religion in the former novel:

> The commentary on religion is not subtle. Gissing attacks English Puritanism with special vigour. Miriam, in early sections of *The Emancipated*, is his exemplar of the perils of puritanism. Repressed, cold, joyless, she refuses to open herself to literature, art, music, or other "frivolous" amusements. This is the result of the training she received during her youth in Yorkshire; she has been an apt pupil [*Gissing* 123].

Two of Gissing's early novels, *Demos* and *Isabel Clarendon*, nevertheless, suggest by religion's near absence and the thinness of its impact on the characters' lives, that a shift in the role of religion has occurred. Both published in 1886, these novels have varied and overlapping class representations. In *Demos*, the middle class and working class mingle throughout the marriage of Adela Waltham and Richard Mutimer while in *Isabel Clarendon*, middle-class and upper-middle-class characters are the focus. In the former novel, Richard Mutimer, a working-class engineer and labor leader, initially inherits his grandfather Mutimer's fortune and promptly begins to turn the still rural Wanley Valley into New Wanley. (See Chapter 3.) A later will disinherits Mutimer in favor of Hubert Eldon. What is important is Adela Waltham Mutimer's moral rejection of her husband's desire to suppress the new will. She does not suggest that her moral position has any religious basis, though she attends church as a regular part of her life. The ironic discovery of the will in a church is as immaterial as if it were found in a book in the family library. No reference is made to Adela's being led by a higher power to find it. The simple idea of honest fairness controls Adela's beliefs about what Mutimer should do just as the general reaction against Mutimer's breaking his engagement to Emma Vine once he inherits money is a moral condemnation. He is wrong on both counts without benefit of clergy.

The Rev. Wyvern is the only clergyman involved with the principal characters in *Demos*. He appears in the novel in a way that has little or nothing to do with his profession. While visiting his son in Germany, he awakes one morning before dawn and goes for a walk. He hears a pistol shot and discovers the wounded Hubert Eldon. He informs Hubert of seeing in Paris two days after the incident his dueling adversary and the lady over whom they quarreled. He adds, "'I was a man of the world before I became a Churchman; you will notice that I affect no professional tone in speaking with you, and it is because I know that anything of the kind would only alienate you'" (74). Mr. Wyvern performs his duties in Wanley but appears more of a friend to Hubert than a clergyman. He shares the same class and that colors his actions:

"But surely you are not a Socialist, Mr. Wyvern?" cried Mrs. Mewling, after doing her best to pump the reverend gentleman, and discovering nothing. "I am a Christian, madam," was the reply, "and have nothing to do with economic doctrines" [87].

After marrying Richard Mutimer, Adela Waltham declares herself a socialist to her friend Letty Tew. Not only that, she tells Letty that the Rev. Wyvern thinks, like her, that "'all Christians ought to be Socialists [...]'" (252). Letty seems surprised:

> "But does Mr. Wyvern thinks so?"
> "Yes, he does; he does indeed. I talk with Mr. Wyvern frequently, and I never knew, before he showed me, how necessary it is for a Christian to be a Socialist."
> "You surprise me, Adela. Yet he doesn't confess himself a Socialist."
> "Indeed, he does. When did you hear Mr. Wyvern preach a sermon without insisting on justice and unselfishness and love of our neighbour? If we try to be just and unselfish, and to love our neighbour as ourself, we help the cause of Socialism. Mr. Wyvern doesn't deal with politics — it is not necessary he should. That is for men like my husband, who give their lives to the practical work. Mr. Wyvern confines himself to spiritual teaching. He would injure his usefulness if he went beyond that" [252].

However, Wyvern appears in complete agreement with Eldon's actions in uprooting all traces of the industrial activities that Mutimer established in the Valley. The loss of work and the destruction of the homes in which the workers lived does not disturb Wyvern. Even Adela, when she and Hubert confess their love to one another, puts aside her past socialist aims: "'There *was* a distance between us, and my ends were other than yours. That is the past; the present is mine to make myself what you would have me. I have no law but your desire — so much I love you'" (477).

Isabel Clarendon's Rev. Vissian plays a role similar to the Rev. Wyvern's in religion's absence as a fundamental orientation in his relations with the main characters. In his introduction to *Isabel Clarendon*, Pierre Coustillas remarks:

> In Gissing's gallery of clergymen [Rev. Vissian] is the only truly bookish one; that is why he is also the most congenial. [T]he Reverend Wyvern plays the part of the chorus in *Demos*, distilling his wise comments on modern society [xl-xli].

Vissian performs an act of kindness when he loans Bernard Kingcote money after someone steals his wallet. That act reflects the essential nature of both the reverend and his wife. After Kingcote settles in the Cottage at Wood End, he regularly visits the Rev. Vissian to talk about literature. This and Vissian's bibliomania seem to be their chief connection. Kingcote meets and falls in love with Isabel Clarendon, the Lady of Knightswell. The Rev. Vissian highly esteems her, and while he is in no sense her private chaplain, Gissing makes it clear that their class relationship supports an easy intercourse. She invites the reverend and his wife to her home on social occasions, and he later talks with her about Kingcote's move to Norwich from London in order to take over his father's bookstore. Gissing mentions three situations that involve Vissian's profession. After Isabel is hurt in a hunting accident, the reverend offers a prayer for her at a church service. Shortly afterward, she asks Kingcote, somewhat ironically, to come see her if he can for once miss the Reverend Vissian's sermon. During their discussion of religious topics, Kingcote indicates he is a freethinker. Finally, the reverend has to rush to a church service when he strongly wishes to discuss his Shakespearean criticism with Kingcote. Gissing, subtly if comically, shows him torn between his parish duties and his apparently real desire to talk about literature. The Rev. Vissian is a social and cultural figure who inhabits a nominally religious space, but neither he nor any other character gives a substantive sense to that space. In Gissing's fiction, the institutional church fades in importance as the century ends.

Two of Gissing's principal characters, along with older women who influence the direction of their lives, demonstrate a fervent religious or moral belief that curbs and limits their more secular inclinations. Helen Norman in *Workers in the Dawn*, discussed above, is not an older woman, but she has elements in her character that render her a semi-archetypal figure for religious and moral types. While she is a freethinker, Helen dedicates her life to serving the poor. And, she denies her own happiness when she rejects Arthur Golding as a lover because he is married, if only in name, to the dissolute Carrie Mitchell. Thus, Helen has two qualities that later fit Maud Enderby in *The Unclassed* and Jane Snowdon in *The Nether World*, i.e., a life dedicated to religious and/or moral service with a philanthropic focus and one in which self-denial is a powerful theme. Maud is the main example of this life in Gissing's fiction and surpasses her model Helen Norman. Michael Collie calls Maud, in her rejection of life's pleasures, "the Helen Norman of *The Unclassed*" (*Alien Art* 55). As a young girl, Maud goes to live with her aunt, Miss Theresa Bygrave, a devout, ultra-respectable woman, after a scandal in her parents' lives. Her father, the Rev. Paul Enderby, steals money from a disaster relief fund that he administers, and her mother attempts to hang herself (146–47). Miss Bygrave defines every feeling of delight and happiness as originating in sin and implants feelings of guilt in Maud at any later recurrences of these emotions. She speaks to Maud about why they do not indulge in "'eating and drinking and all sorts of merriment'" (33) during Christmas. She tells her that she will come to understand why these things are "'sinful'" [34]. Miss Bygrave states:

> "In the true Christian, every enjoyment which comes from the body is a sin. If you feel you *like* this or that, it is a sign that you must renounce it, give it

up. If you feel fond of life, you must, you must force yourself to hate it; for life is sin" [35].

She finishes by telling Maud that the only joy that one must pursue is "'sacrifice'" (35) and that "'perfect happiness'" comes with "'death'" (35). This calmly stated belief system, one that she consistently inculcates in Maud, eventually dominates Maud's life, and she gives up all possibility of personal happiness in this world. Gissing describes Miss Bygrave's home in a way that matches her religious philosophy, "There was no sign of lack of repair; perfect order and cleanliness wherever the eye penetrated; yet the general effect was an unspeakable desolation" (32).

Before Maud completely separates herself from the world and what it has to offer, she goes through several stages as she reaches adulthood. Maud struggles to merge into the world and live a normal life, but this merger ultimately leads to retreat. Maud is seven years old when she first goes to live with Miss Bygrave in the above-described household. At the time, Maud attends Miss Rutherford's school at which she meets Ida Starr and Harriet Smales. These two characters, especially Ida, play a significant role in Maud's life. When Maud is eighteen or nineteen years old, she takes a position at Dr. Tootle's school as governess to his children. Maud meets Osmond Waymark, an aspiring novelist, who holds a teaching position there. Waymark subsequently encounters Ida who has become a prostitute like her mother. Ida, Waymark, and Maud form the main source of interest in the novel with Maud's religious extremism determining the direction of the action. However, Osmond initially falls in love with Maud, and they plan to marry, but beyond his ability to understand, if not beyond Maud's, Miss Bygrave's influence reaches a point at which Maud's love for Osmond becomes nothing but sin. Foreshadowing the conclusion of the novel, Maud stops in a Roman Catholic church on her way home from a solitary London walk:

> One evening, wending wearily homewards, she was attracted by the lights in a church in Marylebone Road, and, partly for a few minutes' rest, partly out of a sudden attraction to a religious service, she entered. It was the church of Our Lady of the Rosary. She had not noticed that it was a Roman Catholic place of worship, but the discovery gave her an unexpected pleasure. She was soothed and filled with a sense of repose. Sinking into the attitude of prayer, she let her thoughts carry her whither they would; they showed her nothing but images of beauty and peace [*The Unclassed* 218].

Gissing does not directly return to this effect on Maud's life until the last page of the novel when Miss Bygrave informs him that she and Maud "having become members of 'the true Church,' were about to join a sisterhood in a midland town, where their lives would be devoted to work of charity" (312). Previously, Maud asked to be released from her engagement to Waymark, and he tells Miss Bygrave if she is certain six months after her request, he will do so. No one unduly influences Maud, but she learned her aunt's religious views from an early age and was of a temperament to respond to them. These views seem to reflect her true adult self.

Jane Snowdon's choice of morally based charity work near the end of *The Nether World* is not as dramatic as Maud's nor as long in gestation. Her father abandons her and her mother when she is seven. Four years later her mother dies, and Mrs. Peckover keeps her as a servant. When Jane is thirteen, her grandfather returns to England from Australia and finds Jane of whom Mrs. Peckover says, "'I've been a mother to her an' a good mother — though I say it myself— these six years or more'" (44–45). In reality, Mrs. Peckover and her daughter Clem have underfed and abused her so that when Michael Snowdon arrives at the house, Jane lies ill in an upstairs room. Michael takes her away and raises her to adulthood. While in Australia, Michael inherited money from a son, also named Michael. With this money he intends to put into action a plan to help the unfortunate, and he hopes Jane will serve as his instrument in doing so. Gissing states that he "professed no formal religion. He attended no Sunday service, nor had he ever shown a wish that Jane should do so" (151). Nonetheless, he uses the Bible "as a source of moral instruction" (151). He and Jane read it together but only passages "as had a purely human significance" (151). Michael hopes that Jane "should possess the religious spirit" (151) but rejects any religious "formalism" (151). Gissing describes Jane: "Sensitive to every prompting of humanity, instinct with moral earnestness, she betrayed no slightest tendency to the religion of church, chapel, or street-corner" (152). Jane's attempts to accept Michael's ideas on serving the poor founder when Sidney Kirkwood, who loves Jane and is loved by her, doubts her capability to run such a project. Instead of marrying Jane, Sidney pulls back, and Jane herself realizes that even with the help of Miss Lant, who has devoted her life and modest means to charity, she cannot give up the hope of love for a "higher reward" (307) through charity work. In *George Gissing: Grave Comedian* (1954), Mabel Collins Donnelly notes the incompatibility of Michael's and Jane's ends; he

> has dwindled into a fussy old man with a religious mania that his granddaughter should save the world at the expense of her own happiness — this despite the fact that she has neither the intelligence nor the drive to accomplish the purpose [118].

All prospects for the project unravel when Michael destroys a will leaving most of his money to Jane and dies before he can write another. His disreputable son Joseph James Snowdon, Jane's father, inherits but squanders the money. Jane realizes she is "no saviour of society" (391) but helps others one person at a time. Such a method suits her personality, and she finds peace in the activity and uses some of her little money from work to relieve others. Simon J. James states, "Philanthropic projects can provide only partial or temporary relief against the totality of the social forces ranged against them, and may cause more harm than good" ("How to Read" 18). Among other novels, James applies this statement to *The Nether World*, and Jane, before she rejects her grandfather Michael's plans for her life and comes to a clearer understanding of her temperament and abilities, exemplifies it. Jane compares with Maud Enderby in feeling a "gleam of hope in renunciation" (318) but does not go so far as Maud and her aunt in connecting her modest, morally based charity work to a religious organization.

Gissing was a Positivist early in his career. He actually became a good friend of Frederic Harrison, one of the leading English Positivists. After he had *Workers in the Dawn* published, Gissing sent Harrison a copy. He received a kind and interested response, and soon after, Gissing began to tutor his sons. Eventually, Arthur Schopenhauer's outlook on life appealed more to him. In 1882, he wrote a long essay entitled "The Hope of Pessimism" which remained unpublished until 1970. As early as *Workers in the Dawn*, Gissing was moving away from Positivism. Arthur Golding, Will Noble, and a few others meet to discuss social and political problems. The tone of these talks is both intellectual and practical. However, when Golding receives his legacy from the Rev. Norman, he does not invest it in practical plans to improve society but rather uses it to train as an artist. David Grylls remarks:

> Much later, the account of Noble's library — no poetry, no works of imagination — reveals a man immersed in the "savage facts" of political economy. Eventually, breaking from Arthur Golding, Noble condemns his commitment to art as "devotion to a mere unreasoning passion." Even the most worthy and blameless reformers betray some lack of fineness [*Paradox* 29].

Golding not only rejects the promises of religion but also sees no point in improving the masses. Darwin's ideas regarding evolution in the natural world seep into nineteenth-century thought on social change. Gissing reflects the language of Darwinism and social Darwinism in his novels, e.g., struggle for survival and survival of the fittest, but does not believe in any general tendencies toward human betterment. Only in the personal area does Gissing consider anything worth struggling for.

Gissing dramatizes few positive developments in people's lives in his early fiction. Critics and reviewers frequently attack him for his grim and gloomy portrayals of society. As a realist, he sees himself showing life as it is. While it may suit his personality to see the world largely in negative terms, Gissing can also point to the pain and suffering in nineteenth-century London as justification for his views. Further, he demonstrates no sense that he bears any responsibility in his fiction to make things come out right. Some characters in his novels have happy endings, but not all who undergo trials succeed in overcoming them. Death and loss, thus, parallel a certain stoicism that dramatizes the manner in which certain characters sort out difficulties they encounter and accept what they get from life. Stoicism, a Greek and Roman philosophical system probably best known through Marcus Aurelius's *Meditations*, offers no such succor as does Christianity. However, it suggests a way of going on with expected pains and disappointments one experiences. It would take approximately one hundred and fifty years before Christianity became the official state religion under the Emperor Constantine. In Gissing, Mr. Gammon in *The Town Traveller* is a clear example of one who hopes for happiness and satisfaction in life and who, even if some avenues close off, gratefully takes what remains. He might represent the sunny side of a stoical outlook, but he is remarkable for focusing on this world and not overreaching in his engagements with others. He and Polly Sparkes agree to disagree and decide not to marry. Subsequently, he suggests to Mrs. Louisa Clover that he would like to marry her daughter Minnie, but she very kindly turns him away from that idea, and they wind up marrying one another. Mr. Gammon expresses no clear philosophy on how to cope with disappointment, but he does cope satisfactorily. By staying on an even keel and not expecting too much, he is able to accept a positive development with Mrs. Clover when it comes. As a town traveler, Mr. Gammon is familiar with the world and, without making difficulties, he bends under Louisa's soft yoke by giving up his dogs and planning more thoroughly about the work he will do. Reflecting a stoical attitude, Mr. Gammon neither bemoans his losses nor exaggerates his gains. The moral impact of Mr. Gammon's stoicism comes from the social harmony he helps establish, and while one might assume some formal religious observance, Gissing does not center anyone's hopes in the novel on what religion has to offer.

In character after character, Gissing makes clear that religion is not a necessary part of everyone's life. Some, to their loss, at least in the eyes of others, make it central to their lives. Others repudiate any idea that religious concepts guide their behavior, morally, socially, or personally. Characters in some novels for the most part go about their religious observances as they have in the past, accepting it in the flow of their lives. As a social and psychological realist, Gissing, no matter his personal beliefs, attempts to show what a given personality in a given family or social group will do when religious decisions have to be made and not just accepted as part of the fabric of things. A Maud Enderby and a Jane Snowdon and a Godwin Peak and a Sidwell Warricombe reveal the different outcomes of these dramatic situations, outcomes that Gissing does not claim will necessarily be repeated by anyone else.

18

The Natural World in Human Time

On the surface, Gissing's fiction presents no obvious conflicts with nature. His novels predominantly deal with an urban world and its many struggles, especially those between people intimately connected to one another. Emotional upheavals would be a better description, from *Workers in the Dawn* and *The Unclassed* on, of the tensions that continually arise between various characters. London, with its large population, extremes of wealth and poverty, and disease, provides a perfect backdrop to this human drama. However, in almost every novel, the natural world or at least rural or semi-rural environments intermix with the characters' lives.

Among Gissing's novels, *Workers* probably has the least amount of suggestion that the grim world that his protagonist Arthur Golding experiences is not the sole framework within which his life can unfold. Yet, some tendrils of a nonurban existence insert themselves into the novel; however, his wife Carrie Mitchell has no such connection to an alternative environment and lifestyle. Bounded by the streets and vice, pregnant and abandoned by her lover, and having a taste for alcohol and friends who encourage her indulgence before and after she meets Arthur, Carrie knows little of any other existence. She inhales the fumes of an atmosphere resembling that which Inspector Bucket and Dr. Alan Woodcourt in Charles Dickens' *Bleak House* experience while seeking Jo in Tom-all-Alone's. The rural world, of course, is often more a suburban one in Gissing's fiction offering trees and grass but not a country atmosphere where the rhythms of nature prevail. In *Isabel Clarendon, A Life's Morning, The Odd Women,* and *The Paying Guest,* the rural world is nearby but only weakly hinted at or made secondary in Gissing's seeming resistance to its thematic possibilities. Small towns are by definition closer to the country than larger ones, but as Gissing moves his individual and social concerns to these venues in *Denzil Quarrier* and *Our Friend the Charlatan*, the natural world still has little effect on the action. Finally, nature plays a major role in *The Private Papers of Henry Ryecroft* and with the urban world then no more than a memory. However, it is a memory that dominates the novel equally with his present experience of the Devon countryside near Exeter. Gradually, one realizes that in his fiction Gissing generally minimizes and thus constrains the natural world but makes an unusual exception in *The Private Papers of Henry Ryecroft*.

Gissing lived and wrote in the last half of the nineteenth century and the first few years of the twentieth. All his novels were published from 1880 onwards. Thus, at the end of the first industrial century, he participated realistically in his life and imaginatively in his art. When he moved to London after returning in 1877 from his year of exile in America, an America substantially changed from Dickens' 1842 portrait in *American Notes*, Gissing responds creatively both to the city and the country in his many novels and short stories. His time at Owens College in Manchester may have pointed him towards Cambridge and an academic career, but the sheer amount of his published and unpublished fiction, his essays, and his critical work on Charles Dickens strongly suggest that far from a disappointed academic, Gissing displays his real desire to encompass and analyze modern culture through narrative fiction.

As his creative energies moved toward fiction, his many novels set in urban environments, especially London, reveal a major theme in the inevitable human conflicts. And, this theme revolves around the city as a force that directly weakens the power of the natural world to dominate the ebb and flow of human life. Henry Fielding was a man of the city — dramatist, essayist, novelist — but the setting in which *The History of Tom Jones: A Foundling* (1749) begins and to which it returns is the country. Country and land mattered greatly before the 1832 Reform Act began to alter the political structure of the nation, but by the 1880s and 1890s, the urban worlds of London, Birmingham, Liverpool, Manchester, Leeds, and Sheffield dominated the social, political, and cultural influences. The omnipotence and omnipresence of nature and religious myths partially disappear, framed and made into aesthetic objects in the age of evolution, steamships, railroads, telegraphs, gas and electric lighting, typewriters, bicycles, and the first motor cars.

One question the above statement raises is whether it is a too-extreme position and that, rather than an aesthetic object, the natural world is only more restrained than heretofore in its bursting life and growth. In other words, does man's actions circumscribe nature, creating a smaller sphere in which natural processes still strongly unfold? *Workers in the Dawn* gives a curious, even paradoxical example of this idea in America, a country with an image of a still-expanding, open experience of nature. At the end of the novel, Arthur Golding journeys to Niagara Falls in order to end his life. The waters pour over the Falls, overwhelming one's sense the closer one approaches. However, as Dickens reflects in *American Notes*, Niagara Falls during his trip was already a tourist attraction. Dickens' anticipation of seeing the "Great Falls" and his first experience of them sets the scene:

> It was a miserable day; chilly and raw; a damp mist falling; and the trees in that northern region quite bare and wintry. Whenever the train halted, I listened for the roar; and was constantly straining my eyes in the direction where I knew the Falls must be, from seeing the river rolling on towards them; every moment expecting to behold the spray. Within a few minutes of our stopping, not before, I saw two great white clouds rising up slowly and majestically from the depths of the earth. That was all. At length we alighted: and then, for the first time, I heard the mighty rush of water, and felt the ground tremble underneath my feet [228].

In *Workers*, the Niagara River still rushes to the edge and over with all the accompanying sights and sounds, but it has become a spectacle, an aesthetic object to a certain extent bounded and curtailed rather than only a natural, open-ended wonder. In contrast, when the Rev. Edward Norman takes young Arthur home to his country parish after Arthur's father dies in a London slum, he sees a natural world, but not an aesthetic object, enclosed and bounded even more than by the effect from the Enclosure Acts in the latter part of the eighteenth century. Man and nature have made contact, and especially in southern England there are fewer rural areas that, uninhabited, create buffers between settled and unsettled areas. When Arthur runs away from the Rev. Norman's home and care and manages to find his way back to London and the slum room in which his father died, the city closes around him. After many difficult experiences, the kindly Mr. Tollady raises him, and a subsequent legacy from the Rev. Norman allows him to cultivate his abilities as an artist. All of Arthur's conflicts, except for the last scene at Niagara Falls and the earlier rejected refuge at the Rev. Norman's, occur in the city. Gissing gives him no sustaining hope that a benevolent power, revealed through the natural world, will aid him. Unlike the young Wordsworth in Books One and Two of *The Prelude*, Arthur hears no breathing spirits from nature and receives no revivifying power from its communications that enable him to persevere with life. The city abandons him just as, ironically, nature abandons the unhappy Margaret in "The Ruined Cottage," Book One of Wordsworth's *The Excursion*. Armytage, the poem's sympathetic peddler, records her disintegration and death and the natural growth that later over-whelms her roadside cottage and garden.

The natural world and its processes in Gissing's fiction intermix in odd ways with the characters' lives. He does not repeat anything like the dramatic action at Niagara Falls that ends *Workers*. However, one aspect of that inci-dent reappears on occasion, suggesting echoes of natural forces. The scene in *The Unclassed* at Hastings in which the heroine Ida Starr wades in the sea at night and then swims in the nude (145) is such a suggestion or reminder that not everything occurs within civilization's circle. This is not to deny the moral aspect of the episode. Michael Collie writes, "Sin for Ida Starr, the sometime prostitute, is a moral repugnance from which she can free herself by her own decision, represented in the novel by her night swim: this is the humanist solution, as it were" (*Alien Art* 56). Further on, Collie discusses it as an act of purification (66). However, what connects this scene to the one at Niagara Falls is the idea of edges or frontiers. The dark sea that opens out beyond Ida and the immense vista from the Falls, both countering in some sense man's aestheticization of the natural world, represent instances that occur in many of his works. The re-naturalizing of Wanley Valley in *Demos* is a curious example of this combination of nature's aestheticization by humans and its natural state. (See Chapters 5 and 14.) But can one put this genie back into the bottle? However satisfied Hubert Eldon and the Rev. Wyvern are at the removal of every trace of the Mutimers' industrial efforts, could one look at the Valley without at least remembering what occurred there? David Grylls notes, "Throughout the book the purity of nature is praised and the filth of the factories associated with Mutimer" (*Paradox* 43). Theirs is not the shock of the new as in Cortez's (Balboa's) sighting of the Pacific Ocean in Keats' "On First Looking into Chapman's Homer" (1816). For all that Eldon is "aes-thetically sensitive" and "has no doubt that Mutimer's ugly factory must be closed" (40), does Eldon see nature's rhythms undisturbed when he gazes on his work? For, the scene is partially his work and not nature's alone. Adrian Poole offers a possible synthesis in the person of Adela Waltham: "Adela, the well-bred girl, is in a sense an analogue for the inherent 'culture' of the val-ley, and of Nature itself" (*Gissing in Context* 72).

Gissing not only mixes the natural world and human lives, but he also does it in creative ways. In *The Crown of Life*, he performs this mixing in a literal manner by placing the writer Jerome Otway, Piers Otway's father, at Hawes, "a little stony town at the wild end of Wensleydale" (9) with his wife. Mr. Otway has withdrawn from the hurly-burly of life. One can also sequester oneself from life in the city, but the country seems the more logical place to choose if one wishes to be away from it all. In Gissing's novels, romantic and sexual relations generally occur in the city, but in *In the Year of Jubilee*, Nancy

Lord and Lionel Tarrant meet at Teignmouth while Nancy is vacationing with Jessica Morgan and Mrs. Morgan. One afternoon she and Lionel take their second walk alone in the country. At one point, Tarrant and Nancy return to the lovely hollow he discovered. They go to this hideaway, and Tarrant supposedly seduces her. Gissing is fittingly, for his Victorian audience, ambiguous about her acquiescence and the physical details, but Nancy subsequently becomes pregnant. (See Chapters 13 and 14.) Gissing has set this natural bower as a place apart for their unconventional behavior. Soon, however, society's conventions and strictures loom, and though they marry, Nancy must conceal from her friends both her pregnancy and marriage because of the terms of her father's will. The idyllic setting for their lovemaking is Gissing's only instance of a sexual union in a natural setting that suggests Edenic echoes. Finally, *New Grub Street* provides something closer to a clash between nature and man on Jasper Milvain and Marian Yule's country walk soon after they meet. Milvain is visiting his mother and sisters' home in the small village of Finden near Wattleborough. Marian and Jasper are attracted to one another, and their walk is the first instance of their being alone together. Gissing sets a harmonious scene until they pause on a bridge over the mainline railroad track. Milvain says he wants to show Marian something. Soon the train comes thundering under the bridge, exhilarating Jasper but dismaying Marian in its ferocious display of power (32–33). (See Chapter 2.) Not only is the train a discordant element in the bucolic setting, but it sets them, for the first time, apart. This much-referred-to scene has the feeling of a set-piece with its symbolic connections to later events, but it is, at the same time, a superb mixing of natural processes, broadly considered, and human desire.

The natural world — grass, trees, flowers, streams — is often nearby but only briefly hinted at. Gissing frequently resists its thematic possibilities unless it is constricted, constrained, or owned. In *New Grub Street*, two important events occur in parks, i.e., Harold Biffen's suicide on Putney Heath and Jasper Milvain's manipulation of Marian Yule in Regent's Park to force her to break their engagement. The human drama dominates the parks' natural setting just as human society also surrounds them, lessening their naturalness. Gardeners plant the flowers, tend them and the trees, and cut the grass. One either sees or infers fences and gates. Roads circle the park, and across the roads, buildings rise up, deflecting or impeding one's view. In *The Paying Guest*, Clarence and Emmeline Mumford live with their young son in a house in one of the new suburbs south of London. Open land lies a short walk from their home, but it functions more as a break in the housing patterns than as a natural expanse. One gets only a little bit of the natural world, the little bit that will soon disappear as the city expands. The Mumfords' home is an outpost of civilization placed close to the natural world and its many rhythms.

It is fitting that the would-be educated and refined Louise Derrick and her even more vulgar father and stepmother should soon follow, disrupting whatever harmony the Mumfords have hoped to achieve by living there. Ironically, it takes engineer Tom Cobb's successful pursuit of Louise to bring a simulacrum of the Mumfords' former peace. Man builds the parks in London, and its suburbs fast become part of the city. Posted regulations adorn the park entrances, and thus man stamps his seal on nature.

In *Isabel Clarendon* and *Our Friend the Charlatan*, the country homes of Isabel and Lady Ogram, respectively, radiate into the natural world with few barriers that enclose their grass and trees from nature's. The characters in the two novels view it or use it, especially in the fox hunting episode in *Isabel Clarendon*. But, nature in the latter, through Mrs. Clarendon's accident, is a scene for human drama but of a social class higher than in Gissing's earlier work. Jacob Korg states that it is mainly about "aristocratic country scenes where poverty and social evils never appear" (*George Gissing* 79). Isabel joins the chase and falls, thus canceling out any other possible interest in the environment. As expected, they bring her home, pulling the focus back to human concerns and interests. She may as well have slipped on the pavement in a city. Gissing could reply to these observations that nature is not here his concern but rather character and its motivations to action. And, he would be right to say so, but what he leaves out or "glances off" as he pursues his themes tells one about his conception of the world and culture before him. *Our Friend the Charlatan* is instructive here. Dyce Lashmar, the charlatan of the title, seeks political help from Lady Ogram at her country home near Hollingford through the auspices of his friend Constance Bride. Lashmar grew up in the country at his father's rectory at Averholme in Northamptonshire. Constance lived near him, and they had a rather disappointing relationship, especially for her, as young adults and then lost touch with one another. Lashmar later discovers that Constance is Lady Ogram's secretary. Neither when Dyce and Constance were younger nor in the present does the natural world play on their feelings, provide images of beauty that lift them out of themselves, or offer moral instruction. Examples of these kinds of interaction with nature from classical and English, especially Romantic, literature were part of Gissing's education and would have been part of these characters' educations as well. Lashmar, Bride, and Lady Ogram do not contemplate nature nor must they do so. Of course, in the midst of London one does not expect it, but in the country with the natural world at least present, the near absence of any awareness of nature leaves a gap in their understanding. The juxtaposition of Thomas Hardy's novels, especially *Tess of the D'Urbervilles* (1891), with Gissing's concerning the use of nature shows that the latter has often dropped, left out, and even abandoned a concern that functions as part of his literary heritage.

The above is not to suggest the unimportance of nature to Gissing's fiction but rather its marginalization. *A Life's Morning* is instructive in the way that Gissing introduces the Surrey landscape as backdrop rather than forefront. Near the beginning of the Trinity term at Balliol College, Oxford, Wilfred Athel falls ill and must leave. His father takes him to the "Firs, a delightful house in the midst of Surrey's fairest scenery" (3). Gissing's comments about the countryside are not always so general, but the role of people as spectators is to subjugate it by their presence and to incorporate nature's qualities into their concerns and interests. Writing about a print of a Wakefield scene made a decade before Gissing's 1857 birth, Gillian Tindall suggests a reason for his attitude toward nature: "It was then a sylvan landscape, the very prototype of that rural England — decorated with the odd venerable pile — which Gissing was later to enthuse over in his writings but never gave the impression of knowing deeply" (*Born Exile* 30). Tindall remarks a few pages later, "When he first saw the more picturesque parts of his native country he saw them as 'landscape' or as settings for portions of history which had fired his imagination" (32). The Firs in *A Life's Morning* takes its name from the nearby trees. Gissing states:

> We find the family assembling for breakfast at The Firs one delightful morning at the end of July. The windows of the room were thrown open, and there streamed in with the sunlight fresh and delicious odours, tonics alike of mind and body. From the Scotch firs whence the dwelling took its name came a scent which mingled with wafted breath from the remoter heather, and the creepers about the house-front, the lovely bloom and leafage skirting the lawn, contributed to the atmosphere of health and joy [5].

The people in the room take in nature's sights and smells, in the process improving mentally and physically. Nature is not passive but rather bends to do service to the inhabitants. Not only does Philip Athel, the father, enter the house from the lawn and garden, but nature appears to exist as a garden. However, this allusion to the biblical Garden of Eden is heavily ironic given the present and larger industrial world in which Gissing sets the novel.

Returning to his home from an invigorating ride on the downs, Wilfred catches "a glimpse of a straw hat moving into a heath-clad hollow a hundred yards from the road" (*A Life's Morning* 9). He follows and soon encounters Emily Hood, the two younger children's governess. Gissing thus sets Wilfrid and Emily, the protagonists, in the natural world for their first talk. As in the breakfast room, all the world around serves them. Specifically, Gissing introduces a bee, a butterfly, a cloud, and a spray Wilfrid offers Emily. The bee fills up a pause in their conversation while the butterfly represents an alteration in his treatment of the natural world. When he was ten years old, he would have stuck it on a pin, but now it is "that glorious butterfly." The butterfly leaves but the bee remains. It now hums "about them" (13) rather than formerly "between them" (12). The offer of the spray by Wilfrid and its acceptance by Emily, their fingers touching in the process (13–14), signals the beginning of intimacy between them. As well as the bee, a cloud that Wilfrid remarks on before giving her the spray (13) has hardly changed its shape. On their rising to return to the house, Emily destroys the pastoral dream with nature open and attendant on them. Wilfrid suggests he will see such a cloud in the Alps in a week, and inquiring what she will see in Dunfield, Yorkshire, she says, "'No, there we have only mill-smoke'" (19). This moment presages Gissing's initial ending of the novel when Emily rejects Wilfrid's offer of marriage after her father's theft of £10 from his employer Richard Dagworthy and his suicide. She feels unworthy of Wilfrid after these two events. However, as Pierre Coustillas states in the introduction, James Payn, the publisher's reader, demanded "a happy ending" (xxiv), thus marring the novel's structure.

   Denzil Quarrier's Polterham and *Our Friend the Charlatan*'s Hollingford are not discovered places but rather occupied space. Quarrier comes from Polterham, and thus, it does not offer a newfound retreat for him and Lilian. She has a residual anxiety about the discovery of her previous marriage to Arthur James Northway, but even though they are not divorced, time has somewhat allayed her fears. The turmoil of a parliamentary election furnishes background to Eustace Glazzard's betrayal of his friend and his friend's supposed wife. (See Chapter 10.) In describing Lilian's suicide, Gissing does not sentimentalize the image of a lost bucolic peace nor hint at any sense of desecration in the natural world turned into a scene of self-destruction. The Wordsworthian image of the harmony of nature and its use as a moral example has faded in a century of industrial expansion and empire. Gissing's neutral picture of this near-country setting neither adds to nor takes away any of its parts. The fields are empty of houses or streets, the pond has water deep enough to drown Lilian, and Mrs. Wade has the fortitude to watch.

   The town of Hollingford in *Our Friend the Charlatan* has a significance of its own apart from Lady Ogram's nearby residence. The parliamentary election in which Dyce Lashmar participates takes place there. Since Lady Ogram is the grande dame of the area, despite her somewhat scandalous past as a model, she represents Lashmar's hope of winning the seat until Lord Dymchurch exposes his plagiarism and she withdraws her support. However, the Conservative incumbent decides to run after all and has enough votes to succeed. Gissing does not develop this potential political theme between town and landed gentry. Yet, he does connect them and the natural world in interesting ways. Hollingford is small enough to be accessible to the countryside, but what emerges is an image of the town and country estate connected by a thread that passes through but often ignores the countryside. It barely exists in the novel whether from the town's or Lady Ogram's perspective. Human concerns and conflicts pass along this road and minimize the nonhuman. Neither in figurative language nor descriptive sketches of the rural world through which the characters move does Gissing suggest the natural world as a support or illustration of the characters' lives. Not a dead world, nature is largely absent from the characters' thoughts, though near.

It is not that events do not happen in the natural world in *Our Friend the Charlatan* or at least in the garden or the enclosed park surrounding Rivenoak, Lady Ogram's country home. Dyce Lashmar and May Tomalin, Lady Ogram's recently discovered great-niece, scheme to marry against Lady Ogram's wishes. She plans for Lashmar to marry her secretary Constance Bride and for Tomalin to marry the relatively poor Lord Dymchurch. Lashmar and Tomalin arrange their deception in a secluded area of the park. Lord Dymchurch accidentally overhears them and decides against proposing to May when they meet in the garden near the house. After the debacle at Rivenoak when Lord Dymchurch suddenly leaves and the ill but determined Lady Ogram forces Dyce, May, and Constance to reveal what they have said, planned, and done against her wishes, Dyce goes to Yarmouth on the east coast to see Iris Woolstan. She is his lifeline, and later they plan to marry and live on her small income until Dyce can succeed in some field. Formerly he served as her son Leonard's tutor, and she fell in love with him. Finally, Lord Dymchurch, who has returned to his home in Somerset to look after his two unmarried sisters, walks the nearby lanes at peace with "nature's beauty." This is the principal sustained incorporation of nature into a character's life; it is a solace to Dymchurch, foreshadowing the more important example in *The Private Papers of Henry Ryecroft*. Gissing writes of the now-alone Dymchurch since one sister died shortly after he returned to Somerset and the other soon afterward entered a religious community:

> He lived on in the silent house, quite alone and desiring no companionship. Few letters came for him, and he rarely saw a newspaper. After a while he was able to forget himself in the reading of books which tranquillised his thought, and held him far from the noises of the passing world. So sequestered was the grey old house that he could go forth when he chose into lanes and meadows without fear of encountering anyone who would disturb his meditation and his enjoyment of nature's beauty. Through the mellow days of the declining summer, he lived amid trees and flowers, slowly recovering health and peace in places where a bird's note, or the ripple of a stream, or the sighing of the wind, were the only sounds under the ever-changing sky [363].

The Private Papers of Henry Ryecroft shows the protagonist gratefully experiencing, even luxuriating in, the natural world surrounding his home near

Exeter and remembering with feeling his urban struggles. He acknowledges his hope for a few more years of peace and the profound quiet with only Mrs. M., his housekeeper, in attendance. His memories of London and the hardships of his writing career wash over him. Wisely, on his walks in the nearby country lanes he makes no attempt to repress them. Thus, they mingle in the sights and sounds of the natural world, a world that daily offers emotional balm and sustenance. Gissing published the autobiographical novel from 1902 to 1903 in the *Fortnightly*. At that point, he entitled the work *An Author at Grass*. It suggests being put out to pasture, in his case the immense, garden-like world of the Exeter countryside. However, far from vegetating, Ryecroft attunes himself both to the present and past. He occasionally has one friend to stay for a few days and then returns to his solitary bliss. The natural world does not energize Ryecroft, but it does sustain him. He has not gone to the country with his pension of £300 per annum from an admirer of his work to gain spirit to return to the literary grind. Yet, bemused by his desire to write, he begins his work, his *Papers*, purely for his own pleasure. Gissing poses as his editor and takes responsibility for arranging the book by the seasons.

The autobiographical novel commences with Spring, almost as if Ryecroft fears delaying the delights it offers. Yet, he does not immediately turn outward but rather inward to his immediate task of writing. Spring, Part One, begins: "For more than a week my pen has lain untouched" (*Private Papers* 23). He calls his pen, "Old companion, yet old enemy!" (24) In Part Two, he takes note of the room in which he sits and his garden. His home is especially important:

> To me this little book-room is beautiful, and chiefly because it is home. Through the greater part of life I was homeless. Many places have I inhabited, some which my soul loathed and some which pleased me well; but never till now with that sense of security which makes a home [26].

In Part Three, Ryecroft describes a walk. Three paragraphs later he tells of replacing a boy's lost sixpence. From this, he writes of the effects of poverty and his refusal to dwell on it. However, he cannot escape his past and the thoughts it brings. His present peace, quiet, and security enable him to contemplate what he and others endured without undue disturbance. He writes, "Everyday the world grows noisier; I, for one, will have no part in that increasing clamour, and were it only by my silence, I confer a boon on all" (29). Without this stoical attitude, Ryecroft confesses that his conscience would disturb him too much to enjoy his own comfortable existence (28). However, a surfeit of past pain and suffering buffer him from foolishly giving way to these feelings. Ryecroft evinces a hard awareness of the world's difficult choices and accepts those he has made.

Ryecroft balances his present joy with memories of the past that are not all bad. Nature and memory intertwine. Except for his youth and the memory of one year spent in Devon years before, a place that he did not then expect to be his future home, Ryecroft knows that these two concepts, nature and memory, have separate existences for him. Nature is now; memory is London and the struggles of the writing life. London does have parks, but he dismissively refers to them as "but pavement disguised with a growth of grass" (*Private Papers* 34). Turning inwardly was one way he survived. He describes "what was perhaps the worst London fog I ever knew" and one that lasted "three successive days" (39). He kept mostly to his room but, paradoxically, he felt "only the more cosy. I had coals, oil, tobacco in sufficient quantity; I had a book to read; I had work which interested me; so I went forth only to get my meals at a City Road coffee-shop, and hastened back to the fireside" (39). He writes, "Nature took revenge now and then. In winter time I had fierce sore throats, sometimes accompanied by long and savage headaches" (39). That is nature in London, but he ends Spring on a predominantly joyful note. He multiplies references to the discovered valleys, birds, trees, blossoms, and the silence of his home to which he awakes each morning. The subsequent seasons duplicate this balance between present and past with the first part of the equation dominating the discourse. The only flaw in the developing, but positive, imbalance is the short time Ryecroft has in which to enjoy his discovered haven.

The Private Papers of Henry Ryecroft is an oddity in Gissing's fiction. He was raised in Wakefield in Yorkshire and had easy access to the countryside. Thomas Gissing, his father, was an amateur botanist and wrote two books on the flora surrounding Wakefield (Selig 121n.1). Yet, Gissing instinctively turns to the city for the majority of his settings, knowing that there the battle for existence will be fought. Social Darwinist terminology and imagery permeate his fiction and reveal that the struggle for existence is not between humans and nature but now largely between humans. The natural world, for the most part tamed, shows its beauty along with its macro elements of rain, wind, snow, sleet, and storm.

Outside Africa and the Poles, there are few frontiers left. H. G. Wells writes of space and time travel, and Arthur Conan Doyle, H. Rider Haggard, and Jules Verne create unknown worlds. In England the Georgian Poets J. C. Squire and W. H. Davies and in America Robert Frost and Robinson Jeffers remind one that nature is still there. However, Gissing and other late-nineteenth-century writers often seem to avert their gaze from nature, caught up in the human dilemma and compelled to explore it beyond all else. Fiction in the twentieth century that looks back to an earlier time like in Willa Cather's American prairie novels, *O Pioneers!* (1913) and *My Antonia* (1918), might be the only way a modern sensibility can recapture nature. Gissing, writing into the early years of the twentieth century, appreciates nature but does not contemplate it with much hope that it will provide any answers. At best, it is a pleasant image, an enhancer of his former life in Devon and other venues.

19

The Late-Victorian Detective

In 1887, Sir Arthur Conan Doyle published his first Sherlock Holmes story, *A Study in Scarlet*. With this novel, Doyle continued the tradition begun forty-six years earlier with Edgar Allan Poe's "The Murders in the Rue Morgue" (1841). Although Dr. John Watson reports in *A Study in Scarlet* that Holmes thought little of the methods of Poe's detective, C. Auguste Dupin (24), Holmes continues the focus on the detective's reasoning powers as the principal way to solve cases. Five years later in *Denzil Quarrier*, George Gissing begins to use private inquiry agents or private detectives as a means of finding out crucial information needed for the development of his plots. Two other novels, *The Odd Women* and, especially, *The Town Traveller*, continue this practice. The latter novel employs Greenacre, the private detective, as a significant factor in the conclusion of the plot. Other Gissing novels in the 1890s and on into the early twentieth century use certain characters as ad hoc detectives, e.g., Buckland Warricombe in *Born in Exile* and Maurice Hilliard in *Eve's Ransom*, that parallel the private detectives in the above-mentioned novels.

Corresponding to the New Woman *fin-de-siècle* feminist movement, *Denzil Quarrier*, *The Odd Women*, and *The Town Traveller* focus for the most part on marital situations and, with the exception of *The Town Traveller*, show men investigating women. Thus, Gissing reflects, in part, the unease men felt toward the increasing assertion of female independence and the need for professional help in discovering their actions and intentions as well as a broader social discontinuity that allows the contravention of social practices, particularly with regard to marriage.

197

Gissing's first use of a private detective arises from the desire of Eustace Glazzard in *Denzil Quarrier* to expose the Quarriers' pretended marriage. In the novel, the inexperienced Lilian Allen marries Arthur James Northway when she is seventeen years of age. On the day of the ceremony, Northway's cast-off mistress informs the police that he is a forger, and they arrest him. He and Lilian never see one another again until Eustace has detectives track him down to confront her. In telling Glazzard of Lilian's past, Quarrier remarks, "'She understood that Northway was really nothing to her'" (109). They are two individuals who only relate through the social and legal contract of marriage. When Lilian meets Denzil Quarrier and they fall in love, her former marriage becomes a minor obstacle to their union. Quarrier, an independently wealthy writer, has no overbearing family connections either; they only become important when he decides to return to Polterham and stand for Parliament. Lilian is a governess and former teacher and otherwise independent, Northway's absence being total and leaving her to rely for survival on her inheritance of £100 per annum and her ability to work. As one can see, the institution of marriage is not a controlling one for either Lilian or Quarrier. Their solution to her former marriage is, ironically, not to hire a detective, track down Northway, and have Lilian divorce him but rather to go to Paris and there pretend to marry. The distance between London and Paris is not great, but the difference in the languages, cultures, and dominant religions is sufficient to make any effort to trace their activities in Paris not an obvious consideration. England is where the complication originates, and England is where the protagonists play out the tragic events.

Trouble comes to Denzil and Lilian Quarrier when he not only reveals their secret to Eustace Glazzard but also to Mrs. Wade only to be betrayed by both. Glazzard is a longtime friend of Quarrier who has secret political ambitions of his own. When Quarrier speaks first of standing as a candidate, he cannot decide on whether to run as a Radical-Liberal or Conservative. Glazzard is jealous of Quarrier's position in the world and feels his candidacy as an additional goad. As another spur to act against Quarrier, the latter laughs when Glazzard suggests that he run for Parliament instead of his friend (*Denzil Quarrier* 114). When Quarrier explains that he and Lilian are not married but plan to go to Paris and pretend to marry and that her husband is still alive, Glazzard sees a chance to destroy Quarrier's reputation with the Polterham electorate. He hires Tulks and Crowe, a detective agency, to find Northway. When they do, they confirm Quarrier's revelations about Lilian's marriage. More than three weeks after he hires the firm Glazzard hears from them. The letter has the businesslike tone of a solicitor. Gissing writes, "Long before this he had grown careless whether they succeeded or not. An impulse of curiosity; nothing more" (203). Glazzard's reaction reveals the weakness of his character, a weakness tinged with malice. He knows that these secrets, a means "to get power into his hands" (203), are dangerous but proceeds anyway in contacting Northway, now living in Bristol.

Secrets held and disclosed are not unknown plot elements, but the use of a detective in their discovery in 1892 is a fairly recent phenomenon. The February 13, 1892, *Chicago Tribune* review of *Denzil Quarrier*, interestingly, refers not to the business like Tulks and Crowe but rather to "Nemesis" and the "Detective Bureau of Olympus" (Coustillas and Partridge 189). However, a post–Holmesian novelist could easily turn to a professional solution. Gissing was aware of and knew most English novelists during his career from 1880 to 1903. H. G. Wells was a special friend of his, and he admired his science fiction. He also knew Sir Arthur Conan Doyle and E. M. Hornung, the creator of A. J. Raffles, first appearing in *The Amateur Cracksman* (1899). In contrast to Glazzard's use of detectives to betray the Quarriers, Mrs. Wade needs nothing more than jealousy to motivate her. After Quarrier confides his and Lilian's circumstances in order for her more easily to help the despondent Lilian, Mrs. Wade persuades Lilian that by committing suicide she would best help her husband and thus remove any impediment to his political career. Mrs. Wade stands and watches while Lilian walks into a pond and drowns herself.

All three of Gissing's uses of detectives involve marital situations. However, none of them reflects an identical set of circumstances, and though no protagonist hires a detective, Edmund Widdowson in *The Odd Women* is married to one of the principal characters. His pursuit of his wife Monica and his hiring a detective to find out if she is having an affair with Everard Barfoot mysteriously lead to her death following childbirth. Widdowson suspects but never knows whether the child is his or Barfoot's. Unlike in the case of the Quarriers, Widdowson and Monica's mismatched marriage results in her demise. Published one year after *Denzil Quarrier*, *The Odd Women* provides an equally fertile plot for an unhappy denouement. None of Gissing's three uses of detectives starts with a murder, but they do involve death, even in the case of the unfortunate Mark Clover–Lord Polperro in *The Town Traveller*. The Widdowson marriage is a clash of wills between the male who attempts to dominate and the female who passively sets her will against his. A growing antipathy on Monica's part and a rigidity on Widdowson's prevent them from living peacefully together. Since his ideal union is one in which they largely isolate themselves from the world, every move of hers to attain some sense of independence sparks a jealous resistance on his part. At one point, Widdowson tells her, "'I want to keep you all to myself'" (190). Weakly incapable of discovering what she does and where she goes when she leaves home and unable to fathom that she just desires to be free for a while, Widdowson, as Maria Teresa Chialant states, "vicariously controls Monica by

setting a private detective on to her" ("Feminization of the City" 64). John
Goode argues that Widdowson is as flawed as his wife:

> He too is reduced to stealth, having to maintain his tyranny by using a
> detective, that is by exploiting the impersonality of London which makes it
> possible to set up what is explicitly, in a telling analogy, termed an "ambush"
> [*Ideology* 154].

Although Gissing's aim in *The Odd Women* is not to write a detective story,
he seems singularly inept in employing that character type. With Poe's creation of Dupin, Conan Doyle's Holmes, Charles Dickens' Development of
Inspector Bucket in *Bleak House* and Wilkie Collins' Sgt. Cuff in *The Moonstone* (1868), along with the fictive detectives of numerous minor novelists,
many writers were eager to explore the possibilities in the detective fiction
genre. In *The Odd Women*, Widdowson's detective apparently disguises himself as a mechanic and follows Monica into the building in which Barfoot
inhabits the flat below Bevis's, Monica's putative lover. Robert L. Selig states,
"Widdowson suspects the wrong man, Barfoot, and hires a detective to trail
Monica, but, by knocking at the wrong door, she deliberately misleads him"
(*George Gissing* 63). In fact, she does not wish to be observed knocking at
Bevis's door, so she stops at Barfoot's when she hears the "mechanic" come up
behind her and continue upstairs. Monica knows that Barfoot is out of town
and so feels relatively confident that no one will be in his flat. She leaves the
building, stops at a shop and has tea. When she returns to the building, the
mechanic waits outside and fails to discover an important difference between
the two visits. Gissing observes, "Acting on very suggestive instructions, it
never occurred to the worthy man that the lady's second visit was not to the
same flat as in the former instance" (284). Since Widdowson suspects Barfoot
as Monica's lover, the "suggestive instructions" apparently allude to her possible relationship with him and thus distort the information Widdowson ultimately receives. He violently castigates Monica when she returns home, and
she subsequently abandons him (285–88). Gissing leaves the dilemma ambiguous, as well, with Monica pregnant and in despair, Widdowson rigidly certain
of what he knows, and Barfoot protesting his innocence. Bevis, much to his
relief, is never suspected as Monica's lover and Widdowson's real rival. The
detective's entrance into the lovers' triangle provides no more accurate knowledge as to the real state of affairs than do the principal characters.

Edgar Allan Poe and Sir Arthur Conan Doyle introduce their detectives
at the very beginning of their tales, focusing the reader on the central protagonist whose profession gives rise to the various works. In addition, these
two archetypal figures in the nineteenth-century detective story often use the
police as clients. Poe and Doyle accomplish several things with this plot device.
First, they quickly bring to the fore the underlying conflict between the pri-

vate and public detectives, a conflict that resonates to the present. However, the sense of superiority that Dupin and Holmes feel and demonstrate regarding the sometimes bumbling but generally competent official detectives is not a path that many twentieth-century hard-boiled detective writers allow their private detectives to follow. True, some private detectives show that they are more intelligent and more clever than the police, and some police bring puzzling cases to their acknowledged superiors, witness Agatha Christie's Hercule Poirot and Detective Chief Inspector Zapp's relationship in the early twentieth century. However, the private investigator and the police detective relapse in the twentieth century into an uneasy alliance in which the private citizen resists and/or thwarts the bureaucrat in order to serve his or her client. By coming to Dupin or Holmes, the police share elements of their work usually held back from the public. When this for the most part changes in the twentieth century, suspicion on both sides becomes the norm even when the private detective establishes a friendship with a police detective. Bill Pronzini's Nameless and San Francisco Police Department's Lt. Eberhardt are good examples of this uneasy connection.

Gissing employs Greenacre in *The Town Traveller* in a way that simultaneously uses and rejects some of these nineteenth-century features. First, Greenacre is not a major character in the novel, but he is crucial to solving the puzzle of the missing Mark Clover and revealing his startling past. While it is possible that the man Mr. Gammon, the town traveller, sees is Greenacre on the night early in the novel as he leaves Mrs. Louisa Clover's home, it turns out to be the missing Mark Clover himself who is in fact Lord Polperro. Greenacre's mysterious comings and goings, his refusal to tell Mr. Gammon where he lives, and his sudden appearance as the representative of Mark Clover–Lord Polperro in his dealings with his "supposed" wife unnecessarily complicate the plot and make it difficult to untangle the various threads of the story. A review of the novel in the September 2, 1898, *Pall Mall Gazette* notes, "Suspicion of blackmail attaches to him" (Coustillas and Partridge 339). The *Morning Post*, September 8, 1898, review refers to "the queer hobby of the impecunious Greenacre" (Coustillas and Partridge 342). The New York *Critic* review in December 1898 alludes to "the mysterious Greenacre" (Coustillas and Partridge 345). Gissing's inexperience in writing detective fiction leads to some of the awkward aspects of the novel. A good example is Greenacre's interest in genealogy (the "queer hobby" above) that is referred to on several instances but never displayed in any detail or effectively integrated into the story. Gissing rejects using the police in any form but does show Greenacre's feelings of superiority toward Polly Sparkes, who first discovers the missing Mark Clover, and Mr. Gammon, who traces the older woman, first seen by Polly with Clover at the theater where she works, to her daughter-in-law's home. They turn out to be sister and niece to Clover–Polperro. After Mr. Gammon tells Polly's and his stories to Greenacre, the latter connects Clover to Lord Polperro, and Mr. Gammon works out the subsequent reconciliation between Clover and his "wife" Louisa. Of course, Clover's title, revealed to Polly and Mr. Gammon, and Clover's bigamous marriage to Louisa, discovered by Greenacre but revealed to her by Mr. Gammon (*The Town Traveller* 274), are additional complications. In sum, the various strands of the plot jostle uncomfortably with one another in a novel unlike most of Gissing's other fiction, both in the use of a detective and the comic tone that often leads to unexpected exuberance. Mr. Gammon's surrealistic night adventures with Clover–Polperro as they wait for Greenacre to return from Ireland with news as to whether his first wife is still alive and their desperate attempt to track down Cuthbertson, Lord Polperro's lawyer, in order to change his will are examples of this energy. Gissing's novels in the 1890s largely focus on the middle class, but *The Town Traveller* juxtaposes and interrelates the working class, the lower-middle class, and the minor aristocracy. Lord Polperro's desire for a "humbler station" (269), and Mr. Gammon's interactions with all three classes hold the novel together.

Gissing seems hardly aware that he uses private detectives in his fiction, and, except for Greenacre, gives none of them a prominent role. In *The Private Life of Henry Maitland* (1912), a biographical novel based on Gissing's life, Morley Roberts states that the Owens College "authorities set a detective" to catch the thief who was stealing from the students (31). Gissing was the thief and spent a month in prison. One would think, incorrectly as it turns out, that this experience would give him an acute awareness of detectives. But with Doyle and other writers, mystery and detective fiction are prominent features in late nineteenth-century fiction. Part of this stems from the prominence of crime in more traditional fiction, especially in Gissing's work. (See Chapter 3.) Some authors, such as Wilkie Collins in *The Woman in White* (1860), blur the distinction between mystery and detective fiction and novels of manners and morals, a pattern that continues to the present. It is in this border area that Gissing could have more effectively explored the use of the private detective.

20

Frontiers, Edges, and Boundaries

George Gissing frequently depicts characters divided emotionally and intellectually. Being in one place and imagining another more desirable, wanting one thing and somehow missing one's aim, starting one path in life and turning to another — these are just some of the separations of self that Gissing explores. These inner conflicts underscore the characters' humanity and tie them to those they might wish to avoid or escape. Gissing's early novels deal with the poor and their seemingly eternal and ineradicable problems, but the personal element marks his work regardless of the social and cultural dimensions and emphasizes the crucial importance of his characters' individual strivings and their often deflected aims. For example, Bernard Kingcote in *Isabel Clarendon* struggles to separate Isabel from her friends and social acquaintances. The stages of her initial possession of wealth (to Kingcote's understanding), its temporary loss, and its final re-possession through the agency of Ada Warren, her ward, do not sufficiently engage Kingcote to tempt him to accommodate his feelings to her situation. Kingcote's rejection of the idea of their marriage appears unconnected to any deep set of principles. Rather, he relapses into a despondent acceptance of his lot and disappears into the wilds of Norfolk. In *Thyrza*, Walter Egremont, Thyrza Trent, and Gilbert Grail form a triangle that suggests the limits and gulfs implied in this chapter's title. *Born in Exile* captures these same concepts in the relationship between Godwin Peak and Marcella Moxey, the woman who leaves him a surprise legacy. The fruitful themes of frontiers, edges, and boundaries reveal Gissing's imaginative grasp of the social dynamics of his culture's layered personal and communal complexities.

Certain of these themes' opposing ideas, e.g., success and failure, hope and disappointment, suggest, paradoxically, a quality of overlapping that is more image than substance. Thus, the barriers and gulfs in Gissing's novels become reinforced rather than mitigated as his realistic social and psychological probings work themselves out in his fiction. *Thyrza* demonstrates important aspects of overlapping and the dire consequences that can flow from them. Since many philanthropic efforts were underway in the late nineteenth century, it is not inevitable that the likes of Walter Egremont, Gilbert Grail, and Thyrza Trent meet. Egremont wishes to help raise the cultural level of the working classes. He comes to the East End of London, gives lectures, and opens a library with the candlemaker Grail in charge. But, Gissing moves away from types to individuals in delineating the passions and hopes of these characters. Grail is supremely happy to be in charge of a library. A man who, under narrow circumstances, still reads widely, he feels liberated by the chance. He loves Thyrza and proposes marriage to her. She accepts but subsequently falls in love with Egremont who has helped her to a singing career. Whatever distance initially separates these two characters from Egremont, they unconsciously reach across it. Yet, Egremont ultimately pulls back from Grail and Thyrza. Mrs. Ormonde, with whom Thyrza goes to live as she pursues her career, suggests a two-year trial separation when she learns that Egremont and Thyrza love one another. During this time, Egremont's passion for Thyrza cools. Somewhat melodramatically, Thyrza falls ill and dies, presumably of a broken heart. Although Egremont and Grail are estranged, he continues to support the library with Grail as its head. Rather than a reaching across class lines as equals, Gissing appears to argue that the gap between them is too wide and that what is covered over by the overlapping is more important than the unsubstantial surface.

The contrasting pictures in *Thyrza* of the working- class and middle-class characters suggest part of the difficulty in these characters' abilities to make connections. However, *Demos*, published only the year before, in part breaks down the class divisions. Adela Waltham, the bridge between the working class and the middle-class with her marriage to Richard Mutimer, ultimately comes to despise him and returns to Hubert Eldon after Mutimer's death. Gissing attempts to balance the middle class portraits with those of the working class but except for Richard, who becomes economically middle class when he inherits his great-uncle's estate, and Emma Vine, the working-class characters do not function at the same level of complexity. Mrs. Mutimer, Richard's mother, and Hubert symbolize class divisions as states of nature, a position that Gissing, while deploring the effects of poverty, often seems to support. John Goode links Adela, Emma, and Mrs. Mutimer in the sense of oppression that each endures, the latter two more lastingly:

What is important about *Demos* in the development of Gissing is something
that is continued and extended from *A Life's Morning,* the foreshortened
awakening of the oppressed woman, Adela, into the trammels of social actu-
ality. It is extended importantly because Adela's sense of oppression is linked
with the oppression of the working-class girl Emma Vine, and the
spokesman for both is, as it were, the mother of the oppressor, Mrs.
Mutimer [*Ideology* 89].

For some characters, reclamation or recovery occurs, as if a bridge suddenly provides a successful crossing point. Of course, much happens in their
lives before they see the way to another, happier life. Miriam Baske in *The
Emancipated* crosses this bridge from her sterile life in the English Midlands
to her eventual liberation in Italy. The Victorian novel is replete with the grim
picture of the industrial heart of England, especially in novels of Dickens,
Mrs. Gaskell, and Benjamin Disraeli. The flight by Little Nell and her grandfather through the burning waste lands in *The Old Curiosity Shop* or the dominant image of Coketown in *Hard Times* with Josiah Bounderby as the
capitalist bully who lauds the very smoke as healthy exemplifies the dangers
of this environment. If one adds Thomas Gradgrind and his reverence for facts
as opposed to fancy or the imagination, one can understand Gissing's instinctive realization that the opening up of a human mind to the world's possibilities could not easily happen in the mill towns.

Of course, it does not always happen even in Italy. Reuben Elgar,
Miriam's brother, and Cecily Doran, Ross Mallard's ward, fall in love and
elope. Full of energy and plans, they marry, but regardless of their appreciation of art and literature, Reuben's weak character is not equal to their hopes.
Everything seems to beckon them to a bright future, but neither youth nor
love can counter the downward pull of Reuben's nature. In her chapter on
Reuben Elgar and Lionel Tarrant (*In the Year of Jubilee*) in *Masculine Identity
in Hardy and Gissing,* Annette Federico widens the focus on male weakness:

> It is a paradox of sexual stereotyping in Victorian Society that women are
> imaged as indecisive, fickle, and contradictory, though the men who have
> created that image display the very faults they project on the social-sexual
> Other [29].

From another viewpoint, one possible model for Reuben's behavior is Richard
Carstone's inability to withstand the lure of the Jarndyce case in Dickens' *Bleak
House.* As David Grylls observes:

> Reuben Elgar [in contrast to Miriam and Ross], is both unwholesome and
> pretending; but what makes him most inadequate is his failure in work and
> duties. Elgar is presented as a man of talent who fatally — and fatalistically —
> lacks will power. The reasons for his failure feed into the theme of genuine
> and spurious emancipation [*Paradox* 10].

Miriam and Cecily, after her recovery from her relationship with Reuben, represent the former theme and Reuben the latter. In *The Emancipated*, Gissing underscores the idea that nothing is guaranteed, that crossing into a happier, more hopeful existence requires work and effort that still might not meet with success. Gissing's later novels will emphasize this point time and time again. Further, some characters achieve a better life and find a bridge over difficulties without talent or ability, clarifying even more Grylls' statement about the talented Ross Mallard, that the words of his self-written epitaph "epitomize perfectly the paradox of pessimism and will" (12).

The desire to dominate can be an unsettling element in a love affair, but sometimes the effects of this emotion can lead to sustainable relationships. Characters recover a sense of balance in their lives either by abandoning the attempt to dominate another or by finding a more pliable target. In *The Odd Women*, Rhoda Nunn rejects Everard Barfoot and returns to her career; he equally shifts his marital intentions to the more traditional Agnes Brissenden. Since both Polly Sparkes and Mr. Gammon in *The Town Traveller* want to dominate one another, they also part and look for more suitable mates. Polly finds the clerk Christopher Parrish to control, and Mr. Gammon comes to an understanding with Mrs. Louisa Clover that suits both. In addition, London has the anomalous Mark Clover, aka Lord Polperro, who attempts to live in two or more worlds and survives in none. He returns sick and dying to his supposed wife Louisa, thinking or hoping that his previous wife was dead when he married Louisa. This is not his first return to her, but his failure to find any balance in life arises from his character and not the environment. (See Chapter 14.)

Gissing's fiction reveals instances of overlapping ideas, events, and actions while also demonstrating reclamations or recoveries from separations or barriers that bridge gulfs opening between individuals or groups. However, Gissing explores other manifestations that disclose more negative experiences. People plunge into abysses of various types, within themselves or between themselves and others that either widen slowly or dramatically. *The Unclassed* offers examples that do not allow any escape from the crisis. No one suffering such a fall climbs back from the depths. Julian Casti, trapped as he feels, into marriage with Harriet Smales, sees his fall but cannot affect the course of it. He is as bewildered as Harriet who suffers from some sort of dementia that admits no positive interference or alleviation. Osmond Waymark, his friend and fellow teacher and writer, cannot help him even though he knows the danger his poet-friend faces. Nature offers parallels to Harriet's actions in deadly snakes, encircling vines, and quicksand. Casti loses heart and eventually dies from Harriet's fatal embrace. Jacob Korg writes, "If the feelings Julian Casti expresses in *The Unclassed* can be attributed to the young Gissing, what he responded to in Roman history were its episodes of heroism" ("Gissing and Ancient Rome" 225). Unfortunately, Casti cannot live up to these heroic images. In the same novel, Slimy takes no one with him as he plunges over the edge through drink and ends his life. Collecting rents for Abraham Woodstock, Ida's estranged grandfather, Waymark goes to Slimy's hovel where the latter attacks him and steals the money Waymark has received. Slimy leaves Waymark tied up and dies in an orgy of drink, an orgy that he predicts will occur. Those left behind, even by the behavior of a Slimy, know an experience both severe and unexpected. Waymark is the unasked-for witness to the suffering of this repulsive human being. (See Chapter 4.)

For different reasons, neither Casti nor Slimy feel he has any choice in the matter. Both know, however, that what they do leads to a closing down of hope and the ability to go on living. Whether it be someone or some thing, internal or external in origin, they not only die but also disappear into death, the hopeless foreknowledge of which leaves those behind stunned. Slimy does not function at Casti's intellectual level, but he shares the sense of an unavoidable ending. Gissing has explored this nightmarish mental state from his first novel. Often characters who experience this condition are minor yet still observed and therefore preserved in different ways. In *Workers in the Dawn*, Samuel Tollady has two friends he tries to help, even to rescue, but fails. John Pether and Mark Challenger fight against life but know its pressing, unchangeable nature. They are more sketches than fully realized characters. Andrew Whitehead observes of them, "They are portrayed as a sinister pair, whose radicalism is based not on intellectual persuasion but on their personal miseries and misfortunes" ("'Against the Tyranny'" 21). John Hewett in *The Nether World* is the more extensively drawn portrait of this type, one of uncontrollable anger and rage. (See Chapter 4.) Sidney Kirkwood and the young Jane Snowdon helplessly watch the disintegration of the Hewett family, mirroring the greater suffering of Hewett, his wife, and his two grown children, Clara and Bob. Because of his inability to control his passions, Hewett cannot help himself or his family. In contrast, Mrs. Peckover and her daughter Clem, primarily due to their treatment of Jane Snowdon, live in the abyss. Their moral failure comes from their natures and not from outer circumstances. They are not poor, in fact, Mrs. Peckover owns her own home and rents to the Hewletts. Clem is, as it were, in training to be another Mrs. Peckover and her mother encourages in her harshness toward Jane and self indulgence.

What of those on the farther side of divisions, gulfs, or abysses? As noted earlier, *Thyrza*, Thyrza Trent escapes her background with none too happy results. Neither she nor Walter Egremont, who initially helps her and who loves her, is able to act independently regarding their relationship. In one of Gissing's novels of misunderstandings and missed opportunities, they drift away from one another. One thinks that Thyrza would have been happier in marrying Gilbert Grail. For Egremont, he appears headed for a loveless marriage with Annabel Newthorpe. He crosses back over the class divide but finds no happiness on either side. Of course, not all who reach a farther shore wind up unhappily. Will Warburton's seemingly disastrous move behind the counter in the 1905 novel of that name frees him from the mistaken assumption that Rosamund Elvan is worthy of his love, but his courage and hard work gain the admiration of Bertha Cross, a woman of a more solid character than Rosamund. A possibly too idealized figure, Bertha loves Warburton for who he is and not his class position. (See Chapter 4.) Irene Derwent in *The Crown of Life* is an earlier figure who similarly decides to follow her own wishes when she breaks her engagement to the surprised and angry Arnold Jacks and marries Piers Otway. Bertha and Irene are women who put personal desires above social or class distinctions. It is not what others think but what they themselves think that matters.

It is possible that someone like Irene Derwent might go against both social and class expectations to marry the man she loves. But, how probable is it in any socially or psychologically realistic novel? After all, Piers Otway is both illegitimate and saddled with a set of disreputable brothers. Writing of Piers, Robert L. Selig states, "The novel's portrayal of romantic love seems less an 'ideal' than a sexual daydream" (*George Gissing* 89). However, this applies equally to Irene once she realizes her love for Piers, former complications notwithstanding. Initially, Piers has not the means to marry. Gissing solves this problem by having Piers serve his apprenticeship as a lover and prospective husband by going into international business and also becoming a writer. Piers acquires a greater degree of culture and personal assurance than heretofore, and Irene now finds him not only worthy of her but also an object of desire. Miriam Baske in *The Emancipated* raises similar questions as to the probability of her conversion from her rigid chapel-going faith to what appears as an aesthetic-based appreciation of art and life. Does she remain a Christian? If so, is her former ardor attenuated to that of a modern-day Unitarian? Gissing obscures these questions in the crisis that precedes her falling in love with Ross Mallard. Miriam has come to Italy to recover her health. She has not cut her ties to her past and intends to build a chapel for her religious sect. Of course, the reader understands that it is her religious practice that has effaced her own personality and desires and only its rejection, wholly or in part, leads to her recovery. However much she initially resists Mallard and his ideas, Miriam unconsciously knows that she must accept a new worldview.

Thyrza Trent fails, Will Warburton succeeds, both Irene Derwent and Piers Otway succeed, and Miriam Baske at least partially converts to a new belief system and finds love and happiness. With four other characters, Gissing employs a variation of the farther shore as possibility. Sidwell Warricombe in *Born in Exile* and Rhoda Nunn in *The Odd Women* pull back from the brink while Adela Waltham in *Demos* and Walter Egremont in *Thyrza* go back to their former side and condition. The first pair experience some of what another life would be like with Godwin Peak and Everard Barfoot, respectively. They have emotionally crossed over, but examining their potential mates and their former lives and conditions, they cross back, choosing the known for the unknown. Their present lives have purpose and meaning and the unknown cannot, ultimately, compete. As for Adela, she was unhappy with her choice long before Mutimer's death, but the event liberates her, and she willingly embraces her old life, station, and lover. Egremont projects the image of someone who has no meaningful role left in life. His rejection of Thyrza is an indication that henceforth his life would have less passion or purpose, symbolized by his projected marriage to Annabel Newthorpe who exudes a feeling close to indifference toward him. In contrast, Everard Barfoot's marriage to Agnes Brissenden seems a positively healthy development, emotionally and socially. Willingly joining as class equals, they seem pleased with their choices.

These three interlinked themes, i.e., frontiers, edges, and boundaries, similar but also distinct, reveal, through Gissing's imaginative force, the mixture of personal and fictional elements that are a hallmark of his work. Of course, Gissing is not alone in this, but from his first novel, *Workers in the Dawn*, anyone familiar with his life finds many poignant reminders of his experiences, hopes, and regrets. Gissing lived on the periphery of his world and could discover no easy way to move to its center. Yet, one must recognize the fact of his accomplishments and realize the creative power it took to produce them. From those emotional, psychological, and physical impediments to a happier life, he could observe himself and his society and explore both with little interference to his art. The lack of money disturbed him, but he was, paradoxically, free to focus his talents on whatever subject interested him. His work is more than an extended autobiography and even in *The Private Papers of Henry Ryecroft*, Ryecroft separates himself from the author and becomes a character in his own right. One sees this most powerfully in *New Grub Street* as Gissing works out the details of Edwin and Amy Reardon's failed marriage. While their relationship was never Gissing's, except in the element of failure in his two marriages, Reardon portrays some of Gissing's anxieties and fears as a writer. In addition, his life represents some of the barriers and limits with which Gissing, and through him many other characters, have to contend.

21

Conclusion

The previous chapters reflect George Gissing's focus on the external world and his narrative needs. He best understood and explored the world around him through fiction. Little more than twenty years of age when he returned from America in 1877, Gissing knew something of the hard side of life. He began writing about the London poor in *Workers in the Dawn* and *Demos*, but as early as *The Unclassed*, he expands his focus to the lower-middle class and middle class as well as the world of art and literature. Even *Workers in the Dawn*, with Arthur Golding and Gilbert Gresham as artists and Samuel Tollady and Helen Norman interested in books and ideas, lifts Gissing's vision from the intractable problems of the poor to a wider vision of society and culture. In *Isabel Clarendon*, *Thyrza*, and *A Life's Morning*, one can see Gissing's imaginative engagement with a wider cast of characters and new narrative possibilities. *The Nether World* demonstrates Gissing at his most pessimistic view of social and cultural prospects. Nothing can lift the characters out of the life they endure, neither money nor education. However, *The Emancipated* does just that with a leavening of art and culture, represented initially by Ross Mallard and Italy itself. In the same novel, Gissing balances Miriam Baske against her brother Reuben Elgar. While Miriam grows and changes, Elgar turns inward, declines, and eventually dies, leaving behind his wife Cecily Doran who successfully copes with life's demands.

With *The Emancipated*, Gissing never looks back to the themes of the struggling poor. He has other narrative interests such as those reflected in *New Grub Street*, *Born in Exile*, and *The Odd Women*. Even when he writes predominantly about the working class in *The Town Traveller*, his characters seem almost unrecognizable as coming from the lower class. Their level of energy is greater than most of the lower-class characters in *Workers in the Dawn* or

The Nether World. Gissing traveled during the 1890s, married again and had children, and met other writers, but the change in his novels comes through an intensification of his artistic development. His imaginative exploration of his culture achieves a breadth and depth hard to explain. *The Whirlpool, The Crown of Life, Our Friend the Charlatan,* and the elegiac *The Private Papers of Henry Ryecroft* reveal a sustained level of creativity and craft that in their variety, enhances one's lived feel of his world. What Gissing's novels show is that while his imagination creates these works, the reader must engage as well in order to open up his long-gone world.

One way to understand the function of the imagination in Gissing's creative work is to contrast his letters, diary, and notebooks with his novels and short stories. In the former, one sees the man living and struggling with his life and those with whom he intimately relates. One can say that these are not the forums for the exercise of the imagination. When one turns to his fiction, the power of the imagination, with some exceptions, consistently manifests itself. Whatever Gissing lived of what Reardon and Whelpdale experience in *New Grub Street* or Ryecroft reflects back on in *The Private Papers of Henry Ryecroft* transforms itself in the telling. It is not just the compelling stories one reads but rather the crafted and compelling stories. And, the degree to which the imagination operates is the mark of the writer's craft. With his many novels and short stories, Gissing wrote an enormous body of work from 1880 to his death in 1903, and it is the relatively short time period coupled with the quality of his work, almost all set in the modern world, that makes possible a twenty-first-century reader's comprehension of his culture. Nothing is guaranteed in life, but Gissing sets the late-Victorian culture before his readers and offers them an opportunity, through his imagination, to see, feel, and recover it, however partially.

Bibliography

Abrams, M.H., and Stephen Greenblatt, eds. *The Norton Anthology of English Literature*. 7th ed. Vol. 2. New York and London: Norton, 2000.

Allen, Walter. *The English Novel: A Short Critical History*. New York: Dutton, 1954.

Beckson, Karl. *London in the 1890s: A Cultural History*. New York and London: Norton, 1992.

Bergonzi, Bernard. *The Turn of a Century*. New York: Barnes & Noble, 1973.

Bishop, Morchard, ed. Introduction. *The Private Life of Henry Maitland: A Portrait of George Gissing*. 3rd ed. London: Richards Press, 1958. 1–18.

Bloom, Harold. *The Western Canon: The Books and School of the Ages*. New York and London: Harcourt Brace, 1994.

Bowlby, Rachel. *Just Looking: Consumer Culture in Dreiser, Gissing and Zola*. New York and London: Methuen, 1985.

Bradbury, Malcolm. *The Social Context of Modern English Literature*. Oxford: Blackwell, 1971.

Briggs, Asa. *Victorian Cities*. 1963, 1968. London: Penguin, 1990.

_____. *Victorian People: A Reassessment of Persons and Themes: 1851–1857*. Harmondsworth, England: Penguin, 1954, 1955, 1965.

Caird, Mona. "The Emancipation of the Family." In *The Morality of Marriage and Other Essays on the Status and Destiny of Woman*. London: George Redway, 1897. 21–59.

Calder, Jenni. *Women and Marriage in Victorian Fiction*. London: Thames and Hudson, 1976.

Carey, John. *The Intellectuals and the Masses: Pride and Prejudice among the Literary Intelligentsia: 1880–1939*. London and Boston: Faber, 1992.

Carlyle, Thomas. *Sartor Resartus & Selected Prose*. Intro. Herbert Sussman. New York and London: Holt, Rinehart, 1970.

Chialant, Maria Teresa. "The Feminization of the City in Gissing's Fiction: The Streetwalker, the *Flâneuse*, the Shopgirl." In *A Garland for Gissing*. Ed. Bouwe Postmus. Amsterdam and London: Rodopi, 2001. 51–65.

Coleridge, Samuel Taylor. From *Biographia Literaria*. Richter,1998.321–32.

Collie, Michael. *The Alien Art: A Critical Study of George Gissing's Novels*. Folkestone, England: Dawson, 1978, 1979; Hamden, CT: Archon, 1978, 1979.

213

_____. *George Gissing: A Biography*. Folkestone, England: Dawson; Hamden, CT: Archon, 1977.

Collins, Wilkie. *The Moonstone*. 1868. Intro. Frederick R. Karl. New York and London: Signet-Penguin, 1984.

Conan Doyle, Sir Arthur. *A Study in Scarlet*. 1887. *The Complete Sherlock Holmes*. Pref. Christopher Morley. New York and London: Doubleday, 1930. 15–86.

Cope, Jackson I. "Definition as Structure in Gissing's *Ryecroft Papers*." *Modern Fiction Studies* 3(1957): 127- 40.

Coustillas, Pierre. "Gissing the European." In *A Garland for Gissing*. Ed. Bouwe Postmus. Amsterdam and New York: Rodopi, 2001. 1–10.

_____. "Gissing's Feminine Portraiture." In *English Literature in Transition* 6.3 (1963). Rpt. *George Gissing: Critical Essays*. Ed. Jean-Pierre Michaux. London: Vision, 1981; Totowa, NJ: Barnes, 1981. 91–107.

_____, ed. Introduction. *Isabel Clarendon*. By George Gissing. 1886. 2 vols. The Harvester Press Society & the Victorians. Gen. Eds. John Spiers and Cecil Ballantine. Brighton, England: Harvester, 1969. xv-lx.

_____, ed. Introduction. *A Life's Morning*. By George Gissing. 1888. Brighton, England: Harvester, 1984. xi-xxix.

_____, and Colin Partridge, eds. *Gissing: The Critical Heritage*. The Critical Heritage Series. Gen. ed. B.C. Southam. London: Routledge, 1972.

Cross, Nigel. *The Common Writer: Life in Nineteenth-Century Grub Street*. New York: Columbia University Press, 1985.

Davis, Oswald H. *George Gissing: A Study in Literary Leanings*. Intro. Pierre Coustillas. Dorking, England: Kohler and Coombes, 1974.

Dickens, Charles. *American Notes*. 1842. Intro. Christopher Lasch. Premier Americana. Gen. ed. Henry Steele Commager. Greenwich, CT: Premier Americana-Fawcett, 1961.

_____. *Bleak House*. 1853. Afterword Geoffrey Tillotson. New York: Signet-New American, 1964.

_____. *David Copperfield*. 1850. Afterword Edgar Johnson. New York: Signet — New American, 1962.

_____. *Hard Times: For These Times*. 1854. Afterword Charles Shapiro. New York and Scarborough, Canada: Signet-New American, 1961.

_____. *Nicholas Nickleby*. 1839. Intro. Edgar Johnson. Toronto and New York: Bantam, 1983.

_____. *The Old Curiosity Shop: A Tale*. 1841. Ed. and intro. Norman Page. London and New York: Penguin, 2000.

Donnelly, Mabel Collins. *George Gissing: Grave Comedian*. Cambridge: Harvard University Press, 1954.

Dowling, Andrew. *Manliness and the Male Novelist in Victorian Literature*. Aldershot, England and Burlington, VT: Ashgate, 2001.

Ettorre, Emanuela. "Sensational Gissing? *Denzil Quarrier* and the 'Politics' of Dissimulation." In *A Garland for Gissing*. Ed. Bouwe Postmus. Amsterdam and New York: Rodopi, 2001. 67–80.

Federico, Annette. *Masculine Identity in Hardy and Gissing*. Rutherford, NJ: Fairleigh Dickinson University Press; London and Toronto: Associated University Presses, 1991.

Fernando, Lloyd. "Gissing's Studies in 'Vulgarism': Aspects of His Anti-Feminism." *George Gissing: Critical Essays*. Ed. Jean-Pierre Michaux. London: Vision; Totowa, NJ: Barnes, 1981. 108–20.

Fletcher, Ian, ed. Introduction. *The Paying Guest*. By George Gissing. 1895. Brighton, England: Harvester, 1982. ix-xxxii.

Gissing, George. *Born in Exile*. 1892. Intro. Gillian Tindall. London: Hogarth, 1985.

_____. *Charles Dickens: A Critical Study*. 1898. London and Glasgow: Blackie & Son-Casket Library Edition, 1929.

_____. *Commonplace Book: A Manuscript in the Berg Collection of the New York Public Library*. Ed. and intro. Jacob Korg. New York: New York Public Library, 1962.

_____. *The Crown of Life*. New York: Frederick A. Stokes, 1899. Facsimile ed. Elibron Classics-Adamant Media. <http://www.elibron.com. [2003?]>.

_____. "The Day of Silence." In *The Day of Silence and Other Stories*. Ed. Pierre Coustillas. London: Dent; Rutland, VT: Tuttle, 1993. 14–24.

_____. *Demos: A Story of English Socialism*. 1886. Ed. and intro. Pierre Coustillas. Society & the Victorians. Gen. ed. John Spiers. Brighton, England: Harvester Press, 1982.

_____. *Denzil Quarrier: A Novel*. 1892. New York: AMS Press, 1969.

_____. *The Emancipated*. 1890. Intro. John Halperin. London: Hogarth, 1995.

_____. *Eve's Ransom*. 1895. New York: Dover, 1980.

_____. "The Hope of Pessimism." In *Essays and Fiction*. Ed. and intro. Pierre Coustillas. Baltimore and London: Johns Hopkins Press, 1970. 76–97.

_____. *In the Year of Jubilee*. 1894. Ed. Paul Delany. London: Everyman-Dent; Rutland, VT: Tuttle, 1994.

_____. *Isabel Clarendon*. 1886. Ed. and intro. Pierre Coustillas. 2 vols. The Harvester Press Society & the Victorians. Gen. Eds. John Spiers and Cecil Ballantine. Brighton, England: Harvester, 1969.

_____. *A Life's Morning*. 1888. Ed. and intro. Pierre Coustillas. Brighton: Harvester, 1984.

_____. "Lou and Liz." 1927. In *The Day of Silence and Other Stories*. Ed. Pierre Coustillas. London: Everyman-Dent; Rutland, VT: Tuttle, 1993. 1–13.

_____. *The Nether World*. 1889. Ed. and intro. Stephen Gill. Oxford and New York: World's Classics-Oxford University Press, 1992.

_____. *New Grub Street*. 1891. Ed. and intro. John Goode. Oxford and New York: World's Classics-Oxford University Press, 1993.

_____. *Notes on Social Democracy*. 1880. Intro. Jacob Korg. London: Enitharmon Press, 1968.

_____. *The Odd Women*. 1893. Intro. Elaine Showalter. London: Penguin, 1993.

_____. *Our Friend the Charlatan: A Novel*. 1901. New York: AMS Press, 1969.

_____. *The Paying Guest*. 1895. Ed. and intro. Ian Fletcher. Brighton, England: Harvester, 1982.

_____. *The Private Papers of Henry Ryecroft*. 1903. Foreword V.S. Pritchett. New York: Signet-New American Library, 1961.

_____. "The Sins of the Fathers." 1924. In *The Sins of the Fathers and Other Tales*. Chicago: Pascal Covici, 1924. 1–31.

_____. *Sleeping Fires*. 1895. Lincoln: U of Nebraska P, 1983.

_____. *Thyrza: A Tale*. 1887. Ed. and intro. Jacob Korg. Brighton, England: Harvester, 1974.

_____. *The Town Traveller*. 1898. Ed. and intro. Pierre Coustillas. Brighton, England: Harvester, 1981.

_____. *The Unclassed*. 1884, 1895. Ed. and intro. Jacob Korg. Brighton, England: Harvester, 1976.

_____. *Veranilda: A Romance*. London: Archibald Constable, 1904.

_____. *The Whirlpool*. 1897. Intro. Gillian Tindall. London: Hogarth, 1984.

_____. *Will Warburton: A Romance of Real Life*. 1905. New York: AMS Press, 1969.

_____. *Workers in the Dawn*. 1880. Ed. and intro. Pierre Coustillas. 2 vols. Brighton, England: Harvester, 1985.

Goode, John. *George Gissing: Ideology and Fiction*. Barnes & Noble Critical Studies. Gen. ed. Anne Smith. New York: Barnes — Harper, 1978, 1979.

_____, ed. Introduction. *New Grub Street.* By George Gissing. 1891. Oxford and New York: World's Classics-Oxford University Press, 1993. vii–xxi.

Greenslade, William. "Writing against Himself: Gissing and the Lure of Modernity in *In the Year of Jubilee.*" In *A Garland for Gissing.* Ed. Bouwe Postmus. Amsterdam-New York: Rodopi, 2001. 271–77.

Grylls, David. *The Paradox of Gissing.* London: Allen & Unwin, 1986.

Guillaume, André. "The Jamesian Pattern in George Gissing's *New Grub Street.*" *Gissing Newsletter* 20.1 (1984): 28–33.

Halperin, John. *Gissing: A Life in Books.* 1982. Oxford: Oxford University Press, 1987.

Henkin, Leo. *Darwinism in the English Novel: 1860–1910. The Impact of Evolution on Victorian Fiction.* New York: Russell & Russell, 1963.

Ingham, Patricia. *The Language of Gender and Class: Transformation in the Victorian Novel.* London and New York: Routledge, 1996.

James, Simon. "Experiments in Realism: How to Read a George Gissing Novel." In *A Garland for Gissing.* Ed. Bouwe Postmus. Amsterdam-New York: Rodopi, 2001. 11–21.

James, Simon J. *Unsettled Accounts: Money and Narrative in the Novels of George Gissing.* London: Anthem, 2003.

Jameson, Fredric. *The Political Unconscious: Narrative as a Socially Symbolic Act.* Ithaca, NY: Cornell University Press, 1981.

Johnson, Samuel. *The History of Rasselas: Prince of Abissinia.* 1759. Ed. J.P. Hardy. London: Oxford University Press, 1968.

_____. *The Lives of the English Poets.* 1779–81. 2 vols. Garden City, NY: Dolphin-Doubleday, [n.d.].

Keating, Peter. *The Haunted Study: A Social History of the English Novel 1875–1914.* London: Secker, 1989.

Keats, John. "The Eve of St. Agnes." 1820. Abrams and Greenblatt 834–44.

Korg, Jacob. "Division of Purpose in George Gissing." In *Collected Articles on George Gissing.* Ed. Pierre Coustillas. London: Frank Cass, 1968. 64–79.

_____. *George Gissing: A Critical Biography.* 1963. Seattle: University of Washington Press, 1979.

_____. "George Gissing: Humanist in Exile." In *The Victorian Experience: The Novelists.* Ed. Richard A. Levine. Athens, OH: Ohio University Press, 1976. 239–73.

_____. "Gissing and Ancient Rome." In *A Garland for Gissing.* Ed. Bouwe Postmus. Amsterdam and New York: Rodopi, 2001. 225–33.

_____. "The Spiritual Theme of George Gissing's *Born in Exile.*" In *From Jane Austen to Joseph Conrad: Essays Collected in Memory of James T. Hillhouse.* Ed. Robert C. Rathburn and Martin Steinmann, Jr. Minneapolis: University of Minnesota Press, 1958. 246–56.

Korg, Jacob, and Cynthia Korg, eds. and intro. *George Gissing on Fiction.* London: Enitharmon, 1978.

Lawrence, D.H. *Sons and Lovers.* 1913. Intro. Benjamin DeMott. New York and London: Signet-Penguin, 1985.

Mattheisen, Paul F., Arthur C. Young, and Pierre Coustillas, eds. *The Collected Letters of George Gissing.* 9 vols. Athens, OH: Ohio University Press. 1990–97.

Michaux, Jean-Pierre. "Names in *New Grub Sreet.*" In *George Gissing: Critical Essays.* Ed. Jean-Pierre Michaux. London: Vision; Totowa, NJ: Barnes & Noble, 1981. 204–11.

Miller, J. Hillis. *The Form of Victorian Fiction: Thackeray, Dickens, Trollope, George Eliot, Meredith, and Hardy.* 1968. Case Western Reserve University. Cleveland: Arete, 1979.

Ogden, Stephen. "Darwinian Scepticism in George Gissing's *Born in Exile.*" In *A Garland for Gissing.* Ed. Bouwe Postmus. Amsterdam and New York: Rodopi, 2001. 171–78.

Orwell, George. "George Gissing." In *Collected Articles on George Gissing.* Ed. Pierre Coustillas. London: Frank Cass, 1968. 50–57.

_____. "'Not Enough Money': A Sketch of George Gissing." *Gissing Newsletter* 5.3 (1969): 1–4.

Peck, John. "*New Grub Street*: An Approach through Form." In *George Gissing: Critical Essays*. Ed. Jean-Pierre Michaux. London: Vision; Totowa, NJ: Barnes & Noble, 1981. 144–54.

Poe, Edgar Allan. "The Murders in the Rue Morgue." 1841. In *Complete Stories and Poems of Edgar Allan Poe*. Garden City, NY: Doubleday, 1966. 2–26.

Poole, Adrian. *Gissing in Context*. London: Macmillan, 1975.

Rawlinson, Barbara. "Devil's Advocate: George Gissing's Approach to the Woman Question." *Gissing Journal* 33.2 (1997): 1–14.

_____. *A Man of Many Parts: Gissing's Short Stories, Essays Other Works*. Amsterdam and New York: Rodopi, 2006.

Richter, David H., ed. *The Critical Tradition: Classic Texts and Contemporary Trends*. 2nd ed. Boston: Bedford, 1998.

Roberts, Morley. *The Private Life of Henry Maitland: A Portrait of George Gissing*. Ed. & intro. Morchard Bishop. 3rd ed. London: Richards Press, 1912, 1958.

Saint, Andrew, and Gillian Darley. *The Chronicles of London*. New York: St. Martin's, 1994.

Selig, Robert L. *George Gissing*. Rev. ed. Twayne's English Author Series No. 346. Ed. Herbert Sussman. New York: Twayne-Simon; London: Prentice Hall International, 1995.

_____. "'The Valley of the Shadow of Books: Alienation in Gissing's *New Grub Street*." In *George Gissing: Critical Essays*. Ed. Jean-Pierre Michaux. London: Vision; Totowa, NJ: Barnes, 1981. 162–73.

Shelley, Mary. *Frankenstein or the Modern Prometheus*. 1818. Oxford and New York: World's Classics-Oxford University Press, 1994.

Shelley, Percy Bysshe. From *A Defence of Poetry*. 1840. Richter 339–56.

Showalter, Elaine. *Sexual Anarchy: Gender and Culture at Fin de Siècle*. London: Bloomsbury, 1990, 1991.

Sidney, Sir Philip. *An Apology for Poetry*. Richter, 1998. 134–59.

Sjöholm, Christina. "*The Vice of Wedlock*": *The Theme of Marriage in George Gissing's Novels*. Uppsala: Acta Universitatis Upsaliensis, 1994.

Sloan, John. *George Gissing: The Cultural Challenge*. New York: St. Martin's, 1989.

Spiers, John, ed. "Introduction: Why Does Gissing Matter?" In *Gissing and the City: Cultural Crisis and the Making of Books in Late Victorian England*. Basingstoke and New York: Palgrave Macmillan, 2006. 1–29.

Sutherland, John. Foreword. *Rereading Victorian Fiction*. Ed. Alice Jenkins and Juliet John. Basingstoke,Hants: Macmillan, 2000; New York: St. Martin's, 2000. xi–xiii.

Swafford, Kevin. "Mourning, Pleasure and the Aesthetic Ideal in *The Private Papers of Henry Ryecroft*." *The Gissing Journal* 38.3 (2002): 1–13.

Swinnerton, Frank. *George Gissing: A Critical Study*. 1912. New York: Doran, 1923.

Symons, Julian. *Bloody Murder: From the Detective Story to the Crime Novel: A History*. 1972. 3rd ed. London: Pan, 1992.

Tennyson, Alfred Lord. *In Memoriam*. 1850. In *The Poems and Plays*. New York: Modern Library, [n.d.]. 294–374.

Tindall, Gillian. *The Born Exile*. New York and London: Harcourt, 1974.

Whitehead, Andrew. "Against the Tyranny of Kings and Princes: Radicalism in *Workers in the Dawn*." *Gissing Newsletter* 22.4 (1986): 13–28.

Wilde, Oscar. Preface to *The Picture of Dorian Gray*. 1891. In *The Works of Oscar Wilde*. Ed. and intro. G.F. Maine. London and Glasgow: Collins, 1948. 17.

Williams, Raymond. *Culture and Society: 1780–1950*. New York: Harper, 1958.

Woods, Sandra R. "Dangerous Minds: The Education of Women in Gissing's Marriage

Quartet." In *A Garland for Gissing.* Ed. Bouwe Postmus. Amsterdam and New York: Rodopi, 2001. 107–14.

Wordsworth, William. "Lines Composed a Few Miles above Tintern Abbey." 1798. Abrams and Greenblatt 235–38.

_____. *Preface to Lyrical Ballads.* 1802. Richter 302–14.

_____. *The Prelude or, Growth of a Poet's Mind: An Autobiographical Poem.* 1850. Abrams and Greenblatt 305–83.

_____. "The Ruined Cottage." 1814, 1949. In Book One *The Excursion.* Abrams and Greenblatt 259–70.

Yates, May. *George Gissing: An Appreciation.* Manchester: The University Press, 1922.

Young, Arlene. *Culture, Class and Gender in the Victorian Novel: Gentlemen, Gents and Working Women.* Basingstoke And London: Macmillan; New York: St. Martin's, 1999.

Zola, Emile. *L'Assommoir.* Trans. Leonard W. Tantock. New York: Viking, 1970.

_____. *Nana.* 1880. Trans. Douglas Parmee. Oxford: Oxford University Press, 1999.

Index

Afghanistan 171
Africa 195
"Against the Tyranny of Kings and Princes: Radicalism in *Workers in the Dawn*" 207
The Alien Art: A Critical Study of George Gissing 2, 12, 26, 76, 96, 114, 150, 156, 157, 160, 168, 180, 188
Alienation 108, 114, 115, 131, 135, 138, 141
Allen, Walter: *The English Novel: A Short Critical History* 155
Alps 192
Alverholme 148
The Amateur Cracksman 199
American Notes 146, 186, 187
Amsterdam 1
Anglicanism 100, 176
An Apology for Poetry 13
Arnold, Matthew: "The Function of Literature at the Present Time" 18
As You Like It 5
L'Assommoir 30
Atheism 89, 110, 151, 175, 176
Aurelius, Marcus: *Meditations* 184
Austen, Jane: *Emma* 125
Australia 36, 137, 170, 182
Author at Grass 194

Babbitt 80
Bailey, Benjamin 13
Balliol College 191
Beckson,Karl: *London in the 1890s: A Cultural History* 172
Bentham, Jeremy 50
Bentley, George 16

Bergonzi, Bernard: *The Turn of a Century* 24, 25
Bertz, Eduard 26, 30, 150, 162, 171
Biographia Literaria 13
Birmingham 186
Bishop, Morchard: Introduction to *The Private Life of Henry Maitland* 164, 165
Bleak House 95, 185, 200, 205
Bloody Murder: From the Detective Story to the Crime Novel 10
Bloom, Harold: *The Western Canon: The Books and School of the Ages* 15
The Born Exile 2, 39, 79, 125–26, 127, 149, 162, 164, 191
Born in Exile 10, 17, 29, 30, 38, 39, 41, 45, 57, 60, 69, 71, 78, 88, 98, 104, 107, 115, 118, 119, 130, 138, 151, 152, 156, 163, 166, 175, 176, 178, 203, 209, 210
The Bostonians 77
Bowlby, Rachel: *Just Looking: Consumer Culture in Dreiser, Gissing, and Zola* 96, 148
Bradbury, Malcolm: *The Social Context of Modern English Literature* 54
Briggs, Asa: *Victorian Cities* 12, 146; *Victorian People: A Reassessment of Persons and Themes: 1851–1857* 11
Brighton 55, 96, 97
Bristol 199
British Library 3, 55, 86, 87, 115, 118, 157, 158
Browning, Robert 12
Business 40, 41, 65, 71, 72, 77, 78, 79,

219

80, 81, 87, 89, 96, 102, 111, 115, 120, 132, 138, 154, 169, 170, 171, 198, 199, 208
Butler, Samuel: *The Way of All Flesh* 57
Byronic 133

Caird, Mona: "The Emancipation of the Family" 61
Calder, Jenni: *Woman and Marriage in Victorian Fiction* 119
Camberwell 154
Cambridge 186
Candide 72
Carey, John: *The Intellectuals and the Masses: Pride and Prejudice Among the Literary Intelligentsia: 1880–1939* 79
Carlyle, Thomas: *On Heroes, Hero-Worship and the Heroic in History* 12; *Sartor Resartus* 72–73
Cather, Willa: *My Antonia* 195; *O Pioneers!* 195
Chance 64, 98
Charles Dickens 30
Chialant, Maria Teresa: "The Feminization of the City in Gissing's Fiction: The Streetwalker, the *Flaneuse*, the Shopgirl" 199
Chicago Tribune 199
Children 6, 57, 58, 59, 60, 62, 64, 67, 70, 78, 101, 108, 177
Christianity 156, 168, 172, 175, 176, 177, 179, 184, 208
Christie, Agatha 201
The Chronicles of London 55
Church of England 75, 151
Church Times 175
The City 52, 102
Class 5, 10, 17, 29, 31, 32, 37, 38, 39, 40, 42–48, 51, 52, 58–62, 63, 64, 65, 67, 68, 69, 71, 72, 75, 79, 80, 82–86, 88, 89, 90, 93, 98, 100–2, 104, 108, 109, 110–11, 115, 117, 120, 121, 124–27, 128, 129, 130, 133, 135, 145, 146, 148, 152, 153, 157, 163, 169, 176, 177, 178, 180, 190, 202, 204, 205, 208, 209, 210
Coleridge, Samuel Taylor 3, 6; *Biographia Literaria* 13
Collie, Michael: *The Alien Art: A Critical Study of George Gissing* 2, 12, 26, 76, 96, 114, 150, 156, 157, 160, 168, 180, 188
Collins, Wilkie: *The Moonstone* 200; *The Woman in White* 202
Commonplace Book 26
Comte, Auguste 173

Conan Doyle, Sir Arthur 10, 195, 199, 200, 202; *A Study in Scarlet* 197
The Confidence-Man: His Masquerade 73
Conrad, Joseph 30
Emperor Constantine 184
Cooper, Rev. Theodore 175
Cope, Jackson I. 28
Cortez (Balboa) 188
Coustillas, Pierre 2; *Gissing: The Critical Heritage* 1, 101; "Gissing the European" 174; "Gissing's Feminist Portraiture" 36, 126; Introduction to *Isabel Clarendon* 179; Introduction to *A Life's Morning* 192
Partridge, Colin: *Gissing: The Critical Heritage* 1, 101
Crime 29, 30, 37, 39, 40, 63, 153, 202
Crimea 120
Critic (New York) 201
Criticism 14
The Crown of Life 15, 38, 45, 58,63, 71, 77, 79, 87, 89, 94, 119, 122, 130, 149, 166, 167, 168, 169, 170, 172, 172, 188, 208, 211
Crystal Palace 29
Culture 2, 6, 7, 10, 15, 16, 18, 42, 43, 46, 51, 70, 81, 82, 83, 88, 89, 106, 108, 117, 130, 136, 146, 151, 156, 158, 163, 166, 168, 169, 185, 198, 203, 205, 210, 211
Culture and Society 15, 40, 50
Culture, Class and Gender in the Victorian Novel: Gentlemen, Gents and Working Women 106

"Dangerous Minds: The Education of Women in Gissing's Marriage Quartet" 129
Dante, Alighieri 55, 149
Darley, Gillian: *The Chronicles of London* 55
Darwin, Charles 23, 96, 99, 183
Darwinism 99, 100, 115, 183
Darwinism in the English Novel: 1860–1910: The Impact of Evolution on Victorian Fiction 23
"Darwinism Scepticism in George Gissing's *Born in Exile*" 115
David Copperfield 36, 57, 93, 164
Davies, W.H. 195
Davis, Oswald H. 21
"The Day of Silence" 82
Deception 30, 38, 39, 99, 104
A Defence of Poetry 14
Delphi 107
Demos: A Story of English Socialism 14, 15, 16, 17, 29, 31, 33, 37, 40, 42, 50, 52, 53,

57, 59, 63, 65, 68, 71, 72, 85, 101, 112, 116, 134, 141, 145, 151, 152, 154, 169, 175, 178, 188, 204, 205, 209, 210

Denzil Quarrier 17, 32, 33, 71, 73, 74, 104, 105, 119, 132, 147, 168, 186, 192, 197, 198, 199

Descartes, René 107

Detective 129, 197–202

Determinism 37, 53, 107, 207

"Devil's Advocate: George Gissing's Approach to the Woman Question" 85

Devon 39, 95, 133, 145, 149, 161, 186, 195, 196

Dickens, Charles 9, 11, 30, 205; *American Notes* 146, 186, 187; *Bleak House* 95, 185, 200, 205; *David Copperfield* 36, 57, 93, 164; *Great Expectations* 95; *Hard Times* 52, 53, 56, 177, 205; *Little Dorrit* 95; *Martin Chuzzlewit* 95, 124; *The Mystery of Edwin Drood* 30; *Nicholas Nickleby* 77, 95; *The Old Curiosity Shop* 56, 205; *Oliver Twist* 95, 124; *Our Mutual Friend* 141; *Sketches by Boz* 12

Disraeli, Benjamin 205

Dissenting Churches 176

"Division of Purpose in George Gissing" 9

Donnelly, Mabel Collins: *George Gissing: Grave Comedian* 1, 182

Dowling, Andrew: *Manliness and the Male Novelist in Victorian Literature* 104

Dreiser, Theodore: *Sister Carrie* 54

Dryden, John 2

Dunfield 192

Dyer, John: "Grongar Hill" 163

Eagleton, Terry 14

Eden 189, 191

Education 10, 34, 37, 41, 48, 62, 65, 67, 79, 82–84, 85, 86–89, 90, 93, 98, 110, 115, 121, 128, 129, 146, 159, 190, 210

Education Act, 1870 82

Egypt 45

Eliot, George 11

"Elegy Written in a Country Churchyard" 82

The Emancipated 17, 41, 57–58, 65, 83, 84, 105, 112, 114, 130, 168, 169, 175, 177, 205, 206, 208, 210

"The Emancipation of the Family" 61

Emma 125

Enclosure Acts 187

England 6, 11, 15, 30, 73, 83, 86, 94, 117, 120, 128, 145, 157, 166–71, 174, 182, 187, 191, 195, 198

The English Novel: A Short Critical History 155

Escarpit, Roland 14

Ettore, Emanuela 106

Europe 139

"The Eve of St. Agnes" 109

Eve's Ransom 125

Evolution 23, 96, 100, 115, 183, 186

Exeter 89, 108, 109, 110, 118, 161, 172, 173, 176, 186, 194

"Experiments in Realism: How to Read a George Gissing Novel" 183

Family 6, 47, 57–70, 71, 78, 79, 85, 93, 96, 104, 108, 109, 110, 116, 123, 128, 132, 134, 135, 137, 139, 140, 151, 157, 159, 177, 184, 198, 201, 207

Fate 64, 98, 105, 107

Federico, Annette: *Masculine Identity in Hardy and Gissing* 87, 93, 151, 205

Feminism 33, 77, 106, 119, 123, 197

"The Feminization of the City in Gissing's Fiction: The Streetwalker, the *Flâneuse*, the Shopgirl" 200

Fernando, Lloyd: "Gissing's Studies in 'Vulgarism': Aspects of His Anti-Feminism" 128

Fielding, Henry: *The History of Tom Jones: A Foundling* 186

Finden 116, 159, 189

Flaubert, Gustave 153, 155

Fletcher, Ian: Introduction to *The Paying Guest* 102

Foerster, Dr. Friedrich Wilhelm 171

Fortnightly 194

Framley Parsonage 176

France 129

Frankenstein, or the Modern Prometheus, a Gothic Tale of Terror 54, 55

Free will 52

Frost, Robert 195

"The Function of Literature at the Present Time" 18

Gandhi, Mahatma 171

Gaskell, Elizabeth 205

Geneva 169

George Gissing 2, 27, 29, 40, 50, 73, 74, 95, 98, 103, 123, 129–30, 132, 139, 154, 156, 158, 172, 200, 208

"George Gissing" 15

George Gissing: An Appreciation 1

George Gissing: A Critical Biography 1, 2,

38–39, 51, 71, 82, 83–84, 95, 145, 162,
  167, 175, 177, 190
George Gissing: A Critical Study 1, 165
George Gissing: The Cultural Challenge 2,
  36, 38, 93, 135, 147, 160, 168–69, 171
George Gissing: Grave Comedian 1, 182
"George Gissing: Humanist in Exile" 176
George Gissing: Ideology and Fiction 2, 21,
  23, 33, 47, 95, 134, 154, 160, 170,
  199–200, 204–5
George Gissing on Fiction 12
Georgian poets 195
Germany 146, 168, 169, 171, 176, 178
Gissing 1, 157, 162, 164–66, 202
Gissing, Algernon 21
Gissing, Ellen 11
Gissing, George: *Author at Grass* 194; *Born
  in Exile* 10, 17, 29, 30, 38, 39, 41, 45, 57,
  60, 69, 71, 78, 88, 98, 104, 106, 115, 118,
  119, 130, 138, 151, 152, 156, 163, 166, 175,
  176, 178, 203, 209, 210; *Charles Dickens*
  30; *Commonplace Book* 26; *The Crown of
  Life* 15, 38, 45, 58, 63, 71, 77, 79, 87,
  89, 94, 119, 122, 130, 149, 166, 167, 168,
  169, 170, 172, 172, 188, 208, 211; "The
  Day of Silence" 82; *Demos: A Story of
  English Socialism* 14, 15, 16, 17, 29, 31, 33,
  37, 40, 42, 50, 52, 53, 57, 59, 63, 65,
  68, 71, 72, 85, 101, 112, 116, 134, 141, 145,
  151, 152, 154, 169, 175, 178, 188, 204,
  205, 209, 210; *Denzil Quarrier* 17, 32,
  33, 71, 73, 74, 104, 105, 119, 132, 147,
  168, 186, 192, 197, 198, 199; *The Emancipated* 17, 41, 57–58, 65, 83, 84, 105, 112,
  114, 130, 168, 169, 175, 177, 205, 206,
  208, 210; *Eve's Ransom* 125; "The Hope
  of Pessimism" 28, 51, 133, 183; *In the
  Year of Jubilee* 17, 29, 40, 41, 50, 54, 55,
  56, 58, 61, 63, 64, 71, 72, 78, 87, 101,
  102, 105, 112, 120, 138, 141, 154, 166, 205;
  Isabel Clarendon 17, 57, 58, 68, 78, 118,
  127, 139, 166, 175, 178, 179, 186, 190,
  203, 210; *A Life's Morning* 37, 58, 85, 89,
  132, 141, 186, 191, 205, 210; "Lou and
  Liz" 101; *Mrs. Grundy's Enemies* 16; *The
  Nether World* 5, 15, 16, 29, 37, 40, 41, 43,
  50, 56, 57, 58, 59, 62, 63, 69, 71, 72,
  98, 101, 112, 114, 124, 136, 137, 151, 152,
  170, 173, 175, 180, 182, 183, 207, 210, 211;
  New Grub Street 1, 6, 10, 15, 16, 17,
  21–28, 32, 38, 46, 54, 55, 58, 60, 64,
  66, 71, 73, 84, 86, 87, 88, 89, 94, 95,
  96, 97, 103, 104, 105, 115, 118, 132, 133,
  139, 140, 141, 147, 148, 151, 153, 156,

157–61, 166, 168, 170, 189, 209, 210, 211;
  Notes on Social Democracy 26; *The Odd
  Women* 10, 54, 55, 65, 69, 71, 76, 77, 78,
  98, 104, 110, 112, 115, 120, 123, 128, 135,
  136, 141, 150, 152, 170, 186, 197, 199, 200,
  206, 209, 210; *Our Friend the Charlatan*
  10, 17, 29, 30, 36, 38, 58, 64, 66, 68, 69,
  71, 73, 87, 98, 99, 100, 102, 117, 118, 134,
  148, 168, 175, 177, 186, 190, 192, 193, 211;
  The Paying Guest 10, 17, 38, 41, 52, 60,
  87, 100, 101, 102, 134, 148, 152, 186, 189;
  "The Place of Realism in Fiction" 12; *The
  Private Papers of Henry Ryecroft* 1, 5, 17,
  28, 30, 51, 64, 94, 100, 111, 133, 145, 149,
  152, 154, 156, 161, 162, 163, 168, 169, 172,
  186, 193, 195, 209, 211; "The Sins of the
  Fathers" 83; *Sleeping Fires* 102; *Thyrza: A
  Tale* 10, 16, 40, 57, 59, 68, 71, 83, 98,
  115, 136, 137, 152, 173, 203, 204, 207,
  209, 210; *The Town Traveller* 17, 38, 59,
  64, 79, 86, 100, 101, 124, 125, 134, 151,
  152, 184, 197, 201, 202, 206, 210; *The
  Unclassed* 16, 34, 35, 36, 39, 43, 57, 58,
  62, 65, 67, 68, 71, 77, 85, 87, 88, 100,
  112, 114, 125, 147, 152, 156, 157, 173, 175,
  177, 180, 181, 185, 188, 206, 210;
  Veranilda: A Romance 5, 9, 155; *The
  Whirlpool* 30, 31, 43, 58, 65, 68, 81, 84,
  127, 136, 150, 152, 153, 168, 171, 211; *Will
  Warburton: A Romance of Real Life* 43, 51,
  71, 77, 79, 80, 132, 151, 152, 208; *Workers
  in the Dawn* 5, 10, 15, 16, 29, 30, 32, 33,
  34, 35, 39, 40, 42, 50, 57, 58, 59, 61,
  62, 67, 68, 70, 71, 72, 75, 77, 82, 84,
  85, 87, 88, 94, 95, 100, 101, 112, 114, 117,
  124, 127, 132, 139, 145, 147, 151, 152, 167,
  157, 167, 168, 169, 175, 176, 177, 180, 183,
  185, 187, 188, 207, 209, 210
Gissing, Marianne Helen "Nell" (née Harrison) 100
Gissing, Thomas 195
Gissing, Walter 173
Gissing: A Life in Books 2, 6, 10, 25, 33,
  39, 53, 80, 85, 93, 102, 111, 119, 132–33,
  145, 161, 169, 175, 178
"Gissing and Ancient Rome" 20607
*Gissing and the City: Cultural Crisis and the
  Making of Books in Late Victorian
  England* 11
Gissing in Context 2, 27, 75, 149, 158, 159,
  163, 188
Gissing Journal 1
Gissing Newsletter 1
Gissing: The Critical Heritage 1, 101

"Gissing the European" 174

"Gissing's Feminist Portraiture" 36, 126

"Gissing's Studies in 'Vulgarism': Aspects of His Anti-Feminism" 128

Goldmann, Lucien 14

Goode, John: *George Gissing: Ideology and Fiction* 2, 21, 23, 33, 47, 95, 134, 154, 160, 170, 200, 204–5; Introduction to *New Grub Street* 153

Gray, Thomas: "Elegy Written in a Country Churchyard" 82

Great Britain 45, 169, 171, 172

Great Expectations 95

Greece 168, 184

Greenslade, William: "Writing Against Himself: Gissing and the Lure of Modernity in *In the Year of Jubilee* 166

"Grongar Hill" 163

Grub Street 48, 149, 160

Grylls, David: *The Paradox of Gissing* 98, 100, 101, 108, 109, 146, 161, 166, 183, 188, 205, 206

Guillaume, André: "The Jamesian Pattern in George Gissing's *New Grub Street*" 26

Gunnersbury 128

Haggard, H. Rider 195

Hallam, Arthur Henry 162

Halperin, John: *Gissing: A Life in Books* 2, 6, 10, 25, 33, 39, 53, 80, 85, 93, 102, 111, 119, 132–33, 145, 161, 169, 175, 178

Hamlet 5

Hard Times 52, 53, 56, 177, 205

Hardy, Thomas 93; *Tess of the D'Urbervilles: A Pure Woman* 190

Harrison, Frederic 183

Hastings 188

The Haunted Study: A Social History of the English Novel 1875–1914 17, 30, 96, 151

Henkin, Leo: *Darwinism in the English Novel: 1860–1910: The Impact of Evolution on Victorian Fiction* 23

Henley, W.E. 171

Henry IV Part I 5, 124

Henry VI Part I 5–6

The History of Rasselas: Prince of Abissinia 154

The History of Tom Jones: A Foundling 186

Hollingford 148, 192

Homer 55

"The Hope of Pessimism" 28, 51, 133, 183

Hornung, E.M.: *The Amateur Cracksman* 199

Humanism 177

Identity 133, 138, 139, 140

Imagination 2, 3, 5, 67, 9–12, 13–14, 15, 16, 18, 40, 60, 66, 67, 98, 141, 164, 191, 203, 205, 209, 210, 211

Imperialism 11, 121, 122, 130, 167, 168, 169, 171, 172, 174

The Importance of Being Earnest 17, 53

In Memoriam 162

In the Year of Jubilee 17, 29, 40, 41, 50, 54, 55, 56, 58, 61, 63, 64, 71, 72, 78, 87, 101, 102, 105, 112, 120, 138, 141, 154, 166, 205

India 118, 127, 171

Indian Mutiny, 1857 171

Individual 6, 105, 107, 108, 132–141, 147, 173, 203, 204

Ingham, Patricia: *The Language of Gender and Class: Transformation in the Victorian Novel* 126

The Intellectuals and the Masses: Pride and Prejudice Among the Literary Intelligentsia: 1880–1939 79

Internationalism 167

Ireland 202

Isabel Clarendon 17, 57, 58, 68, 78, 118, 127, 139, 166, 175, 178, 179, 186, 190, 203, 210

Italy 83, 130, 161, 172, 205, 208, 210

James, Henry 30; *The Bostonians* 77

James, Simon J.: "Experiments in Realism: How to Read a George Gissing Novel" 183; *Unsettled Accounts: Money and Narrative in the Novels of George Gissing* 2, 108, 109

"The Jamesian Pattern in George Gissing's *New Grub Street*" 26

Jameson, Frederic: *The Political Unconscious: Narrative as a Socially Symbolic Act* 14

Jeffers, Robinson 195

Johnson, Samuel 2; *The History of Rasselas: Prince of Abissinia* 154; *The Lives of the English Poets 1779–81* 160

Jonson, Ben: "To Penshurst" 163

Jubilees 56, 171

The Jungle 54

Just Looking: Consumer Culture in Dreiser, Gissing, and Zola 96, 148

Keating, Peter: *The Haunted Study: A Social History of the English Novel 1875–1914* 17, 30, 96, 151

Keats, George 13

Keats, John 3, 6, 13; "The Eve of St. Agnes" 109; "On First Looking into Chapman's Homer" 188
Keats, Thomas 13
Kew 150
King Lear 5
King's College–Cambridge 177
Kipling, Rudyard 171
Knightswell 179
Korg, Cynthia: *George Gissing on Fiction* 12
Korg, Jacob: "Division of Purpose in George Gissing" 9; *George Gissing: A Critical Biography* 1, 2, 38–39, 51, 71, 82, 83–84, 95, 145, 162, 167, 175, 177, 190; "George Gissing: Humanist in Exile" 176; *George Gissing on Fiction* 12; "Gissing and Ancient Rome" 206–7; "The Spiritual Theme of George Gissing's *Born in Exile*" 25

Lamarck, Jean Baptiste de Monet, chevalier de 115
The Language of Gender and Class: Transformation in the Victorian Novel 126
The Last Chronicle of Barset 176
Lawrence, D.H.: *Sons and Lovers* 84
Leeds 186
Lewis, Sinclair: *Babbitt* 80
A Life's Morning 192
A Life's Morning 37, 58, 85, 89, 132, 141, 186, 191, 205, 210
Little Dorrit 95
Liverpool 167, 186
The Lives of the English Poets 1779–81 160
London 1, 3, 5, 24, 29, 30, 31, 36, 40, 42, 46, 55, 56, 56, 59, 64, 65, 75, 76, 78, 79, 85, 86, 88, 89, 100, 101, 108, 110, 115, 116, 118, 121, 128, 129, 130, 135, 136, 138, 145, 146, 147, 148, 149, 150, 151, 152–54, 157, 158, 159, 160, 163, 168, 170, 173, 176, 177, 180, 185, 186, 187, 189, 190, 194, 195, 200, 204, 206, 210
London in the 1890s: A Cultural History 172
London Underground 54, 55
"Lou and Liz" 101
Love 32, 33, 39, 42, 44, 46, 48, 58, 60, 62, 63, 67, 68, 69, 86, 87, 88, 93, 94, 98, 102, 104, 108, 109, 110, 114, 115, 116, 118, 120–122, 126, 127, 129, 135, 136, 137, 146, 147, 169, 171, 176, 179, 181, 182, 193, 198, 204, 205, 206, 207–9

Luddite 52
Lukacs, Georg 14

Malthus, Thomas 50
A Man of Many Parts: Gissing's Short Stories, Essays and Other Works 2, 157
Manchester 157
Manliness and the Male Novelist in Victorian Literature 104
Manon Lescaut (l'Abbé Antoine-François Prévost) 165
Marriage 6, 31–32, 33, 37, 47, 57, 58, 60, 61, 62, 63, 64, 66, 67–70, 74, 76, 79, 80, 86, 88, 93, 94, 96, 97, 98–99, 101–102, 105, 108, 109, 111, 112, 115, 116, 117, 120, 121, 122, 123, 125–29, 130, 131, 136–39, 146, 147, 148, 152, 154, 157, 159, 160, 161, 169, 170, 172, 176, 177, 178, 179, 180, 181, 184, 192, 193, 197, 198, 199, 202, 203–6, 208, 209
Martin Chuzzlewit 95, 124
Marx, Karl 14
Masculine Identity in Hardy and Gissing 87, 93, 151, 205
Meditations 184
Melville, Herman: *The Confidence-Man: His Masquerade* 73
Memory 195
Meredith, George 93
The Merry Wives of Windsor 124
Michaux, J.P.: "Names in New Grub Street" 27
Midlands 205
Miller, J. Hillis: *The Form of Victorian Fiction: Thackeray, Dickens, Trollope, George Eliot, Meredith, and Hardy* 137, 141
Money 6, 24, 25, 37, 42, 43, 46, 47, 48, 49, 62, 63, 65, 68, 73, 74, 75, 80, 89, 93–103, 111, 115–18, 121, 125, 127, 133, 134, 135, 138–141, 148, 158, 159, 170, 175, 177, 178, 179, 180, 182, 183, 194, 198, 207, 209, 210
The Monument 41, 79, 102
The Moonstone 200
Morality 35, 38, 44, 69, 85, 86, 105, 112, 117, 124, 125, 126, 146, 147, 148, 163, 165, 168, 171, 175, 176, 178, 180, 182, 183, 184, 188, 190, 192
Morning Post 201
"Mourning, Pleasure and the Aesthetic Ideal in *The Private Papers of Henry Ryecroft*" 149
Mrs. Grundy's Enemies 16
Mrs. Warren's Profession 77

"Ms. Found in a Bottle" (Edgar Allan Poe) 154–55
Mudie's 35
"The Murders in the Rue Morgue" 197
My Antonia 195
The Mystery of Edwin Drood 30

"Names in New Grub Street" 27
Nana 30, 35
Napoleonic Wars 50
Nationalism 11, 167, 169, 174
Natural Selection 23
Nature 51, 53, 54, 64, 94, 134, 145, 147, 148, 149, 151, 161, 163, 168, 170, 172, 185–96, 206
Negative Capability 14
The Nether World 5, 15, 16, 29, 37, 40, 41, 43, 50, 56, 57, 58, 59, 62, 63, 69, 71, 72, 98, 101, 112, 114, 124, 136, 137, 151, 152, 170, 173, 175, 180, 182, 183, 207, 210, 211
New Criticism 14
New England 83
New Grub Street 1, 6, 10, 15, 16, 17, 21–28, 32, 38, 46, 54, 55, 58, 60, 64, 66, 71, 73, 84, 86, 87, 88, 89, 94, 95, 96, 97, 103, 104, 105, 115, 118, 132, 133, 139, 140, 141, 147, 148, 151, 153, 156, 157–61, 166, 168, 170, 189, 209, 210, 211
New Testament 100
New Woman 151, 197
New York 146
Niagara Falls 32, 94, 95, 127, 146, 147, 169, 187, 188
Niagara River 187
Nicholas Nickleby 77, 95
Norfolk 64, 203
Norris, Frank: *The Octopus* 54
Norwich 180
"Not Enough Money" 15, 97
Notes from the Underground (Fyodor Dostoyevsky) 154
Notes on Social Democracy 26

O Pioneers! 195
The Octopus 54
The Odd Women 10, 54, 55, 65, 69, 71, 76, 77, 78, 98, 104, 110, 112, 115, 120, 123, 128, 135, 136, 141, 150, 152, 170, 186, 197, 199, 200, 206, 209, 210
Oedipus Rex 135
Ogden, Stephen: "Darwinism Scepticism in George Gissing's *Born in Exile*" 115
Oil! 54

The Old Curiosity Shop 56, 205
Oliver Twist 95, 124
"On First Looking into Chapman's Homer" 188
On Heroes, Hero-Worship and the Heroic in History 12
Orwell, George: "George Gissing" 15; "Not Enough Money" 15, 97
Our Friend the Charlatan 10, 17, 29, 30, 36, 38, 58, 64, 66, 68, 69, 71, 73, 87, 98, 99, 100, 102, 117, 118, 134, 148, 168, 175, 177, 186, 190, 192, 193, 211
Our Mutual Friend 141
Owen, Robert 73
Owens College 157, 186, 202

Pacific Ocean 188
Pall Mall Gazette 201
The Paradox of Gissing 98, 100, 101, 108, 109, 146, 161, 166, 183, 188, 205, 206
Paris 33, 105, 178, 198
Parliament 74, 105, 177, 198
Partridge, Colin: *Gissing: The Critical Heritage* 1, 101
The Paying Guest 10, 17, 38, 41, 52, 60, 87, 100, 101, 102, 134, 148, 152, 186, 189
Payn, James 192
Peck, John 21, 22
Philoctetes 165
"The Place of Realism in Fiction" 12
Poe, Edgar Allan 200; "The Murders in the Rue Morgue" 197
The Poles (North and South) 195
Police 200, 201
The Political Unconscious: Narrative as a Socially Symbolic Act 14
Politics 45, 71, 72, 74, 81, 82, 87, 89, 93, 98, 106, 107, 115, 147, 168, 172, 177, 179, 183, 186, 190, 192, 198, 199
Polterham 147, 192, 198
Poole, Adrian: *Gissing in Context* 2, 27, 75, 149, 158, 159, 163, 188
Pope, Alexander 2; "Windsor Forest" 163
Positivism 173, 183
Post-Modern 5, 14
Postmus, Bouwe 2
Preface to Lyrical Ballads 3, 13, 53
The Prelude: or, Growth of a Poet's Mind: An Autobiographical Poem 13, 54, 56, 171, 187
The Private Life of Henry Maitland 164, 165
The Private Papers of Henry Ryecroft 1, 5, 17, 28, 30, 51, 64, 94, 100, 111, 133, 145, 149, 152, 154, 156, 161, 162, 163, 168, 169, 172, 186, 193, 195, 209, 211

Progress 51, 52, 53
Pronzini, Bill 201
Prostitution 29, 30, 32, 34, 63, 67, 85, 88, 94, 100, 125, 126, 147
Protestant Dissent 168
Puritanism 178
Putney Heath 33, 64, 189
Pygmalion and Galatea 83
Pyrenees 175

The Raj 171
Rawlinson, Barbara: "Devil's Advocate: George Gissing's Approach to the Woman Question" 85; *A Man of Many Parts: Gissing's Short Stories, Essays and Other Works* 2, 157
Realism 12, 105, 107, 176, 183, 184, 208
Redemption 112, 147, 170, 171
Reform Act, 1832 186
Regent's Park 189
Religion 35, 39, 45, 46, 50, 63, 88, 97, 99, 108, 110, 126, 130, 133, 138, 146, 151, 159, 175–84, 186, 198, 208
Rereading Victorian Fiction 11
Richmond 150
Robert Elsmere 164, 176
Roberts, Morley 111; *The Private Life of Henry Maitland: A Portrait of George Gissing* 1, 157, 162, 164–66, 202
Roman 184, 207
Romance 111, 112, 119, 122
Romantics 13, 50, 54, 190
Rome 5, 168
Rosetta Stone 122
Royal Academy of Music 150
"The Ruined Cottage" (Book One of *The Excursion*) 171, 187
Russia 169, 170, 171, 172

Saint, Andrew: *The Chronicles of London* 55
Sartor Resartus 72–73
Satan 107
Savage, Richard 160
Schopenhauer, Arthur 183
Science 52–56
Selig, Robert L.: *George Gissing* 2, 27, 29, 40, 50, 73, 74, 95, 98, 103, 123, 129–30, 132, 139, 154, 156, 158, 172, 200, 208; "The Valley of the Shadow of Books: Alienation in Gissing's *New Grub Street* 27, 95
Sermon on the Mount 99, 100
Sexuality 39, 102, 107, 112–20, 122, 189

Shakespeare, William 13, 15, 180; *As You Like It* 5; *Hamlet* 5; *Henry IV Part I* 5, 124; *Henry VI Part I* 5–6; *King Lear* 5; *The Merry Wives of Windsor* 124; *Titus Andronicus* 6; *Two Gentlemen of Verona* 5
Shaw, George Bernard: *Mrs. Warren's Profession* 77
Sheffield 186
Shelley, Mary: *Frankenstein, or the Modern Prometheus, a Gothic Tale of Terror* 54, 55
Shelley, Percy Bysshe 3, 6, 12; *A Defence of Poetry* 14
Showalter, Elaine 69
Sidney, Sir Philip 2; *An Apology for Poetry* 13
Sinclair, Upton: *The Jungle* 54; *Oil!* 54
Sinister 104–9, 112–13, 207
"The Sins of the Fathers" 83
Sister Carrie 54
Sjöholm, Christina: *"The Vice of Wedlock": The Theme of Marriage in George Gissing's Novels* 2, 67
Sketches by Boz 12
Sleeping Fires 102
Sloan, John: *George Gissing: The Cultural Challenge* 2, 36, 38, 93, 135, 147, 160, 168–69, 171
The Social Context of Modern English Literature 54
Social Darwinism 1, 21, 22, 27, 107, 172, 183, 195
Social dynamic 16, 17, 18, 203
Social structure 14, 34, 105, 106, 107
Socialism 31, 42, 71, 179
Somerset 193
Sons and Lovers 84
Sophocles: *Oedipus Rex* 135
South Africa 171, 172
Southampton 65
Spectator 124
Spencer, Herbert 21, 96
Spiers, John: "Introduction: Why Does Gissing Matter?" in *Gissing and the City: Cultural Crisis and the Making of Books in Late Victorian England* 11
"The Spiritual Theme of George Gissing's *Born in Exile*" 25
Squire, Sir John C. 195
Stasulevich, Mikhail 157
Stoicism 184, 194
A Study in Scarlet 197
Sudan 171
Suicide 29, 32, 33, 49, 63, 65, 74, 94, 104,

107, 116, 128, 132, 140, 147, 150, 153, 169, 189, 192, 199
Surrey 191
Sutherland, John: Foreword to *Rereading Victorian Fiction* 11
Swafford, Kevin: "Mourning, Pleasure and the Aesthetic Ideal in *The Private Papers of Henry Ryecroft*" 149
Swinnerton, Frank: *George Gissing: A Critical Study* 1, 165
Symons, Julian: *Bloody Murder: From the Detective Story to the Crime Novel* 10

Technology 52–56, 101, 186
Teignmouth 189
Tennyson, Alfred Lord: *In Memoriam* 162
Tess of the D'Urbervilles: A Pure Woman 190
Thackeray, William Makepeace: *Vanity Fair* 57
Thyrza: A Tale 10, 16, 40, 57, 59, 68, 71, 83, 98, 115, 136, 137, 152, 173, 203, 204, 207, 209, 210
Tindall, Gillian: *The Born Exile* 2, 39, 79, 125–26, 127, 149, 162, 164, 191
Titus Andronicus 6
"To Penshurst" 163
The Town Traveller 17, 38, 59, 64, 79, 86, 100, 101, 124, 125, 134, 151, 152, 184, 197, 201, 202, 206, 210
Tradition 45, 46, 48, 119, 128, 153, 197
Trollope, Anthony: *Framley Parsonage* 176; *The Last Chronicle of Barset* 176
Tulks and Crowe 198–99
Turgenev, Ivan 157
The Turn of a Century 24, 25
Tutoring 5, 48, 134, 157, 183, 193
Two Gentlemen of Verona 5

The Unclassed 16, 34, 35, 36, 39, 43, 57, 58, 62, 65, 67, 68, 71, 77, 85, 87, 88, 100, 112, 114, 125, 147, 152, 156, 157, 173, 175, 177, 180, 181, 185, 188, 206, 210
Unitarian 208
United States 157, 169
Unsettled Accounts: Money and Narrative in the Novels of George Gissing 2, 108, 109
Utilitarians 50

"The Valley of the Shadow of Books: Alienation in Gissing's *New Grub Street*" 27, 95
Vanbrugh, Sir John 165
Vanity Fair 57
Veranilda: A Romance 5, 9, 155

Verne, Jules 195
"*The Vice of Wedlock*": *The Theme of Marriage in George Gissing's Novels* 2, 67
Victoria, Queen 171
Victorian Cities 12, 146
Victorian People: A Reassessment of Persons and Themes: 1851–1857 11
Vienna 139
Violence 29–33 39, 63, 128 151, 171
Virgil 55
Voltaire: *Candide* 72
Vyestnik Evropy 87, 157

Wakefield 191, 195
Ward, Mrs. Humphry: *Robert Elsmere* 164, 176
Wattleborough 116, 158, 189
The Way of All Flesh 57
Wells, H.G. 195, 199
Wensleydale 188
The Western Canon: The Books and School of the Ages 15
The Whirlpool 30, 31, 43, 58, 65, 68, 81, 84, 127, 136, 150, 152, 153, 168, 171, 211
Whitehead, Andrew: "Against the Tyranny of Kings and Princes: Radicalism in *Workers in the Dawn*" 207
Wilde, Oscar: *The Importance of Being Earnest* 17, 53
Will Warburton: A Romance of Real Life 43, 51, 71, 77, 79, 80, 132, 151, 152, 208
Williams, Raymond: *Culture and Society* 15, 40, 50
"Windsor Forest" 163
Woman and Marriage in Victorian Fiction 119
The Woman in White 202
Woods, Sandra: "Dangerous Minds: The Education of Women in Gissing's Marriage Quartet" 129
Wordsworth, William 3, 6, 192; "Lines Composed a Few Miles above Tintern Abbey" 56; Preface to *Lyrical Ballads* 3, 13, 53; *The Prelude: or, Growth of a Poet's Mind: An Autobiographical Poem* 13, 54,56, 171, 187; "The Ruined Cottage" (Book One of *The Excursion*) 171, 187
Work 44, 45, 47, 48, 52, 59, 61, 62, 66, 71–77, 80, 81, 85, 86, 88, 89, 93, 101, 127, 129, 130, 135–37, 140, 153, 159, 170, 179, 184, 197, 205, 206, 208
Workers in the Dawn 5, 10, 15, 16, 29, 30, 32, 33, 34, 35, 39, 40, 42, 50, 57, 58,

59, 61, 62, 67, 68, 70, 71, 72, 75, 77, 82,
84, 85, 87, 88, 94, 95, 100, 101, 112, 114,
117, 124, 127, 132, 139, 145, 147, 151, 152,
167, 157, 167, 168, 169, 175, 176, 177, 180,
183, 185, 187, 188, 207, 209, 210
World War I 171, 173
World War II 171, 173
Writing 46–48, 49, 51, 60, 66, 67, 75, 86,
88, 95, 104, 116, 118, 127, 133, 134, 138,
139–41, 145, 148, 149, 156, 157, 159, 160,
162, 165–66, 171, 172, 194, 196, 198,
208–10
"Writing Against Himself: Gissing and the

Lure of Modernity in *In the Year of
Jubilee* 166

Yarmouth 193
Yates, May: *George Gissing: An Appreciation*
1
Young, Arlene: *Culture, Class and Gender
in the Victorian Novel: Gentlemen, Gents
and Working Women* 106
Young, G.M. 11

Zola, Émile: *L'Assommoir* 30; *Nana* 30,
35